D1050697

RUNNING GOD'S WAY

RUNNING GOD'S WAY

STEP BY STEP TO A SUCCESSFUL POLITICAL CAMPAIGN

VICKY HARTZLER

Pleasant W rd

A Division of WINEPRESS PUBLISHING

Pleasant Word (a division of WinePress Publishing, PO Box 428, Enumclaw, WA 98022) functions only as book publisher. As such, the ultimate design, content, editorial accuracy, and views expressed or implied in this work are those of the author.

Unless otherwise noted, all Scriptures are taken from the *Holy Bible, New International Version*®, *NIV*®. Copyright © 1995 by The Zondervan Corporation. Used by permission. All rights reserved.

Scripture references marked KJV are taken from the *King James Version of the Bible*.

Also quoted is *The Living Bible* (Kenneth Taylor; paraphrase; NT 1967; OT 1970; also called *The Book*, and later reprinted as *The Way*).

ISBN 13: 978-1-4141-1124-7
ISBN 10: 1-4141-1124-X
Library of Congress Catalog Card Number: 2007907863

This book is dedicated to
Ed Bohl, campaign treasurer 1994–1995,
and Loretta Filer, campaign treasurer 1996–2001.
They were more than my campaign treasurers—they were
my partners in public service and blessings from the Lord.
I miss them both.
I'll forever be grateful for their hours of selfless service,
their wise counsel, and their constant belief in what we were
trying to do for the Lord and for the people of the 124th District.
Their memory lives on in the legacy of their wonderful families
and the grateful hearts of those who had the privilege to
work with and know them, like me.

CONTENTS

THE CALL TO RUN

It was about 7:30 P.M. My husband and I had just finished dinner.

Like many nights at our household, I was sitting at the kitchen table grading papers. The life of a teacher doesn't end with the school bell.

When the phone rang, my husband answered. I heard a lot of "uh-huhs" and then, "Well, I don't think I'm interested, but I think there's somebody else here who might be." He was grinning at me. "You've been talking to the wrong Hartzler." With that, he handed me the phone.

On the other end of the line was our longtime friend, Bill Day. He was an insurance agent for years before his retirement and now enjoyed gardening, taking walks with his wife, and supporting his political party. What he said stumped me. "Would you consider running for state representative? As you know, our current representative is retiring, and we need someone to run who's willing to serve the people of this area. I asked your husband, but he declined and suggested I talk to you. The committee thought of you, too, but thought you wouldn't give up teaching to serve. Will you run?"

My mind swirled with a thousand thoughts. *I can't do this. I just got my Master's degree and I'm making a difference where I am. I don't know a thing about running. I wouldn't know where to start with a campaign. We can't afford to run for office. That takes a lot of money. Politics is an ugly game with a lot of mean people. I don't want to enter that fray.*

Yet amidst it all, I also remembered. My mind went back to the front sidewalk of my childhood home where I was making mud pies. I was nine years old. I was talking with God and asked, "God, what do you want me to be when I grow up? Where could you use me to serve you and help people?"

Of course I wanted to be a wife and mother, but was there something else He wanted me to do? I thought about being a doctor and then said, "No, too much blood!" Then I thought about being a lawyer and quickly ruled that out. "Too much arguing!" Then the idea of being a state representative came to mind and I smiled, "Yeah, that would be a way to serve you, Lord."

I went on with my life, grew up, got married, and became a teacher. Yet over the years I felt drawn to the political process, preferring to watch the evening news or read the newspaper to learn the latest public policy action of elected officials over watching popular sitcoms. I shared with my husband my childhood thoughts but always assumed that if I ever really did run for office, it would be after I had retired from teaching or after we'd had children and they were out of the house. Not now.

Then a surprise. I found myself saying to Bill, "Well, I do remember as a child thinking it would be rewarding to serve God and others by being a state representative. I shared the idea with Lowell several years ago, and we've joked about when I would run for office 'someday,' but we've never really taken it seriously." Then the thoughts of the realities of campaigning came to mind. "Really . . . I can't. I just completed my Masters degree and am enjoying teaching and . . ."

Bill gently interrupted, "Would you at least consider it? Would you pray about it?"

With a hesitant, "Yes," I said I would. What ensued was a month-long, soul-searching journey trying to discern God's will for my life today. To agree to run for office would be a life-changing decision—one I hadn't actually thought I would make, or at least, not make until I was older. Not now. Surely, this wasn't God's timing.

I was thirty-three years old and in my eleventh year of teaching family and consumer sciences. My husband, Lowell, and I had been married ten years and were in the middle of pursuing adoption. Our neat and tidy plans for our lives hadn't unfolded quite like we'd expected and we might get a phone call any day (or never) saying we were going to be parents through adoption. What would running for office (and possibly serving) do to these plans? What was God saying to us through this? And what about teaching? Wasn't I serving Him as a teacher—striving to make a difference in the lives of young people every day? Could this proposal really be from Him?

During the weeks following the phone call, we met with family members, our pastor and his wife, and our most trusted friends, seeking their words of wisdom and asking them to pray for us as we tried to discern God's will. In my heart I wanted to be open to God's will and direction, yet in my head, I resisted leaving everything I'd known to leap off the cliff of faith into the unknown world of politics. Most of all, though, I wanted to be obedient.

To my surprise, friends, family members, and our pastor all said one thing when told about the opportunity: "I believe you should do this. I think you'd be good at this and God has gifted you in a way that could be used for good. This sounds like God's will to me." It wasn't exactly what I wanted to hear. Images of conniving politicians in smoke-filled rooms sitting around playing poker while devising schemes to smear my name or halt my efforts filled my head. Surely God wouldn't call me to be like Daniel and enter the lion's den! Yet time was running out. The filing period was almost over.

The moment of decision came during church one Sunday morning. We were singing praise and worship songs and a familiar chorus, "I Will Rejoice in You and Be Glad," was displayed on the overhead screen. I was singing the words as usual, but in my heart I was asking God, "What do you want me to do? I've got to decide. Is this really you?" As we sang the song, I suddenly noticed the words of the third line as if for the first time. They said, "Draw me unto you and let us run together." At that point, I knew . . . and tears came to my eyes. Not from sorrow or from dread, but from gratefulness and relief. God wouldn't call me to do anything alone. He was saying to draw close to Him and to *run together with Him* for the office of state representative.

The words of Isaiah came to mind, "Then I heard the voice of the Lord saying, 'Whom shall I send? And who will go for us?' And I said, 'Here I am. Send me!'" (Isa. 6:8). If Isaiah was obedient and willing to follow His call, I could say no less.

I would run for state representative. I would stand alone if I had to. I would be obedient. I would trust God to supply all my needs. I would believe His promise to never leave me nor forsake me. I didn't know if it was God's will that I win or not. I only knew I was supposed to run, but I would do it. My future was in His hands.

What I didn't know was that God had prepared one of the greatest blessings of my life by calling me to run: the opportunity to see Him manifest Himself anew through His Word and prove His faithfulness. It is one thing to *know* that God will catch you when you leap off by faith into the unknown. It is another thing to experience it.

As Thomas Paine said, "The harder the conflict, the more glorious the triumph." Doing new things stretches us, changes us, betters us. New beginnings give us opportunities to lean on God more than ever. Challenges allow Him to reveal Himself to us.

Reveal He did. God put His Bible together to speak to every situation in life. I had read my Bible daily and understood that it was "living and active," yet I had no idea how "living" it would become in the months following my decision. I knew it had been helpful to me as a teacher, but could God teach me anything about how to run a campaign or serve in office through His Word? Yes!

The outline of how to campaign for public office came from a most unusual story in the Bible. The account reveals not only an outline of how to campaign, but also, lessons on how to serve in office. Many other Scriptures provide insights and support for running for public office, as well.

This book is a compilation of those insights God shared with me from His Word, along with practical advice learned during the course of that first battle and the myriad of other campaigns I have been involved with since. The suggestions and insights certainly aren't comprehensive, as God reveals Himself to each of His children in individual ways and has a special way of tailoring His instruction perfectly to fit every situation, but it is my prayer that some of these truths could be universal and prove helpful to others who "receive the call." Like Esther, you may face the possibility that your life's experiences have been prepared for such a time as this. If you choose to take the step of faith, be assured you will find that God is faithful and will supply the equipment and strategy you need to bring Him glory as He carries out His plan for your life. You'll find that the key lies in *Running God's Way.*

CHAPTER 1

THE FIRST POLITICIAN

He was young, handsome, and most of all, committed. He was determined to do the impossible: to unseat the powerful, once extremely popular incumbent. The odds looked impossible. The incumbent had all vestiges of power at his disposal—money, manpower, might. Yet he had his weaknesses. He'd become lazy, out of touch. Most of all, he had made a major mistake early in his career. He'd sinned against God, and the consequences were coming back to haunt him.

Despite overwhelming odds, the challenger won. His name? Absalom. The incumbent he defeated—at least for a time? King David.

The accounts of Absalom and David reveal important truths about campaigning and serving. Absalom was the first politician. He sought higher office and actively campaigned for it. Absalom won over the hearts of the people of Israel using time-tested campaign strategies. We, too, can campaign successfully following these same guidelines. In addition, if elected, we can serve honorably, heeding the insights gained from the circumstances behind his victory.

Absalom was able to win not only because he implemented a winning strategy, but also because God allowed it as punishment for

David's sin with Bathsheba (2 Sam. 11). As a result of David's adultery, God said that the sword would never depart from his house and that out of David's own household, God was going to bring calamity upon him (2 Sam. 12:10–11). Absalom's coup was part of that judgment. While the strategies worked, ultimately Absalom's kingdom didn't last, because Absalom had the wrong heart for service, and because he wasn't called by God to serve. David was the anointed king God had chosen. David was a man after God's heart. In the end, his kingdom prevailed.

Their story points us to an important first question for potential candidates: Are you called to run for office? Is this the will of the Lord for your life? Wise candidates will spend time with God seeking His will before filing the candidate papers. They will make sure they and their entire family have peace about it before proceeding.

Whom God calls, He enables. You can move forward in confidence once your heart is right. But how do you get started? Rely on the Lord with the heart of David, and implement the strategies utilized by Absalom. The time-tested blueprint for successful campaigning is revealed in 2 Samuel 15, verses 1–6.

> In the course of time, Absalom provided himself with a chariot and horses and with fifty men to run ahead of him. He would get up early and stand by the side of the road leading to the city gate. Whenever anyone came with a complaint to be placed before the king for a decision, Absalom would call out to him, "What town are you from?" He would answer, "Your servant is from one of the tribes of Israel." Then Absalom would say to him, "Look, your claims are valid and proper, but there is no representative of the king to hear you." And Absalom would add, "If only I were appointed judge in the land! Then everyone who has a complaint or case could come to me and I would see that he gets justice."
>
> Also, whenever anyone approached him to bow down before him, Absalom would reach out his hand, take hold of him and kiss him. Absalom behaved in this way toward all the Israelites who came to the king asking for justice, and so he stole the hearts of the men of Israel.

Absalom's successful campaign reveals several steps which can be employed today:

1. Make a plan;
2. Look the part;
3. Surround yourself with volunteer partners;
4. Go meet the people;
5. Target voters;
6. Have a group of people with you in parades;
7. Ask questions, affirm their concerns, and then present your message;
8. Define the message by presenting the problem, then sharing how you'd solve it;
9. Connect with voters; and
10. Embrace a humble attitude.

The Word shows us that when Absalom did these things, he won over the hearts of the people. We can, too—not in the *self-serving* way of Absalom, but in the *serving others* way of Jesus. It all begins with a good plan.

Make a plan

A campaign plan is vital. Absalom didn't have a written plan that we know of, but he could have. He certainly had a mental plan which he, no doubt, made "in the course of time" (v. 1). He'd thought out what he wanted to do and planned how he was going to do it. The who, what, when, where, why, and how were clear in his mind before he started executing his plan.

I had never heard of a campaign plan before filing for office. In fact, I knew next to nothing about campaigning. I'd noticed the campaign signs dotting the landscape before election day and seen the ads in the newspaper, but I had no idea what it took to get elected.

It was definitely a leap of faith for me to run for office. I took the plunge, and God provided teachers to help me find my way.

One of the first things a politically-minded person told me was that I should make a campaign plan. When he saw my blank expression, he offered to obtain a sample plan for me. What a lifesaver! I had no idea what a plan included and was able to develop my own using the example. While composing a campaign plan wasn't easy to do, it was very beneficial and made a big difference, I believe, on election day.

A campaign plan analyzes your strengths and weaknesses and the strengths and weaknesses of your opponent. It articulates who will be involved in your campaign, specifies their roles, outlines the strategies you are going to employ to get elected, sets a timetable for putting all the pieces together, and projects a budget of necessary expenses. This provides the basis for your fundraising and puts the wheels in motion for your campaign.

It takes time—a good deal of time—to put this document together, but it is a smart investment. By disciplining yourself to sit down and think through these issues early on, you are able to act with a focus and a purpose for the remainder of the campaign. In addition, you can "count the costs" necessary to participate in a campaign.

Jesus extolled His disciples to count the cost of following Him. In Luke 14:28–32 He gave these examples,

> Suppose one of you wants to build a tower. Will he not first sit down and estimate the cost to see if he has enough money to complete it? For if he lays the foundation and is not able to finish it, everyone who sees it will ridicule him, saying, "This fellow began to build and was not able to finish." Or suppose a king is about to go to war against another king. Will he not first sit down and consider whether he is able with ten thousand men to oppose the one coming against him with twenty thousand? If he is not able, he will send a delegation while the other is still a long way off and will ask for terms of peace.

In the same way, candidates need to thoroughly examine all the challenges and opportunities ahead prior to embarking on this new political journey.

Most importantly, everything in the plan should be directed at reaching your goals. The ultimate goal is to serve God through serving others in public service. But to get that done, you have to get elected. That is your first goal.

Prerequisite goals involve: increasing name ID (identification); winning over voters by conveying your message about who you are, why you are running, and what you want to accomplish; and getting your supporters out to vote on election day. Everything you do should be geared to accomplishing these goals.

Too many candidates fall prey to the "I've got to get going—I'll just do it by the seat of my pants" trap. They travel here and there to this meeting and that occasion, always busy but not knowing why they are going to the event or if this is the best use of their time. They buy whatever looks good from the many campaign catalogs that arrive through the mail without thought of whether the purchase fits within the budget or overall plan of the campaign. They pick up some volunteers here and there and obtain some finances but wonder why they run short at the end. They're surprised by what it costs in time, money, and energy. It doesn't have to be this way.

Developing a campaign strategy and writing it down keeps a campaign focused and on track. Every campaign plan needs to be tailored to each candidate's individual situation, but all include some of the same basics. The chapters to follow will give further insights into how to carry out the plan, but the first step is development.

Getting started

To begin, you need to do some research and ask some questions—questions of yourself and of others. Proverbs 20:18 says, "Make plans by seeking advice; if you wage war, obtain guidance."

Proverbs 24:6 shares further wisdom, "For waging war you need guidance and for victory many advisers."

Now is the time to seek advice from others. Talk to people who have been in the trenches of campaigning before—who have seen the battles, endured the rigors, and when the smoke cleared on Election Day, still stood strong. You can glean insights both from candidates who were successful and from ones who were not. Party activists and campaign volunteers can also provide sage advice to help direct your path. Don't be afraid to contact them and ask for their advice. Most will be glad to share their experiences, and you might even win a future supporter in the process.

When I first decided to run for office, one of the first things I did was to meet and visit with former state representatives I knew from my area. Two were from the opposing political party. One had been the last person of my political party to serve in the state capitol, and that had been over twenty years earlier. I learned a great deal from all of these seasoned veterans of public service. When I first called, I asked if I could come over and visit with them about some new things going on in my life. After arriving, I shared with them my decision to run for state representative and how I respected them and wanted them to be among the first to know. I also wanted to get their perspective on what it was like to be a state representative—what they'd learned and what they'd do differently if they had it to over again. What tips could they share on how to get things accomplished to best serve the people of this area? What were their highlights? Their challenges? And how did they overcome them?

One former state representative had enjoyed the distinction of serving our district for sixteen years—the longest time of public service as state representative ever in our area. During that time, he had an impressive reputation for getting things done and was loved by all, although it had been many years since his retirement. I'll always treasure the almost two hours I spent with him and his wife when he shared story after story from campaigns and the battles of the legislature. I learned more in that time than I could have from spending an entire day at a campaign seminar.

Likewise, when I went to visit the former state representative who had been the last person to serve our area from my political party, I was amazed at both his knowledge of campaigning and his wealth of insights about the people of the community—who the key leaders were and what the issues were that needed to be addressed. Even though it had been twenty years since he had served with the title of state representative, he had kept up with the politics of the day and was well aware of what needed to be done.

My notepad filled with page after page of notes as we talked. In the end, I not only found a wonderful resource on topics of importance and campaigning, I also found an important ally. He graciously agreed to serve as my first campaign treasurer, becoming a true partner in the cause.

Your campaign treasurer not only fills out all the campaign reports dictated by your state's campaign laws, but also lends his or her name to all of your campaign materials. It is an honor when someone agrees to this position, because he or she is risking his or her reputation in order to build yours. In addition, this person is committing a great deal of time and effort to ensure your campaign reports are filed in a timely, legal manner. Ask God to give you favor and raise up a person to be your partner in your campaign. He or she will be one of your greatest blessings of your campaign.

After seeking advice, you are ready to ask yourself and your team some questions. Below is a questionnaire to help you focus your campaign and formulate a winning plan. In the upcoming chapters we will be exploring these topics further. Answer the questions you can. Keep the rest in mind as you read the book, and go back later and fill in the details.

CAMPAIGN PLAN QUESTIONNAIRE

1. Why am I running for office?

2. What Scriptural principles/verses will serve as the basis of my campaign?

3. What theme would I like to carry throughout the campaign? (Examples: "Vicky cares about . . .", "Leadership in . . ." etc.)

4. Is there a slogan I want to use like "Proven Leadership" or "Experienced to Lead. Dedicated to Serve." or "Faith, Family, Freedom"?

5. What is the current political climate of your area? What are the "hot topics" of concern for people you will be serving?

6. List the key people who will most likely serve as your core campaign team.

7. Check the campaign tactics you will most likely want to employ and list a person(s) who might be willing to serve as the Chairman for that project:

• Campaign project	Potential Chairman
_____ Yard signs	_____
_____ Big signs	_____
_____ Phone banks	_____
_____ Newspaper advertising	_____
_____ Volunteer Captain	_____
_____ Direct mail	_____
_____ Web site	_____
_____ Parades	_____
_____ Prayer Team Captain	_____
_____ Events	_____
_____ Fundraising	_____
_____ Absentee ballot	_____
_____ Computer work	_____
_____ Thank you correspondence	_____
_____ Election day activities	_____
_____ Headquarters	_____
_____ Other	_____

8. How many registered voters are in the area you wish to represent?

9. Based on the election history of your area from a similar type of election year (presidential, non-presidential but congressional, county-only, etc.), what percentage of voters would you expect to turn out to vote in this election?

10. Based on the above two questions, how many votes do you expect you will need in order to win? (51 percent of no. 9)

11. Lists the strengths and weaknesses of your opponent(s).

	Strength	Weakness
Physical characteristics:	_____	_____
Educational background:	_____	_____
Occupation:	_____	_____
Community involvement:	_____	_____
Political background:	_____	_____
Family:	_____	_____
Name recognition:	_____	_____
Energy/commitment to campaign:	_____	_____
Overall impression:	_____	_____

12. List your strengths and weaknesses.

	Strength	Weakness
Physical characteristics:	————	————
Educational background:	————	————
Occupation:	————	————
Community involvement:	————	————
Political background:	————	————
Family:	————	————
Name recognition:	————	————
Energy/commitment to campaign:	————	————
Overall impression:	————	————

13. What mailing lists will you use for your initial kickoff letter? List every possible source you can think of: Church directories, Christmas card lists, membership lists from organizations you belong to or used to know, Chamber of Commerce lists, neighborhood friends, etc.

14. How many names are on these lists?

15. Research costs for the following campaign items:
    a) Bulk rate for mailings from the post office

b) Yard signs

c) Big signs

d) Newspaper ads in your area

e) Pushcard or brochure you hand out

f) Direct mail piece printing costs

g) Stationery and envelopes

h) Headquarters rent (if applicable)

i) Phone bank charge (if needed)

16. How will you raise the money needed to pay for the expenses of the campaign, and how much money do you expect to raise from each method?

17. What types of direct mail pieces do you plan to use?

18. List the print date, quantity, drop date, and target of each planned mailer.

Direct Mailer	Print Date	Quantity	Drop Date	Target

19. Do you want to survey voters by phone on issues, and/or call them to increase name ID, garner support, or get them out to vote? If so, when?

20. When do you plan to go door to door?

21. Where will you go door to door? List the neighborhoods in order of priority:

FIGURE 1.1 Campaign plan questionnaire

Putting the plan together

Now that you have obtained advice and answered some basic questions, you are ready to put together your first draft of the campaign plan. The plan can be as simple or complex as you like, depending upon your campaign and what meets your needs. Generally, though, the more detailed the plan, the better. Taking time to think through strategy during the early stages of your campaign saves time and headaches later when the campaign is running full steam.

Most campaign plans include some variation of the basic topics listed in the outline below. Use these ideas to help formulate your plan.

OUTLINE OF A SAMPLE CAMPAIGN PLAN

Overview

The overview includes a brief summary of who is running and the current political climate of the district.

Mission Statement

The mission of most campaigns is to get the person elected to the office for which he or she is running.

Guiding Principles

List the principles and/or Scriptures which will guide the behavior and activities of the candidate and the campaign team.

Campaign Objectives

The basic campaign objectives usually involve:

1. increasing name ID;
2. increasing the positive image (favorability) of the candidate;
3. motivating voters to get out and vote for the candidate, and;
4. raising the necessary resources (volunteers and funding) to implement the necessary campaign tactics.

Candidate Analyses

This section reviews the strengths and weaknesses of all candidates, looking at everything including their resumes, public statements, campaign finance reports, voting and attendance records, and issues that the candidates differ on. Make sure to analyze yourself along with all opponents. (See Questionnaire and Chapter 4.)

Issues Analysis

This section summarizes the issues that will be emphasized in the race. Chapter 4 helps you develop these messages.

Campaign Theme, Logo, Slogan, Colors

Decide upon the campaign theme, logo, slogan, and campaign colors based upon your above analyses of your strengths and the issues that will resonate with the voters. See Chapter 6 for more information.

Voting Analysis of District

Chapter 10 explains how to analyze your district to determine the Republican, Democrat, and swing precincts, along with additional information that helps you prioritize the precincts for both your door-to-door schedule and get-out-the-vote efforts. After this analysis is done, list the order of precinct priority to guide your efforts.

Chapter 17 takes the answers to the questionnaire about number of votes needed to win and helps you break that down by precinct. These numbers help you monitor vote counts on election day.

Campaign Tactics

This is usually the largest section of a campaign. List the activities your campaign is going to employ to achieve the campaign objectives. Subsections will probably include:

➢ Meeting the voters—Door-to-door strategies and schedule, parades, public events you will attend, and any other tactics to meet the voters. (Chapters 11 and 12)

➢ Media plan—Strategies for meeting the editors of local media, obtaining cost information, enhancing "earned media" through the use of press releases, letters-to-the-editor, and press conferences, if any, along with an outline of your complete paid advertising strategy. (Chapter 8)

➢ Sign plan—Yard signs, big signs, and traveling signs on buses or pickup trucks—how many, who, and when. (Chapters 6 and 16)

➢ Literature and direct mail—The type of voter contact sheet you will develop (pushcard or brochure) along with the types, numbers, and sizes of direct mail pieces you want to send out during the final weeks of the campaign. (Chapters 7 and 16)

➢ Phone banks—The purposes of any proposed phone bank (to determine issues, to determine candidate favorability, to ID voters, to advocate for the candidate, and/or to get favorable voters out to vote prior to the election). Also list the who, what, when, and how of any proposed phone bank. (Chapters 4, 10, and 16)

➢ Absentee ballot program—What methods will be employed to reach absentee voters. (Chapter 16)

➢ Campaign materials—Any extra campaign materials the campaign hopes to purchase to increase name ID, such as lapel stickers for parades, refrigerator magnets, bumper strips, etc. (Chapter 6)

➢ Internet presence—Possible Web sites, e-mail campaign, and/ or other Internet methods such as blogging, text messaging, and podcasting—the who, what, when, where, and how. (Chapter 9)

➢ Get-out-the-vote program—The strategies that will be employed during the final weeks and days of the campaign to get out the vote. (Chapter 16)

Campaign Organization

List the key individuals on the campaign team and their roles. Determine the campaign structure you will use (see Chapter 3 for examples), along with meeting dates of the campaign team.

Campaign Budget and Fundraising Plan

Generate a budget for the campaign based upon the anticipated costs from the activities listed above. The budget with its corresponding fundraising plan (see Chapter 13) is one of the most important documents developed for any campaign. It lists the individual expenses of the campaign, the total amount of money that will need to be raised, an outline of how the money is going to be spent, and the methods that will be used to raise the funds. These fundraising goals also provide a timeline of when the funds will be needed and when they will be raised.

Contrary to what many candidates believe, raising funds is the primary activity during the early months of a campaign. While it is important to go meet the voters and talk about issues, it is vital that funds are secured *early* so resources are available to convey your message during the critical final weeks of the campaign. This requires discipline—discipline to raise the funds and discipline to not waste funds early in the campaign. A campaign plan and thorough budget help prevent such oversights.

Campaign Calendar and Timeline

Plot the important dates of your campaign on a calendar. Post it on the wall of your home or campaign office. Let everyone know what needs to be done when, and execute. Adjustments can and should be made during the course of a campaign, but developing a plan and then carrying it out is what will help you win on election day.

Chart out the following on your campaign calendar:
1. Campaign planning meeting(s)
2. Fundraising activities (fundraising letter, events, phone calls, appointments with individuals)
3. Door-to-door schedule (days, times, precincts)
4. Parades
5. Speaking engagements
6. Direct mail schedule (writing deadline, to printer date[s], labeling party[ies], drop date[s] in mail, etc.)
7. Public appearance events
8. Yard and big sign schedules (when to put out, take down)
9. Get-out-the-vote activities (phone banks, last minute literature drops to targeted neighborhoods, etc.)
10. Election day
11. Follow-up activities (thank you's, phone calls, appreciation banquet, etc.)
12. Most importantly, important events in your family (birthdays, anniversaries, children's school programs, etc.)
13. Other

Sample campaign timelines are provided in Appendix A. One timeline is designed for local elections and another is for state or county races. Typically, candidates running for local offices, such as city council or school board, need a six-month plan. Races for elective offices that represent a larger number of people necessitate a twelve- to eighteen-month timeline. Use the samples provided to serve as a basis for your campaign plan timeline.

FIGURE 1.2 Outline of campaign plan

Make the plan and work the plan. While the initial research may seem endless while you are putting together your plan, you will be glad you did. The end result is worth the effort.

CHAPTER 2

LOOK THE PART

For all his less than noble motives, Absalom was smart. The first thing he did when executing his plan was to make himself look "kingly." He went out and bought a chariot and horses and got fifty men to run ahead of him. When people saw him, he looked believable, worthy of listening to, capable of leading.

Thankfully, today's candidates can forego the chariot and horses and fifty running men, but they do need to think about image and take stock of the wardrobe. First impressions do count. Global Image Group expert Michelle Sterling tells us that people size us up in the first three seconds of contact.[1] They "categorize" us by our dress, mannerisms, speech, demeanor, grooming, and even our accessories (watch, handbag, briefcase). In today's fast-paced political environment, perception is reality.

With this knowledge, it is easy for candidates to gravitate toward two extremes: the "like me or lump me" philosophy or the "extreme makeover" trap. Either view can have disappointing results. The first philosophy is embodied by a person who stubbornly refuses to do a self-evaluation and take any positive steps to improve his or her image. "If they don't like me the way I am, then fine!"

The other trap snares candidates who take self-improvement knowledge to the extreme and try to create a whole new image, forsaking who they really are. Neither version is beneficial. Many a good person who might have served nobly has been denied the chance because he or she didn't take stock of a few self-image tips. On the other hand, nobody likes a "fake," and people can usually spot one a mile away. Be yourself—but be your *best* self.

During my first campaign, I remember one humorous conversation I had with a lawyer in town who is an avid worker in another political party. He had run unsuccessfully for office several years prior to my decision to run. I had stopped going door-to-door in our mostly rural neighborhood on that hot summer day long enough to have lunch with a friend. I was wearing my usual door-to-door "uniform": a cool, cotton skirt, short-sleeved shirt, tennis shoes, and simple jewelry, which included earrings and a watch purchased at my favorite super center store. When I walked through the restaurant door, the lawyer motioned me over to his table. To my surprise, he started complimenting me on how well I was doing campaigning. As he motioned with his hand, his big gold bracelet slid up and down his arm and his diamond ring caught the sun's glint streaming through the window.

During mid-sentence he stopped his string of compliments. He paused, looked at my watch and said, "See? That's another thing you're doing that's really smart that I didn't. You've bought a plain old watch which looks ordinary. When you go door to door, people think you're one of them. You don't overpower them. I didn't think about it and wore my gold watch here. Too flashy. Good idea."

I smiled and gently said, "Well, this is the watch I've always had. Thanks. It was good talking with you. Have a nice day," and went to join my friend at a nearby table. For one of the first times, I think the lawyer was speechless. In thinking later about that conversation, I realized there was a volume of difference between him and me. I *was* "representative" of the people of my area and that's what it is all about.

Be yourself, but be your *best* self. This entails looking at who you are, building on your strengths, and presenting yourself professionally in a way that will build confidence in others as they begin to perceive you as their representative in government. It takes a shift in people's thinking to stop seeing you as their neighbor, their co-worker, their friend, and start seeing you as someone who is able to be in authority. This shift takes time and is earned. People will be watching you and listening to what you have to say over the next several months. Like Absalom, you, too, can win over the hearts of your constituents. The journey begins with looking the part.

What to wear

So how should you dress when meeting the public? The general rule is:

You should dress one step more formal than the event you are attending. Example: if you are attending a barbeque where everyone is wearing jeans or shorts, you might want to wear casual pants or, if you are a woman, a casual skirt and a knit shirt with sandals. If you are attending church where most will have on dresses or shirts with ties (but no jacket), you might want to wear a dress suit or wear a jacket with your shirt and tie. And even if you are in a parade on a hot summer day, you still want to dress professionally.

State Representative Brian Baker is a friend of mine who projects a positive image in parades. He wears slacks, a shirt, and a tie in contrast to the shorts and polo shirt typically worn by his opponents. His tie and slacks make him stand out. People notice him. He not only looks the part of an elected representative of the people, he also projects his commitment to hard work. He walks the entire parade route shaking hands, with sleeves rolled up and tie on. Looking the part can make you unique and help you relate to the people. They remember you! After he had served for several years in office, people started commenting that they look for him wearing his tie in each parade.

It is imperative that you invest in a few nice outfits for every level of occasion—casual, semi-casual, and formal. You don't have to spend a lot of money, but you do need to look neat and professional. In my opinion, male candidates have it a lot easier than female candidates as far as finding ideal clothes for campaigning. Most men can get by with a few basic pairs of twill-type pants, a couple of nice button-down shirts, and dress shoes. They can add a tie and sports jacket and fit in nicely at most candidate events or convert to a more casual setting by removing their jacket and tie. Women can sometimes find similar attire, but with changing styles, most have to buy separate outfits for casual, semi-casual, and formal settings.

Regardless of the latest trend, some basics remain the same over time. Now is the time to invest in a few *Dress for Success* books or go online to learn the latest tips for "do's and don'ts" of dress. While many of the details will change with the culture and whims of fashion, a few standard guidelines remain. Below is a chart that contains some of the general guidelines to consider, adapted from the Web article, "Dress for Success" from the University of Wisconsin-Milwaukee.[2]

Dress for success for women:

- Look professional. Dress conservatively. You want your personality and ideas to stand out, not your clothing.
- Best suit colors are dark blue, dark green, dark brown, gray, or black. Hem lengths of skirts should stay at knee length or below. The preferred blouse color is white, cream, or one that contrasts with the suit. Ideal choices for blouses have a high neck or jewel neck.
- Ensure clothing is clean, pressed, and fits well. Test clothing out for fit when both sitting and standing. Check fabric for the likelihood of wrinkles by crunching up a fistful of fabric in the store, holding it for a few seconds, and then releasing it. If it wrinkles badly in the store, imagine the wrinkles after sitting at a meeting and then standing up to speak. Quality

fabric is important. One hundred percent wool suits wear better and breathe better than synthetic fibers. Avoid one hundred percent synthetic fiber suits because these look cheap and will not wear well.

- Black is always a safe color for shoes, but navy works, also. The color of the shoes should be darker or match the color of the outfit. Styles change. For the most conservative look, never wear open toe or open heel shoes in professional settings and keep heel height around 1.5" or lower. Consider comfort as you will be on your feet a lot during the campaign. It's hard to project a positive image when your feet are killing you. In the final analysis, I have concluded that comfort trumps style. A wise investment considers both factors.
- Select neutral skin tones, such as taupe for hosiery.
- Avoid conspicuous jewelry and overpowering perfume. Jewelry should be simple, like a single strand of pearls.
- Watch the use of scarfs. They can take away from your image if not done right. Make sure it's silk and tied in a positive way or else skip using one.
- Drop the purse. It is bulky and makes shaking hands awkward. Use your pockets for essentials like car keys, business card, and lipstick. If you need to bring handouts or more items, consider using a black or burgundy leather portfolio, which looks more professional and can easily be set down on a table as you mingle. The portfolio can carry small items, as well, but if you must take a purse, choose a small bag that won't get in the way.

FIGURE 2.1 Dress for success guidelines for women

Dress for success for men:

- Dark-colored, single-breasted suits such as blues, grays, and black are the most professional "power" suits available. Choose quality fabrics, such as 100 percent wool, and avoid synthetic fabrics.

- With a suit, wear a white shirt with an undershirt. White shirts are perceived as conveying honesty, intelligence, and stability. Pinstripes are acceptable if not too "wild." In less formal settings, a solid, light blue shirt can work, but white is best.

- Choose a standard short-sleeve white undershirt with a round collar. V-neck and tank top undershirts are best left for home use.

- Ties allow the expression of your personality, within limits. A 100 percent silk tie is best in a solid color or with muted stripes or paisleys. A tie should extend just to your trouser belt, with the front of the tie always being longer than the back of the tie. Avoid having a tie hang down over the belt or dangle far above it. Knot it properly.

- Dress shoes should preferably be made of black leather, but dark maroon is also acceptable. Make sure your shoes have a nice shine to them. Polish them regularly. The style most noted for professionalism is lace-up wing tips or slip-ons with a tassel that can work in either formal or informal settings. Choose a matching colored belt.

- Socks should be the same color as the trousers, well-fitted, and long enough to not show skin when seated.

- Avoid cologne and make sure you have a fresh shave.

- Wear only a wedding ring and small subdued cuff links, if you like. Leave all other jewelry at home. (I would add my personal opinion here: If you are a married man, wear your wedding ring! I continue to be baffled at the number of good Christian men who refuse to wear a wedding ring. What message are you sending to the women of your district? Send them a message of marital commitment and fidelity by wearing your ring.)

- Invest in several pairs of khaki-colored twill pants and a navy sports coat. They will come in handy on the day-to-day campaign trail of informal meetings and gatherings.

FIGURE 2.2 Dress for success guidelines for men

Besides clothes, now is time to take stock of other aspects of your appearance that make an impression. Look in the mirror. How's the posture? Are you overdue for a haircut or new hairdo? Do you walk quickly or slowly? Do you look people in the eye when talking or look down at your shoes? How's the handshake? Limp? Firm? Pinched? When you speak, what does your voice project? Timidity? Arrogance? Confidence?

Answering these questions takes some honest reflection on your part. Employ close friends and family members who love you enough to tell you the truth to help you fine-tune your image. Details count and can make a big difference in the impression someone gets from meeting you. The goal is to allow your dress and mannerisms to enhance your message rather than to detract. Simple changes can pay big dividends in the end. Look the part.

Do a light check

Assessing and updating your "outside" image may take some time and effort. In the end, though, it will pay big dividends.

But just as important, is assessing and shoring up your "inside" reality. People will meet you and look at you, and as you shake their hands or speak to them, your eyes will be communicating something far more important than your verbal message. They will be revealing who you are, how you feel about yourself, and how you feel about others.

Luke 11:34–35 says, "Your eye is the lamp of your body. When your eyes are good, your whole body also is full of light. But when they are bad, your body also is full of darkness. See to it, then, that the light within you is not darkness."

A sixteenth century proverb was a variation of Jesus' words in Luke, "Eyes are the mirrors of the soul."

A person can pretend to be someone he or she is not by changing his clothes or polishing her style. But rarely can he or she cover up who he or she really is inside. Light (or darkness) shines through the eyes. The values, beliefs, and heart that make us tick are more important than what people see on the outside.

When Samuel went to anoint a new king for Israel and tried to assess which one God had chosen, the Lord said to him, "The LORD does not look at the things man looks at. Man looks at the outward appearance, but the LORD looks at the heart" (1 Sam. 16:7b).

So, what is in your heart? Why are you really running for office? Is it to gain an important title? Increase your fame? Get back at someone? Show someone you can do it who once criticized you? Increase your self-esteem?

Is there sin or darkness inside your "window" that can come forth and needs to be repented of and removed?

Or are you running because you care about an issue and want to take a stand for righteousness? Do you want to impact your culture? Do you genuinely care about the people of your district? Do you like people? Are you willing to sacrifice your time and resources to serve the people of your area? Do you want to serve God and others through public service?

Now is the time to take stock of your motives. James 4:2–3 reveals, "You do not have, because you do not ask God. When you ask, you do not receive, because you ask with wrong motives. . . ."

Everyone wants to win when he or she files for office. Make sure your motives are right and then your eyes will reflect your pure heart. Others will notice. Your eyes will shine forth who you are and, hopefully, be a reflection of the Father's love. There's no greater image than that.

Chapter 3

Putting Together your Team

Absalom had fifty of them. David attracted four hundred. Gideon only needed three hundred. Noah relied on a handful of family members, and Jesus changed the world with the dedication of twelve.

What are we talking about? Volunteers—the basic foundation for all initiatives. Nehemiah accomplished the monumental task of rebuilding the wall of Jerusalem by organizing volunteers. Battles were won, cities were rebuilt, Noah's ark was erected, and the gospel was spread with the aid of ordinary people who were called by God and dedicated to the task. Certainly God is sovereign and can accomplish goals without the use of human intervention, but the Bible shows us that most of the time, He prefers to use people.

We weren't meant to go it alone in this world. No matter what the task, two hands are better than one. Likewise, no candidate can go it alone and hope to win. Volunteers are vital. They are the individuals who provide the hands to get things done, the feet to accomplish tasks, the mouths to help spread the message, the hearts to care about the campaign, and the knees to wrestle in prayer for you. They are the important partners you need to be successful.

With an enthusiastic team of volunteers, much can be gained.

Benefits of volunteers

1. Volunteers multiply your support. Every volunteer translates into from five to one hundred votes on election day. The volunteer will vote for you and usually bring a minimum of five family votes with her. Depending upon her circle of influence, the vote count could go up to as high as a hundred.

Volunteers have to believe in you and your campaign in order to invest their time assisting you. Because of their investment of time and energy, their efforts become the focus of numerous conversations among their peers. This kind of word-of-mouth advertising is the best kind you can get. A person will support you if someone he or she respects knows you and puts in a good word for you. This is ten times better than hearing about you via a newspaper article, advertisement, or direct mail piece.

2. Volunteers save resources. Money and time are the two critical resources of any campaign. You never seem to have enough of either. Volunteers can make the final difference in whether or not a campaign can reach its potential. Allowing others to help organize and oversee projects enables you to have the time to go meet the voters or raise needed funds. Using volunteer teams of partners to stamp and stuff envelopes frees up revenue that might have been lost to big mail-order houses. In addition, utilizing volunteers accomplishes another important function . . .

3. Volunteering garners ownership in the campaign—and its outcome. Investing time, energy, and effort into your campaign enables a volunteer to become a "team member." By spending hours "sweating" and "working out" on individual drills during "practice," volunteers become acutely aware of the nature and importance of the "big game" and care about their fellow "teammates" and "head coach." They want to win just as badly as you do and agonize with you if there is a defeat. These kinds of "teammates" are what every candidate longs for and needs. They are the biggest blessings of a campaign.

I remember the blessing of a volunteer one cold, rainy election day during my fourth year in office when I was running for re-election. The day mirrored the mood of the past few months during which my opponent had chosen to wage a negative campaign filled with half-truths and distortions. I had chosen to not respond and to "stay the course" with my positive message, but it had not been easy.

The ultimate blow came the night before the election when my mother called me to tell me she had just received a horrific piece of campaign literature in the mail directed against me. The 8-1/2" x 11" four-page, color, glossy direct mail piece featured a front-page picture of a pig lying in bed under a red satin sheet with money sticking out from under the mattress, with a bedside table full of books with titles including: *Back Scratching Success, Lobbyists Influential, Government Waste 101, and Personal Pay Raise Journal,* a stack of IOUs on the nightstand, and a To Do List that included: Breakfast with Lobbyist, Brunch with Lobbyist, Lunch with Lobbyist, Nap with Lobbyist, Cocktail Party, Get Elected, and Party with Lobbyists. The title said, "When it comes to helping Missouri families . . . Vicki (spelled wrong!) Hartzler helps herself first." Inside was a picture of a sow with a litter of pigs suckling up to her and paragraphs of text spewing allegations and misrepresentations of me and my voting record. Many have said that it was the worst campaign literature they had ever seen distributed on a candidate. Depending upon where a voter lived, the piece arrived the day before or the day of the election, leaving no chance to respond.

On Election Day I stood at polling sites under my umbrella trying to stay warm and remain positive as voters scurried into the building. One of the biggest blessings of the day occurred in mid-afternoon when Liz arrived. She was one of my volunteers for the campaign and one of the sweetest women I knew. A mother of four young boys and a youth minister with her husband at our church, Liz always exuded such patience, caring, and love of the Lord. I always marveled at her sweetness, compassion, and soft-spoken ways.

I didn't notice her at first as I was facing the opposite direction from the parking lot, but when I turned around, I was shocked by what I saw. A new Liz, filled with righteous anger, was marching toward me with the campaign flier in her fisted hand. When she arrived, her blazing eyes locked mine. She slapped the flier with her free hand and said, "This is the worst piece of campaign trash I have ever seen! I just got home and got it in the mail and I AM SO MAD!"

With that she grabbed me in a bear hug with strength more reflective of a professional wrestler than the petite mother I knew, pivoted, and marched into the election poll.

That kind of volunteer—partners, teammates, and friends—makes campaigning worthwhile. These people are the wind under your wings—the fuel that helps keep your spirits burning brightly no matter what storms come your way. With these types of friends on your side, you are the winner—no matter the final vote tally.

4. Volunteers help share the load. Without volunteers you can easily become buried under the weight of all that must be done. Sharing the load enables big tasks to be broken down into smaller, more manageable pieces. It allows others to contribute their gifts and talents to your campaign. It enables you to have the strength and energy you need to complete the race.

I remember coming home from my first campaign school feeling overwhelmed. In one short day, I had accumulated a four-inch ring binder stuffed with information, a notepad of notes frantically scrawled during numerous lectures by experts, a pocketful of business cards from people who offered to give suggestions and advice if I needed them, and a head full of frazzled knowledge gained from being on the receiving end of a shotgun blast of information.

During the three-hour drive home, my mind swirled. *Where do I begin? What do I do? How do I do it? How can I do it all by myself?* A feeling of vulnerability swept over me, along with a humbling realization that I would need to ask for help. I certainly didn't mind having others assist me, and I welcomed any help I could get, but

I didn't know where to start. Who would want to help me? What jobs could they do? How should I garner their help? During the following weeks, I found out several valuable ways I want to pass along to you.

Ways to secure volunteer partners

1. Develop a prospect list. Think of those who might be willing to help you. Consider recruiting the types of people God brought to Nehemiah to help him complete his task of rebuilding the wall of Jerusalem. In the third chapter of Nehemiah, the writer lists all the individuals and groups of people who made the vision a reality in Nehemiah's campaign. As I looked over this list, I was amazed to see how similar Nehemiah's groups of workers were to the types of individuals who made my campaign work. Consider the following:

*Religious leaders (*priests* in verses 1, 17, 22)—Key pastors in the area, elders, and deacons understood the moral implications involved in elections and were a source of wisdom, encouragement, and help.

*Small business owners (*merchants* in v. 32)—They supported my pro-business convictions and were willing to help.

*Church workers (*temple servants* in v. 26)—Those who gave their time to serve God were willing to share their time as I strove to serve God through answering His call to public service.

*Fellow elected officials (*rulers* in verses 14–17)—People willing to run for office themselves understand the importance of good government policy and what is at stake for their jurisdiction as a result of elections. They are familiar with campaigns and might be willing to help you. Consider enlisting school board members, county officeholders, fire, sewer, hospital, and water district board members, commission members, and other elected officials.

*Law enforcement (*the guard* of v. 29)—While many cannot openly campaign due to non-partisan service laws, they can be tremendous advocates through word-of-mouth campaigning.

*Families (*father and his daughters* in v. 12)—Your family will probably be your number one base of volunteers. More will be said in later chapters about the importance of family in your campaign, but, like David in 1 Samuel 22:1, it is vital that your family be with you throughout this endeavor.

The Bible says, "David left Gath and escaped to the cave of Adullam. When his brothers and his father's household heard about it, they went down to him there." Your family needs to rally around you, too. If your family does not support your efforts, you should rethink your decision to run. You need to be unified to be successful and to honor the Lord.

In addition, consider families you know who share your values and beliefs and who might be willing to work with you. They can be of tremendous help to you when you need it most.

Several families got involved in my campaigns. Some put up yard signs in their neighborhood or walked with me in parades. Others made phone calls. Several families helped label tens of thousands of direct mail pieces during the final days of the campaign. All were a blessing to me. Families working together can accomplish great things.

*Individual workers (numerous "sons of . . ." throughout Nehemiah 3)—Chapter 3 lists two specific occupations—perfume makers (v. 8) and goldsmiths (verses 8 and 31–32), but anyone willing to work hard will be an asset. People who are busy and who get things done are the ones who can "make it happen" for you, too. In addition, individuals who are retired and have more time to devote to other things can be wonderful additions to your team. Consider reaching out to involve them.

*Individuals who might want a change are often motivated to volunteer.

The types of individuals initially attracted to David when he was in hiding are described in I Samuel 22:2. "All those who were in distress or in debt or discontented gathered around him, and he became their leader. About four hundred men were with him." People who recognize a problem through their personal life experiences or who are discontented with the status quo have the motivation to work. Seek them out. Involve them. Give them an opportunity to make a difference for themselves and others. Action is a great anecdote for frustration.

Absalom targeted those who had a complaint and were already concerned enough about their situation to find the courage and energy needed to travel to Jerusalem and present their complaint before the king. They weren't just thinking about doing something to make things better. They had committed themselves to seeking a solution. They were already people of action. They were won over by Absalom because he was out working and promised a better way.

Only you know the current political climate of the office you are seeking, but no doubt there are policies or laws that some would like to see changed and areas of discontent that serve as motivators to get them involved. Now that you are committed to running and want to bring positive change in those areas, find others who share your desires, and recruit them to work together on your team.

*Don't disregard anyone. Nehemiah reached out and included people from all over the area—other towns, the country, and within areas of Jerusalem. Candidates often initially only think of involving close family members or only people in their geographic area, when there are many others who could and should be tapped.

Young people are often overlooked but can be some of the most willing, enthusiastic workers on your campaign. In addition, their involvement gives you the opportunity to make a lasting impression on their young lives. They will always remember helping you in your campaign. Taking the time to invite them to help can boost their self-esteem and even plant seeds of involvement that might reap political benefits in years to come. Who knows but that the twelve-year-old envelope stuffer might become a U.S. senator someday? Or a pastor who encourages his congregation to get involved at election time?

Or a corporate executive willing to contribute needed money to good candidates? Or a housewife willing to help organize a campaign for a friend in the future?

When I was about ten years old, a friend of my mother called and asked if my sister and I would be willing to walk in our local town parade carrying signs promoting a certain man campaigning for state senator. It took a lot of thinking and a lot of questions before I was willing to do it. You want me to do what? Who is he? What does a state senator do? What will carrying a sign accomplish? Why does he want our help? Why is it important that he win?

It was my first political parade. He won the election and years later, after I was elected, I saw him in the State Capitol in his new role as government relations director for an area community college. I often look back on that first political experience as a volunteer and believe it planted seeds of curiosity and knowledge about the importance of the political involvement, which later bore fruit. You, too, can create such a legacy for someone else.

A friend of mine shared a terrific idea: host a lunch for the youth pastors in your district. Use it as an opportunity to bless them for the important work they do in the community and also to let them know about your campaign and your vision of giving area young people an opportunity to learn about the political process. The youth pastors may connect you to some wonderful young people who will become not only energetic volunteers, but also future leaders.

2. Ask! You have not, because you ask not. There are not many people who have actually volunteered with a campaign, but my experience has shown that more would help if asked. Many people are willing to help if they are given the opportunity.

One of your primary tasks as a candidate is to recruit volunteers (partners). Others can ask for you and that might get a handful of willing workers, but you are the one person they need to hear from. You are the one they are working for/with. God can lay the groundwork in their hearts and help them be willing to participate, but it usually takes your intervention before they will get involved.

Jesus recruited His twelve disciples Himself. He personally interacted with them and called them to service. You can do the same.

There are four common ways to recruit: in person, via letter, through a mass invitation at a political event, and by way of another person connected with the campaign.

In person is most effective. Look over your prospect list and contact them. Ask for their help. To be most effective, have a job already in mind which you want them to do and ask them to do it. Tell them four basic things: specific instructions of what the job entails, what is expected, the amount of time and energy which will need to be expended to complete the task, and the expected timeline to accomplish the goal. This helps give a realistic picture of what saying "Yes" will mean to them and their family. Make sure to relate what their involvement means to you and to the campaign and why it is so important they come aboard. You need them, and together you hope to make a real difference.

If you send a blanket letter asking for support and help, include a Volunteer Recruitment Card where individuals can check boxes indicating their willingness to help in various areas. The card can be the size of a postcard with your return address and postage box printed on the back, or the volunteer form can be printed on the back flap of a return envelope which is included with the letter. The envelope serves two purposes: as a volunteer card and as a medium to send a contribution.

In my first campaign, I printed hundreds of cards. These were included in letters and given out at my kickoff banquet. In subsequent campaigns, I utilized the envelope method.

Below is a sample card that could be tailored to your campaign needs:

John Doe for County Sheriff

Volunteer Form

NAME: _____

ADDRESS: _____

CITY, STATE, ZIP CODE: _____

HOME PHONE: _____ CELL PHONE: _____

E-MAIL: _____

YES! John can count on my support in the following ways:

☐ Put a Yard Sign in my yard ☐ Will put up Yard Signs

☐ Help with mailings ☐ Make phone calls

☐ Go door-to-door ☐ Write letters to the editor

☐ Hold a neighborhood coffee ☐ Contribute funds

Paid for by
John Doe for County Sheriff, Susie Smith, Treasurer

FIGURE 3.1 Sample volunteer form

Print a few cards prior to holding a banquet or kickoff rally. They can be distributed and referred to in your speech as you invite people to participate in your campaign.

Any way you do it, the most important thing to remember is to ask.

3. Pay them to work. This appears to be the method Absalom used. Second Samuel 15:1 says, "In the course of time, Absalom provided himself with a chariot and horses and with fifty men to run ahead of him. . . ." The Living Bible says he *hired* fifty footmen to run ahead of him.

While many campaigns do this—and sometimes it is necessary, especially in bigger campaigns—this is the least desirable method in my opinion. Loyalty, dedication, friendship, and the uniting of purpose which comes from working together only occurs if you are giving from your heart.

That's why a volunteer team is often an indication of the health of a campaign. The candidate with an army of willing volunteers will win any day over a candidate with a payroll of workers.

A story from a friend's campaign emphasizes this point. He was running against a very well-funded attorney for state representative. The attorney *paid* young people to be poll workers. Conversely, my friend organized an outstanding volunteer base and had them at the polls at the same time. The two groups began to talk. When the attorney's workers revealed that they were being paid, several voters overheard. They were not impressed. My friend won the race even though he only raised $40,000 compared to his opponent's $100,000. Volunteers can be more effective than dollars.

There are reasons some candidates prefer paying workers, however. As an "employer" you can manage "employees" more easily, ensure higher quality work, and discharge them, if need be.

As a candidate, you have to weigh the advantages and disadvantages of paying workers or utilizing volunteers. For me, the advantages of involving volunteers in my campaign far outweighed any disadvantages. Of course, you also could use a combination. You could involve volunteers whenever possible, and hire mailing houses to do certain projects.

4. Pray for willing workers. You have not, because you ask not. Ask God to provide all that you need, and He will according to His glorious riches in Christ Jesus.

Pray that God would send many "Baruchs." In Nehemiah 3's listing of all the workers, one stands out. Verse 20 says that Baruch son of Zabbai "zealously" repaired another section of the wall. Others may have, too, but Baruch was the only one who joined into the effort with an extra amount of zeal worthy of notation in the Scriptures. Webster's Dictionary defines zeal as, "eagerness and ardent interest in pursuit of something: fervor, passion."[1] Pray God sends many with zeal for your campaign.

Pray that God would send "mighty men (and women)" to fight alongside you like He provided for David in 2 Samuel 23:8–39.

Great things were accomplished by these dedicated warriors. Every candidate needs mighty men and women.

And finally, pray that the volunteer team God helps put together for you would be like Nehemiah's who accomplished things quickly ". . . for the people worked with all their heart" (Neh. 4:6).

With this kind of unity and God's blessing, nothing will be impossible for you.

Jobs for volunteers

There are numerous opportunities to involve volunteers. Committees can be formed around a certain function with a chairman, assistant chairman, and deputy. Titles of workers can be posted on the bulletin board at your headquarters. Typical jobs include:

*Prayer partners—These individuals are perhaps the most important volunteers of your campaign, those saints willing to do battle for you in the heavenlies. These people are the ones who move mountains and enable political miracles to happen.

*Yard sign chairmen—Being in charge of putting up and taking down yard signs on a given list you have put together.

*Mailing team member—Affixing labels to direct mail cards; folding, stuffing, sealing, addressing, and stamping letters; sorting pieces by zip code for bulk mail purposes; counting pieces; filling out the bulk mail form; and transporting the mailings to the post office.

*Phoning—Calling voters to survey their concerns, taking a straw poll, or reminding likely voters of the importance of voting on election day.

*Fundraisers—Volunteering to raise money for you through their contacts.

*Organizers of special events—Whether you are holding a fundraising banquet with a high-profile speaker or a fun barbeque to generate enthusiasm for "the cause," it is extremely helpful to have those who will take charge of planning and securing the meal, decorating, selling tickets, coordinating with speakers/entertainment/emcee, and lining up workers for the event to check people in upon arrival, hand out bumper stickers, and collect volunteer cards.

*Information gatherers—Securing names of individuals in targeted groups (i.e., church rosters, gun owners, pro-life members, children's advocates, senior citizens, organization members) for "list" purposes; getting voting frequency/history of likely voters in your district; clipping newspaper articles, and analyzing voting patterns of your precincts.

*Computer workers—Entering lists of names of potential campaign supporters, typing your campaign plan, and designing brochures, ads, and direct mail pieces. Also, today it's common to have a Web site. You need someone to design and manage your Web site and/or run your e-mail campaign.

*Photographer—Someone knowledgeable with cameras who can take your important photos for the campaign.

*Opposition researcher—Finding out information about your opponent (strengths, weaknesses, past and current jobs, family situation, etc.); exploring voting history if an incumbent; listening for possible hints into what strategy your opponent might employ in his race for office.

*Artist—Design logo, yard signs, brochures, and other artistic endeavors.

*Parade chairmen—Plans theme, obtains decorations and outfits (usually a T-shirt), asks people to walk/participate in parade, secures vehicle, and thanks participants.

*Thank-you coordinator—I recommend writing your thank you's personally, but certainly someone can be given templates of thank you letters you have written for a specific purpose (fundraising, volunteering, etc.) and they can insert the name of the individual you give them and print out the letter for you to sign and address the envelope to save you time.

*Absentee ballot captain—Obtaining the names of individuals utilizing an absentee ballot in the past; sending them campaign information prior to the start of absentee voting asking them to vote for you; securing absentee ballot applications; sending likely individuals (i.e., college students, military officials) a letter from you asking for their support and sending them an absentee ballot application as a courtesy; going to nursing homes to offer the absentee ballot application to anyone interested and providing information about your candidacy.

*Door-to-door canvassers—People willing to go door to door with you or for you. They can also participate in literature drops in the final days of the campaign.

*Press release editor—Someone with writing skills who is able to write press releases for you and your campaign and be in charge of getting them to the local media in a timely, professional manner.

*Campaign headquarters volunteer

*Spokespersons—In the event you cannot make an appearance, someone whom you trust to share your message at an event or with the media.

*TV/radio spot chairman—For campaigns utilizing these mediums, it is vital you have someone else help write these spots if you are not familiar with them.

*Babysitter—For you, if needed, or others working on your campaign.

While not every campaign will need all these positions, the above list outlines typical jobs which are done in campaigns. Prioritize the jobs that are most important to your campaign and recruit volunteers accordingly, disregarding the ones you don't need.

Working with volunteers

As a candidate, you have three primary roles when it comes to volunteers. Your job is to: recruit, inspire/motivate, and thank them.

Recruitment has been discussed. Just as importantly, however, is to keep volunteers motivated. It is always good to remember that volunteers are just that: *volunteers*. They don't have to be there. They don't have to help you. There are many other demands for their time competing against your tasks, which they could just as easily do if they don't believe their efforts are part of something valuable. You must first sell your message to them before you can sell it to voters.

Ways to keep them involved include:

1. Communicate with them as vital partners throughout the campaign—and afterward! They are your inner circle who deserve to know what is going on—and *why* it is going on. This can be accomplished via meetings, a campaign newsletter, letters, in person, or through liaisons.

During my second and third campaigns, I set up volunteer teams with a team leader and head volunteer coordinator to help divide up and accomplish tasks. The team leader was also in charge of relaying information if I needed something shared quickly with my volunteer team. The system worked great and helped spread the load.

Mostly, though, I tried to visit with volunteers on an individual basis as I came into contact with them, which brings me to my second point:

2. Know your volunteers and what they are doing to help you. If someone you don't know (but who was on one of the lists you compiled) sends in a return volunteer card, call him or her and thank him/her for volunteering. Visit with him or her. Find out his/her background and interests. Ask about his or her family. Embrace this person as a new volunteer member and ask God to help you remember his or her name/personal information when you meet at a future volunteer event. Make notes on the card during the conversation to help you. There's nothing like the personal touch to help avoid a candidate's embarrassment when introducing him/herself to someone and asking for his/her support only to have the person tell the candidate he or she helped stuff envelopes for him/her last weekend.

3. Seek their counsel/input as true partners. Proverbs 24:6 says, "For waging war you need guidance, and for victory, many advisors."

Likewise, Proverbs 20:18 says, "Make plans by seeking advice; if you wage war, obtain guidance."

You need your volunteers' expertise, ideas, and advice. Conversely, volunteers feel needed and appreciated when asked for their opinions. It's a win-win.

Holding regular steering committee meetings is a great way to do this. State Representative Brian Baker believes this is a great way to enhance communication, as well. "Six months out I would have staff meetings once a week for four months. Two months out, we would meet every other week. One month out I would meet weekly with my volunteer leaders or staff team. These meetings were a wonderful resource for me and made a tremendous difference on Election Day."[2]

4. Troubleshoot and motivate. Nehemiah did a masterful job of this in Chapter 4. Their project had met opposition like most campaigns do. Nehemiah quickly assessed the situation, took corrective action, and encouraged the workers. When campaign attacks come, it is important to the health and future of the effort that the candidate seek God, take charge, communicate with the volunteers, and encourage them.

Volunteers aren't as prepared for negative attacks as you are. They haven't been privy to all the insider campaign information about likely tactics of your opponent. They want to know what your plan is for dealing with the attacks and what they can do to help. They want to hear encouraging words about your confidence in the final result.

Be ready for this type of communication. It could mean the difference between volunteers becoming discouraged and disassociated or being ready and able to do battle for you in the final days.

5. Make work fun! Having drinks and snacks available makes work projects more enjoyable. Music playing adds to the festive atmosphere. Tell jokes. Laugh a little. While the campaign cause is serious, you don't have to be; nor should assisting you be drudgery.

You are the spark plug others gain energy from. Your attitude sets the tone for their perspective. Think positively. Remember God is in control, remind them of this fact, and enjoy the ride together.

6. Thank them. Thank them. Thank them. Thank them early and thank them often. Try to thank them for each task they do throughout the campaign—not just a blanket letter at the end, although that is certainly better than none.

I tried to send a note card of thanks to all involved workers after each major project. Only a few sentences are needed to let them know you are aware of their efforts, that they are appreciated, and that you couldn't do it without them. If people feel appreciated, they will continue to expend effort on your behalf. If they feel used or ignored, they will find better uses of their time.

It is especially important to thank them after the campaign is over—win or lose. This can be done through a personal letter, note, phone call, or in person. Thanking them is one of the best ways to ensure they will help you again in future campaigns.

7. Recognize them. Pins, certificates, free tickets to fundraising events, invitations to your inauguration, holding a complimentary banquet in their honor, and mentioning them by name/having them stand for recognition at a banquet are some good ways to let team members know they are special to you.

Organization models

Organization is the key to mobilizing volunteers. People need to be divided up and given a leader in order to accomplish tasks.

King David won back the kingdom from Absalom by organizing an army and mounting a military campaign to conquer the incumbent. Second Samuel 18:1–2 shows how he did this:

> David mustered the men who were with him and appointed over them commanders of thousands and commanders of hundreds. David sent the troops out—a third under the command of Joab,

a third under Joab's brother Abishai son of Zuruiah, and a third under Ittai the Gittite.

Your campaign should do the same. There are three models of organizing your campaign volunteer teams that are most commonly used by candidates. One is the precinct approach. Another is the project approach. In addition, there is the combination approach. All can work successfully. You need to decide what approach would work best for you. Then get organized.

The precinct approach

The precinct approach involves finding key people in all the precincts of your political district. You, or a campaign manager, give the precinct captains various duties they are responsible for. They recruit people under them to help carry out the tasks. When a needed project comes up, the campaign manager contacts the precinct captains and shares with them what needs to be done and when. They carry this out. The campaign manager can either be a volunteer or paid campaign staff.

Typical tasks precinct captains are asked to head up include: going door to door during a certain timeframe; working the campaign phone bank certain nights; finding locations for yard signs and big signs and putting them up when the time arrives; getting volunteers to participate in parades and other events; and recruiting volunteers to help put together mailers.

The precinct approach might look like this:

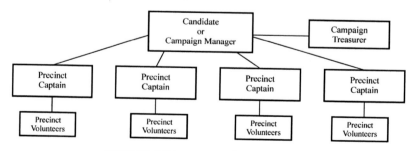

FIGURE 3.2 Precinct volunteer model

The precinct approach also could be modified to involve teams of volunteers with a team leader. The leaders would not need to be from certain parts of your district. They would just be key leaders in your campaign, and volunteers would be assigned to them to accomplish major tasks when called upon.

For example, if it was time to stick mailing labels on your direct mail pieces and the project was going to take three days, a different team leader would be responsible for finding workers and overseeing the project each day.

The project approach

The project approach involves finding a captain or leader for the specific events your campaign wants to conduct. This person's job is to organize and carry out the initiative using the volunteers who have signed up to help with that particular type of project.

The project leaders make up a "Campaign Steering Committee" that meets with you on a regular basis. It is like a Board of Directors in a corporation or organization.

Its structure might look something like this:

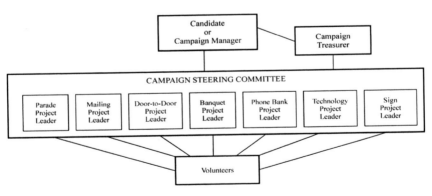

FIGURE 3.3 Project volunteer model

The combination approach

A variation of the above models is to combine them. For instance, leaders would be found for the basic projects like the project approach, but precinct captains would be found and utilized for certain projects such as signage, door to door, and phone banks. This model would look something like this:

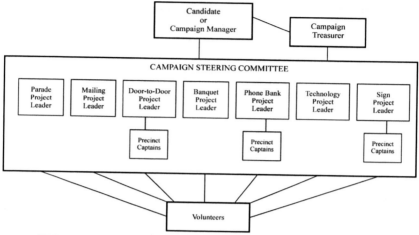

FIGURE 3.4 Combination precinct and project volunteer model

Whichever model you choose, it helps if you use some common sense and biblical advice for working with your volunteers.

With dedicated volunteers you, too, will be able to win battles, complete projects, and change your world for the better.

CHAPTER 4

DEVELOPING YOUR MESSAGE

Campaigns are the same everywhere. You've got to define a message and find a way to communicate it."

These are the words of longtime political consultant Joe Napolitan.[1] His statement conveys long-standing political truth. No matter where you are, or the time in history when you are running for office, the fact remains that the essential elements of a campaign revolve around defining a message and then communicating it.

But what message do you use? Absalom was taking on an incumbent (King David) when he campaigned. His message involved three principles:

1. Affirm people's concerns;
2. Point out opponent's weakness(es); and
3. Tell how you would do things differently if you were in charge.

When people approached Jerusalem with a complaint to be placed before the king, Absalom would say, "Look, your claims are valid and proper, but there is no representative of the king to hear you" (2 Sam. 15:3). He affirmed their concern and then pointed out David's weakness that there was no one available to hear their concerns.

This is one of the most expressed criticisms against politicians today—"They don't listen." "They didn't respond when I wrote them." "They only care about serving themselves." The candidate who truly wants to be responsive to the people (and who hopes to be elected) will listen to his constituents both now during the campaign and later after the election.

After Absalom pointed out his opponent's weakness, he went on to explain how he would do things differently if he were in leadership. "And Absalom would add, 'If only I were appointed judge in the land! Then everyone who has a complaint or case could come to me and I would see that he gets justice'" (2 Sam. 15:4).

He told how he would resolve their problems. He also promised that *everyone* with a complaint or case would get justice. Perhaps this is the first example of an empty campaign promise because the reality of cases and complaints is that one side usually wins and one side loses. Sometimes you can find a compromise that pleases everyone, but usually someone leaves feeling more "justified" than another. As a Christian candidate, make sure you don't fall into the trap of promising *everything* to *everybody*. There is only so much one person can do. Therefore, think through what campaign issues you are going to feature using both knowledge and integrity.

Develop your campaign platform

How do you decide which campaign issues to promote? How do you develop your campaign message? By talking with the people you will represent. As Robert Thomas says in his book How to Run for Local Office, "Don't make the mistake of just automatically thinking that the issues that are important to you are important to the majority of voters."[2] You have to be willing to do what Absalom did: get up early, go meet the voters, and listen to their concerns. Ask people what ideas they have to improve the area of government you would be representing. If running for sheriff, you could ask, "How do you think law enforcement could be improved in our area? What are the concerns you have for the safety of your family? How do you think the sheriff's department could better respond to your concerns?"

Visit with both individual voters you meet and leaders in the community. Make appointments with community leaders to get their ideas for ways to improve the government or hear community concerns. Attend city council meetings and school board meetings to learn what is going on. Ask your friends their opinions on the relevant issues of the day. Stop to talk to strangers at community events or go door to door to get their ideas. Seek out the input from area barbers and hair stylists as they often have a good feel for the concerns of the people in your community.

In addition, drive your district. Chris Benjamin, Chief of Staff for Missouri House Speaker Rod Jetton, advises that one of the best ways to get a visual feel for your district is to drive it. "Get a map of your district and drive around it to familiarize yourself with the people and places you are going to serve. You'll become familiar with the neighborhoods and better understand the issues when you talk with them."[3]

Another way to solicit input is through phone surveys. Campaigns for major offices have made this a science, spending large amounts of money for political firms to survey voters. You don't have to spend thousands, however, to carry out a phone survey. Just develop a small questionnaire and recruit volunteers to call a small sample of voters.

Longtime political consultant S. J. Guzzetta, in his book *The Campaign Manual,* recommends contacting one-tenth of one percent of the district's population in order to get a good sample.[4] So if you are running for sheriff and your county has a population of 65,000, then your goal should be to survey 650 people. He also recommends using female volunteers to do the calling as their voices are less threatening than a male's unknown voice.[5] Call every tenth household in the area phone book[6] or, better yet, use a list of registered voters if you have it.

Below is a sample phone survey which might be useful for John Doe running for sheriff:

Sample Issue Survey Phone Script For Sheriff

"Hello, Mrs. Jones?" (Always verify who you are talking to so you'll know later if the information you obtain matches up with the name and address on your list.)

"This is Karen and we're conducting a short election survey tonight about law enforcement in our community and wondered if we could ask you a couple of questions? It will only take about three minutes."

If "No," then say, "Thank you anyway," and go to the next person.

If "Yes," then say, "Thank you.

1. What do you consider the most important danger to the families in our community?

   _____

2. How could law enforcement in our area do a better job to address this concern?

   _____

3. What needs do you see in the sheriff's department?

   _____

"Thank you for your time. This concludes the survey. Have a good evening."

FIGURE 4.1 Sample phone script to survey issues

Questions could also cover things the governmental entity is doing right or how they would rate the job performance of the person currently in office.

Name ID could also be surveyed at this time. Guzzetta recommends including your name in the list of people you ask about, along with your opponent's name, two or three community leaders, and a couple of fictitious names.[7] Ask whether or not the person has heard of people on a list you have compiled. This gives you an idea of how widely known you are compared to your opponent and how hard you are going to have to work to increase name ID before the election. If 50 percent of the voters surveyed say they recognize your name, then you have a 50 percent name ID. If 75 percent recognize your name, you have a 75 percent name ID. As Guzetta points out, "One of the few axioms in politics, all other things being equal, is that the candidate with the highest name ID rating will inevitably win."[8] Including a name ID question on your voter survey is one way to determine how you are doing compared to your opponent.

Once you have obtained the feedback of area voters, you are ready to choose the messages for your campaign. Candidates should choose three to five primary issues to highlight during the campaign along with three to five secondary issues for each targeted group they are trying to reach.

It is wise to research a variety of issues so that you are knowledgeable about a multitude of topics. Proverbs 24:5 relates, "A wise man has great power, and a man of knowledge increases strength." Knowledge is your strength as a candidate. Generally, a candidate who has more knowledge is more powerful. Bluffing won't carry a person very far. It is imperative to increase your knowledge as much as possible so you will be as strong as possible. Another Proverb reveals a common mistake enthusiastic candidates make: "It is not good to have zeal without knowledge, nor to be hasty and miss the way." Having zeal is not enough. Enthusiasm and commitment to change need to be backed up with knowledge.

Once you have researched the issues and increased your knowledge, pick your primary issues. These three to five primary issues will become the drumbeat of your campaign. They represent the themes you will hit over and over again so your campaign message is understood and heard loud and clear. Examples of primary issues include: "I am for better roads, accountability in government, and more money for our schools," or "If elected, I plan to fight for lower taxes, improved conditions for workers, and safer communities." A candidate for County Clerk might choose a theme like, "When elected, I plan to organize more efficient elections, increase voter registration in the county, and implement a streamlined early voting system."

Along with choosing three to five primary issue goals, you need to develop one to three action items you will implement to carry out these goals. If given a chance to explain your positions further, you can share the action items such as, "For better roads, we need more money and better management. I will introduce legislation to stop the flow of transportation dollars to other programs and make sure highway dollars go into asphalt and concrete. I also support improved auditing of the department to ensure every dollar is used wisely."

In order to be able to develop these all-important themes, you will have to do the research necessary to become an expert in them. The process begins by asking yourself some questions:

1. What issues are of concern to the voters in my community? Perhaps you have a power plant going up in your area that has the community concerned. Maybe there have been a high number of automobile accidents on the dangerous roads in your area or a number of methamphetamine drug busts. Consider problems related to schools, crime, homes, finances, jobs, values, and corruption in government, youth, or the environment. What threats are there to the people of your area? Do they recognize it as a threat? Will they be receptive to your solutions? Use the knowledge you have gained from visiting with the voters to answer these questions.

2. What areas of expertise do you have to offer the community? Are you a teacher who can bring your experience in the classroom to new education policy? Are you a business owner who knows how to balance a budget and believes the

government should do the same? Are you a skilled worker who has seen corruption firsthand in corporate America and wants to speak up for the working man or woman? Are you a parent who understands the threats to the youth of our country and wants to develop policies to protect them? Know your strengths.

3. What will be your opponent's issues? While you may or may not decide to feature the same issues in your campaign, it is important to know your position on your opponent's platform. Voters like a contrast. If you can find an issue where you and your opponent are diametrically opposed, you might consider highlighting it during the campaign.

4. Do a four-corner analysis with your campaign team. Chris Benjamin recommends this method, which is easy to do, yet yields substantial insights.[9] Take a large poster board and divide it into four squares. Brainstorm with the group answering the questions in the squares, then vote on the top three things the group believes should be emphasized in the campaign. These themes not only can become the basis of your campaign message, but also can be helpful in developing your slogan.

The four-corner analysis for Candidate John Doe for Sheriff might look like this:

What we want voters to think of John Doe when they go to vote on election day.	What our *opponent* will want voters to think of John Doe when they go to vote on election day.
What we want voters to think of our opponent when they go to vote on election day.	What our *opponent* will want voters to think about him or her when they go to vote on election day.

FIGURE 4.2 Sample four-corner analysis

5. What do you feel passionately about? You should not rely solely on polls or the newspaper to determine what you want to feature in a campaign or do while in office. You need to know not only the pulse of your district, but also the heartbeat of what makes you tick. What do you care about? You should incorporate your passions, your calling. Promote those things God has laid on your heart and that motivate you, those things you are willing to fight for. Be true to yourself, and your campaign will ring true.

During my first campaign for state representative, my primary issues were stated on the back of my pushcard and repeated throughout my campaign:

"As our representative, Vicky Hartzler will:

- *Push for education reforms which are academically-proven and student-centered.*
- *Speak out for family values.*
- *Promote sensible solutions to health care concerns.*
- *Say NO to taxes without a vote of the people.*
- *Fight for less government in our lives and our businesses."*

Later in the campaign, direct mail cards were developed based on these themes. Each card expounded on the original issue and outlined my action items. The Education card read:

"Vicky's Plan for Improving Our Schools

- *Preserve local control.*
- *Fight for fair education funding.*
- *Raise standards and emphasize basics.*
- *Promote vocational education that prepares kids for jobs upon graduation.*
- *Reward excellence with incentives for schools that improve results and cut dropout rates.*

This is just one example of how to define and articulate campaign issues and action items. List your top campaign issues along with specific action items here:

My Primary Campaign Issues with Action Items

Issue 1: _____

    ACTION ITEMS:

        1. _____

        2. _____

        3. _____

Issue 2: _____

    ACTION ITEMS:

        1. _____

        2. _____

        3. _____

Issue 3: _____

    ACTION ITEMS:

        1. _____

        2. _____

        3. _____

Issue 4: _____

    ACTION ITEMS:

        1. _____

        2. _____

        3. _____

Issue 5: _____

    ACTION ITEMS:

        1. _____

        2. _____

        3. _____

FIGURE 4.3 Primary issue and action item box

Secondary messages are devised for a specific audience rather than the general population. These targeted groups could be senior citizens, the pro-life community, gun owners, families with young children, or businesses, for example. You need to consider what issues these groups might be interested in that differ from your general theme and then have this message prepared in case you have the opportunity to speak with that group or in case you want to send them a specific mailer outlining your platform.

Here are three hypothetical examples of secondary messages and action items developed for the targeted group "senior citizens" that could be used by candidates running for the offices of County Clerk and State Representative.

Example 1:

Election for:	County Clerk
Primary Campaign Issue:	Increase Voter Registration
Secondary Campaign Issue for senior citizens:	Easier Access to Elections
Action Item for this issue:	Ensure all election sites are handicap accessible and at ground level.

Example 2:

Election for:	State Representative
Primary Campaign Issue:	Proven Leadership
Secondary Campaign Issue for senior citizens:	Reduce tax burden for senior citizens
Action Item for this issue:	Propose legislation exempting Social Security benefits from income taxation.

Choose two groups you would like to target. Develop three secondary messages for each group along with corresponding action items and write them in the boxes below.

My Secondary Campaign Issues with Action Items for Targeted Groups

Targeted Group 1: _____

    Issue One: _____

    ACTION ITEMS:

        1. _____

        2. _____

        3. _____

    Issue Two: _____

    ACTION ITEMS:

        1. _____

        2. _____

        3. _____

    Issue Three: _____

    ACTION ITEMS:

        1. _____

        2. _____

        3. _____

Targeted Group 2: _____

    Issue One: _____

    ACTION ITEMS:

        1. _____

        2. _____

        3. _____

```
┌─────────────────────────────────────────────────┐
│                                                 │
│   Issue Two: _____  │
│   ACTION ITEMS:                                 │
│   1. _____   │
│   2. _____   │
│   3. _____   │
│                                                 │
│   Issue Three: _____  │
│   ACTION ITEMS:                                 │
│   1. _____   │
│   2. _____   │
│   3. _____   │
│                                                 │
└─────────────────────────────────────────────────┘
```

FIGURE 4.4 Secondary issues and action item box

Now that you have defined your campaign issues, you need to become an expert on them. Research and study every angle of the issue. Read all you can. Talk to individuals who are working in the areas of concern. Seek out their expertise. Visit with current officeholders. Do your homework. Know the costs, advantages, disadvantages, current policy, and history of the issue. Be able to explain your position and *why* you have that position. Be ready to explain it succinctly and persuasively.

Paul advises Timothy to "Be prepared in season and out of season" (1 Tim. 4:2). Peter writes, "Always be prepared to give an answer to everyone who asks you to give the reason for the hope that you have (1 Pet. 3:15).

This advice not only serves you well while sharing the gospel. It also is important as you hit the campaign trail. People will want to know where you stand on issues and why you believe the way you do. They will notice a difference between a candidate who is just running to get a title and one who knows the issues, has solutions to timely problems, and who will be an effective leader, once elected. Take time now to study and practice articulating your message. Time spent developing your campaign platform will pay off in the end.

CHAPTER 5

SHARING YOUR MESSAGE THROUGH A SPEECH

You are ready to start sharing your message. You have visited with the people of your area, identified the issues, researched the concerns, and developed action items, but where do you begin?

One of the most common methods of conveying your message is through giving a speech. For some people this is fun. But for most individuals, giving a public address is right next to death on the fear index. Diane Ullius in her article, "Crossing a Bridge of Shyness: Public Speaking for Communicators," says even seasoned public speakers get nervous before speaking.[1] Don't sweat it. (No pun intended.) Remember that most people listening to you will be glad it is you up front speaking and not them. They'll be understanding and supportive. Just remember *why* you are running and stick with your message and you'll do fine. Getting up front will get easier and easier the more you do it, so persevere.

God is able to use and speak through anyone. He is not as concerned about *capability* as He is *availability*. He loves a willing, obedient heart and honors that.

Many of us can relate to the feelings of Moses and Jeremiah when God called them to serve Him and to speak out.

Moses responded to the Lord by saying, "O Lord, I have never been eloquent, neither in the past nor since you have spoken to your servant. I am slow of speech and tongue" (Ex. 4:10).

The Lord responded to Moses by reminding Moses of the truth of the situation and giving him a tremendous promise, "Who gave man his mouth? . . . Is it not I, the LORD? Now go; I will help you speak and will teach you what to say" (Ex. 4:11a–12).

Jeremiah raised a similar objection. "Ah, Sovereign LORD," I said, "I do not know how to speak; I am only a child" (Jer. 1:6).

The Lord also encouraged Jeremiah by reminding him that God would always be with him and help him. "But the LORD said to me, 'Do not say, "I am only a child." You must go to everyone I send you to and say whatever I command you. Do not be afraid of them, for I am with you and will rescue you,' declares the LORD" (Jer. 1:7–8). The Word goes on to say that the Lord reached out His hand and touched Jeremiah's mouth and said, "Now I have put my words in your mouth"(Jer. 1:9b).

God understands our fears, our doubts, our objections. He is able to overcome them and speak through us as He spoke through Moses and Jeremiah. He wants to partner with us to help us accomplish His plan. We just need to ask. He will be with us, touch us with His power, provide us with the words, and enable us to speak more powerfully and eloquently than we could have imagined.

The speech

The Bible provides the basic outline of most political speeches in the words of Absalom.

> Then Absalom would say to him, "Look, your claims are valid and proper, but there is no representative of the king to hear you." And Absalom would add, "If only I were appointed judge in the land! Then everyone who has a complaint or case could come to me and I would see that he gets justice."
>
> —2 Sam. 15:3–4

Absalom's basic message involved three principles:

1. Affirm the person's concerns;
2. Point out your opponent's weakness(es); and
3. Tell how you would do things differently if you were in charge.

Likewise, a good political speech contains the elements of:

1. Knowing your audience and affirming their concerns;
2. Stating the problem; and
3. Providing solutions to the problem.

Below are tips to help you incorporate these principles into a winning political speech.

Preparing the speech

In preparing your speech, consider your audience. What will their concerns be? What is important to them? Are they a group of business owners concerned with the escalating costs of health care? Are they senior citizens who are concerned about the increase of crime in the community? Are they a high school civics class concerned about the high cost of college and the increasing drug use among their peers?

If you don't know the concerns of the audience, talk to someone familiar with the group or, better yet, a member of that group. Ask them what they are concerned about. This is your chance to "sell" your case for why they should hire you. You can't do that unless you know what they are interested in.

Next, answer the basic questions of your audience—who you are, why you are running, and why they should vote for you. Highlight your experience and background and share how those will be an asset to your service in office.

Refine your reason for running for office into one sentence and practice it. This is critical for your campaign and can even make or break your chances of getting elected. In 1980, U.S. Senator Ted Kennedy challenged Jimmy Carter in the Democratic presidential contest. His chances were doomed after he gave CBS reporter Roger Mudd a rambling and vague answer as to why he wanted to be president. Kennedy's strong poll numbers began a steady decline after that. People want to know why you are running and expect you to know.

When I first ran for office, I went to a campaign school and was asked to write down the reason I was running for office in one sentence. It was difficult to do, but an excellent exercise. The one-sentence rationale I chose was: "I'm running for office because I believe there's a need for ordinary people to get involved in government—people with morals, values, and common sense who have been living with the laws and understand how they are impacting our lives."

So, why are you running for office? Take a few minutes to refine your message and write it in the box below:

Why I am Running for Office

The next part of your speech will be to state the problems/concerns and then provide your solutions. I have heard it said that all political campaigns revolve around crises of various kinds. There's a lot of truth to that. There's a drug problem. Highways are crumbling. Schools are failing. These crises motivate us to action, whether it is by volunteering for a campaign, deciding to contribute our money, or voting for a candidate. People have to be given a *reason* to get involved. They need to know why supporting you will make a difference.

Tell your issues and what you are going to do to address the problem. If the timeframe allows for a longer speech, spend more time sharing information about the problem. Let your words reflect your knowledge on the subject without belaboring the facts or inciting boredom.

If your race is close, you need to give them a reason to support you versus your opponent(s). This can be risky but necessary if you are in a tight race. If you feel you are doing well in your campaign, I'd avoid bringing up your opponent. Just focus on your campaign messages. But if you are taking on an incumbent or feel the race is too close to call, then, like Absalom, contrast yourself with your opponent. Spend most of the speech highlighting your credentials and how you are going to address the concerns of the audience, if elected, but include a sentence or small paragraph contrasting your position with your opponent's. You are not cutting down your opponent or getting personal. You are *contrasting* your positions on *issues*. This is a valid and necessary part of campaigning.

Don't use your opponent's name. If you do, you are increasing his or her name ID unnecessarily and making your comments seem more personal. Instead, simply say something like, "Unlike my opponent, I support the right of law-abiding citizens to defend themselves through gun ownership," or "My opponent doesn't believe tax reform is necessary. She supports a tax increase to further bloat the government. I believe we need to have better government and will work hard to cut unnecessary spending. The families of this area have to balance their budget and make hard choices. I believe the government should also!" These statements contrast your position with your opponent's. They also leave the audience with a positive statement from you rather than a negative comment about your opponent.

Personalize your message. The difference between a good speech and one that is okay is whether or not the candidate has connected with the audience. One way to do that is to give personal examples showing the impact of the problem or how a solution will matter to the average person. You could say, "Health care costs have risen 48 percent in the past three years, resulting in record costs," or you could say, "Health care costs have made it next to impossible for young families in our area to get the health care they need. I was visiting with one young family the other day while going door to door. Both parents are in their late twenties and work steady jobs. They have a three-year-old and a baby. Unfortunately, they shared with me that when their baby got a high fever, it cost them $90 just for the doctor visit. The antibiotics needed were another $45. The follow-up visit was another $90. That was the amount of money they had budgeted for groceries that week. They just pray that their children don't get really sick. They simply cannot afford the needed treatments and don't know what they would do. We've got to do something about this. That is why I am proposing . . ." Share the reasons the problem needs to be addressed. Do so not only with facts, but with the personal impact of the problem.

Invite them to be part of the team. Use "we" messages rather than "I" messages. This campaign isn't about you. It's about what you can accomplish together as a team. You are their voice. They are the feet and hands that enable you to be their voice. You need each other. Convey the team concept and the message will get through.

Keep your speech short. Fifteen minutes is a good time frame for a political speech. If you are the featured speaker, up to thirty minutes can be acceptable, but generally, people appreciate a well-done fifteen-minute speech. In many forums, talking five to ten minutes is preferable. If you get too long, people tune out and negative feedback begins. If your talk is really long, people will actually dislike you and start painting you as "just another windy politician". Keep it short and people will appreciate you.

After you've decided what you want to say, write it down. Many candidates think they can "wing it," but usually this method shows. Disciplining yourself to write down your thoughts ensures you will narrow the scope of your talk so that you say what you want to say and keep yourself from getting sidetracked by irrelevant comments or extraneous topics.

Your mother always said, "Practice makes perfect" and she was right. Practice giving the speech until you are comfortable with it. You don't have to read the speech word for word when you are in front of the audience. You can talk naturally and just glance at your notes if you have practiced enough that you know what you are going to say.

Before the speech

Rely on the promises in God's Word. The Bible contains many verses related to the topic of speaking. These verses can become your prayers and enable you to speak more eloquently than you ever thought possible. Pray for wisdom, understanding, discernment, and favor. Ask that the Lord instruct you in what to say and show you how to say it. Believe He will use you to inform, inspire, and bless. Here are some of my favorite verses:

"My mouth will speak words of wisdom; the utterance from my heart will give understanding."
—Psalm 49:3

"My tongue is the pen of a skillful writer."
—Psalm 45:1b

"The mouth of the righteous man utters wisdom and his tongue speaks what is just."
—Psalm 37:30

"For in him you have been enriched in every way—in all your speaking and in all your knowledge."
—1 Corinthians 1:5

"The Sovereign LORD has given me an instructed tongue, to know the word that sustains the weary. He wakens me morning by morning, wakens my ear to listen like one being taught."
—Isaiah 50:4

"A wise man's heart guides his mouth and his lips promote instruction."

—Proverbs 16:23

"The mouth of the righteous is a fountain of life."

—Proverbs 10:11

"Wisdom is found on the lips of the discerning."

—Proverbs 10:13

"The mouth of the righteous brings forth wisdom . . . The lips of the righteous know what is fitting."

—Proverbs 10:31–32

"The tongue of the wise brings healing."

—Proverbs 12:18b

"The lips of the wise spread knowledge."

—Proverbs 15:7

"Set a guard over my mouth, O Lord; keep watch over the door of my lips."

—Psalm 141:3

"I have put my words in your mouth and covered you with the shadow of my hand."

—Isaiah 51:16

"May the words of my mouth and the meditation of my heart be pleasing in your sight, O Lord, my Rock and my Redeemer."

—Psalm 19:14

Pay attention to the impression you make. Fair or not, most people assess a speaker not by his or her words, but by the impression they get while watching the person give the speech. Women especially note the dress of the speaker down to the details of hair, jewelry, nails, and clothes. This reality can be intimidating for most speakers, but it doesn't have to be. Remember to be yourself, but your *best* self. If you need some advice on what to wear, ask a friend or someone who is good at putting together clothing choices. Take time to review the state of your shoes and fingernails. This may sound funny, but people notice your hands when you talk because we use them so much in gesturing and making points. Spend a few minutes polishing these and your talk will appear more polished.

Reflect on why you are running. The best way to reflect a positive image in your speech is by thinking about the right things prior to and during your talk. Rather than thinking about details of the words you are going to say, think about the audience and about why you are speaking—not solely to get elected, but because you want to inform them or alert them to problems or because you care about them. If you mentally focus on themes of "Alert them, encourage them, serve them," it will show in your face, voice, and eyes. People will walk away with a good impression of you because they've seen your heart.

Check out the sound system and podium prior to the speech. Walk up to the podium before the event and check out the position of the microphone. Learn how it works. Is there a button you have to push or slide to turn it on? Will the person before you be really tall or short, requiring an adjustment in height? Try adjusting it. Will moving it be easy or create an awkward screech? What does your voice sound like in the microphone? Test it out before, if possible. Nothing marks an amateur speaker like someone who goes up to a microphone and nervously says, "Test? Test?" before clearing his throat and beginning to speak. Do this beforehand.

Also, check out the podium. Is the height correct? Do you want to stand behind it and look at your notes, or do you plan to remove the microphone and walk around while talking? Is there a place for your notes and, if so, will you carry them to the podium or is there a shelf you can keep them on prior to your speech?

Most of these decisions are personal preference, but you need to be flexible, because each situation will be different.

If there is no sound system, be prepared to project your voice. Practice ahead of time at home. You may feel like you are shouting, but your efforts to speak clearly and be heard will be appreciated by all there—especially the senior citizens or others in the audience who often feel isolated at such events because they have difficulty hearing.

Giving the speech

Allow the person introducing you to highlight your qualifications. The best way of communicating your credentials is by allowing the person

FIGURE 5.1 State Representative Brian Baker giving a speech

who introduces you to highlight your attributes rather than your citing them during your speech. Proverbs 27:2 gives wise advice, "Let another praise you, and not your own mouth; someone else, and not your own lips." Provide the emcee with your bio to aid in the introduction. Your bio should include your educational background, work and community experience, honors and awards, and personal and family information. This gives the emcee the tools needed to give a commendable introduction.

Bridge from the introduction to your speech. Thank the emcee for his kind introduction and make a comment about the audience or event that can bridge or transition to your speech. You might want to recognize the leaders who planned the event or comment on the wonderful meal or thank the youth who came to hand out the programs early. Use something that happened at the event to transition to your talk.

An example of a bridge might be something like, "Thank you, Jack, for that kind introduction. I really appreciate it. You've all made me feel so welcome. This is a great event. The meal was wonderful and I am so impressed with these young people handing out programs.

Haven't they done a great job? Let's give them a hand. (clap) They embody the future hope of our country and symbolize the reason I am running for office. I want to bring a better tomorrow to our state (county, city, etc.) and that's why I filed to be your next _____ ."

Use hand gestures with discretion. Using hand gestures can emphasize points and create more interest in your speech. They also make the speaker seem more relaxed, as if she were talking with friends rather than giving a proper speech. But you don't want to overdo it.

I was at a funeral recently and a new, young preacher was giving the address. What he said was very appropriate and befitting the deceased. I could tell he had put a lot of thought and work into preparing his remarks. However, he must have also purposely put into the talk specific hand gestures to emphasize points. Unfortunately, instead of enhancing his remarks, they took away from them because they were so artificial and overdone. "Big" motions are not needed. Just practice talking and using hand gestures naturally and your message will get through.

Let your light shine. Most people aren't expecting a professional speaker; they are looking for someone who is *sincere*. Your words should not just reflect knowledge; they should reflect your *heart*. If you feel passionate about an issue, don't be afraid to sound passionate. If you are outraged, look outraged. If you are frustrated, show it. If you are optimistic, smile. And, most importantly, if you are enthusiastic about running and feel positive about the future, let it shine forth in your eyes and voice.

Introduce family members. Make sure to introduce your family if they are present. They are your partners in this effort and need to be recognized by you. Too many times candidates get caught up the campaign and lose sight of what is most important to them. They forget the people who are enabling them to run for office, to their personal chagrin and their family's detriment. You may not notice if you forget to introduce them, but they will, and chances are the audience will, also. Keep your priorities throughout the campaign. It is good practice for keeping them straight once elected.

Speeches don't have to be feared. They can be enjoyed for the opportunity they are to connect with your audience and, most importantly, to reflect the love and wisdom of your heavenly Father. Focus on *His* objectives for the speech, and you can give Him the glory afterward for a job well done.

Chapter 6

Presenting your Message through Campaign Materials

While conveying your message through giving a good speech is an important aspect of your campaign, it is only one way to get your points across. In reality, a very small percentage of the registered voters will hear you speak. Far more will learn about your message via yard signs, campaign materials, the Internet, newspaper articles and advertisements, direct mail pieces, brochures, and other means. Your themes remain the same; only the vehicle differs. These methods are vital, because they increase your name ID. Name ID is crucial, because most often it determines who will win the election. Taking time to effectively use these alternative methods of communication pays dividends. The next four chapters will give insights into these other important avenues of campaign communication.

Your campaign logo and slogan

Central to getting out your message is finding a way to encapsulate it in the form of a logo. This image will be used over and over in your campaign and can say a lot about you and what you're working for without a lot of words. Once you've developed your basic message, then think how that can be translated to your signs and campaign materials.

The theme of my first campaign was "Vicky Hartzler Cares About . . ." and then I listed education, health care, and family values in my literature. Since my last name has the word *hart* in it, my campaign team and I designed a logo with my name in white on a bright blue background with a red heart around the letters Hart. It looked like this:

FIGURE 6.1 Example of Campaign Logo

The heart symbolized both my name and my theme of caring about issues and people as the motivation for my desire to serve. Think about a symbol for your campaign that could be used as a logo.

Draw your campaign logo here:

FIGURE 6.2 Campaign logo design box

You might also want to develop a slogan based on a theme of your campaign. Slogans can appear on yard signs and advertisements such as, "John Doe for Sheriff—Tough on Crime" or "Julie White for Presiding Commissioner—A Better Government, A Better Tomorrow."

Spend time early in your campaign to plan this important avenue for conveying your message. If you have one, write your slogan below:

What, if any, slogan will be featured in your campaign?

FIGURE 6.3 Slogan box

Yard signs

Most every campaign utilizes yard signs. They are an effective way to increase your name identification and convey the themes of your campaign. There are as many types of yard signs as there are yard sign companies. You will become acquainted with them after you file for office because companies will get your name and send you catalogs selling campaign materials. Local printing companies often offer them, as well. Have a volunteer research the various prices and different options. Your choice should be based on cost, ease of assembly, and durability.

Types

If your budget is tight, you might want to buy low-cost, laminated, paper-type yard signs. These require someone to staple the sides together. They don't hold up well in bad weather and take longer to assemble, but can make do if your funds are limited. You can purchase wires for the signs or make your own.

In my first campaign for state representative, I purchased one-sided 22" x 14" laminated poster-stock paper signs. A friend who worked at a cabinet shop volunteered to secure scrap wood pieces for me and cut them into stakes. Volunteers and I took two signs, stapled them together back to back, and drove the wooden stakes into the ground with a hammer then used a heavy-duty stapler to attach the sign onto the wooden stake.

These signs got the message across with the least amount of money, but getting them out was a lot of work. By the end of the campaign, the signs were torn apart by the winds and the staples were starting to rust. None survived to reuse for the next campaign.

As funds allowed in the next campaign, I switched to corrugated plastic signs and bought metal stakes for yard signs and steel posts for the large signs. These worked much better and most survived for a future campaign. I would recommend plastic corrugated or plastic bag slip on type signs if you can afford them.

If you live in the city, you might consider another form of signage: bus signs. Billboards also increase name ID but can be expensive. Check into these options and, if financially feasible, use them to increase your visibility in the community.

Colors

Decide which colors you want to use in your campaign. You want something that is visible, unique, and economical. Using only one color in addition to white is the most economical way to go, but consider the color carefully. Too many times, all the candidates choose red and white or blue and white and it's hard to distinguish between them.

Consider reverse printing. This involves putting the color as the background with the words showing through white. These signs are a lot more visible and generally don't cost any more than ordering the print in color and leaving the white background. Look at the examples below. Which do you think is more visible?

Traditional:

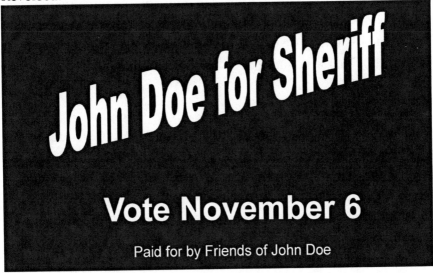

FIGURES 6.4 and 6.5 Examples of yard sign designs

Some colors show up better than others. Green blends in with the landscape. Yellow and white are hard to see. Many candidates choose patriotic colors. This can be good, but redundant. Even wild colors can work. One candidate shocked our community by using neon yellow-green and bright blue as his colors. They really stood out as you drove down the road. Another used neon orange and black. They did the same. Whatever color you choose, stick with it throughout your campaign and in all your campaign materials.

Message

The simpler the better. If you have a short slogan, it could fit on the sign. Otherwise, let your logo convey your message. People have an average of four seconds to look at your sign as they drive by. If the sign is cluttered with too many words or graphics, they'll miss the message. Keep it clean and simple.

Unless you have a primary election opponent, you might want to consider foregoing the printing of your party symbol on your signs as well as printed materials such as any pushcards or brochures. You want people to vote for you because of your qualifications and positions on issues. Depending upon the political makeup of a political subdivision, a party symbol on signs and brochures can unnecessarily cause some voters to be closed to your message. Consider leaving it off and they might be more open to your candidacy.

How many to order?

The number of signs you order will depend upon the size of your district both geographically and population-wise. Obviously, the smaller the size of your district, the fewer signs you will need; the larger the district, the more signs are required.

Signs cost less the more you buy so it makes economic sense to buy what you need up front. However, it is often difficult to gauge how many you will be able to find homes for and some beginning candidates are overly optimistic about how many signs they will be able to utilize. Ask other people who have run for office in your area previously to see how many signs they would recommend. Their experience is probably the best barometer for determining a realistic number.

My state representative district served a population of roughly 32,000 people and was comprised of a combination of small towns and rural areas. When I first ran, I ordered five hundred yard signs and seventy-five big signs. I found homes for all of them, but it took work for an entire six months to secure these locations. When I ran again as an incumbent, I ordered a thousand yard signs and a hundred big signs. It is easier to get them out once you are elected because more like-minded people know you and want to support your re-election.

Buy enough signs for the initial blitz three weeks out from the election and enough for replacement of signage due to damage or disappearance. Also, save some to put out at the polling sites on election day.

Big signs

Every campaign needs a combination of big signs and yard signs. Big signs attract attention and increase name identification along major thoroughfares or other visible locations. They are the "high-powered bullets" of your campaign, producing a major impact. Yard signs gain their impact by "peppering" the neighborhood with a large spray of buckshot of name recognition. Both leave an impression. Large signs can be 4' x 8' or 3' x 5' or 8' x 10' or even billboards. What combination you choose will depend upon your budget and the physical landscape of your area.

Timing

Large signs can go out earlier in the campaign than yard signs. They take longer to set up due to their size. They also can provide the first wave of name recognition strategies of your campaign. Yard signs are part of the last wave and their distribution will be discussed more in Chapter 16.

I usually set up my big signs in mid-July prior to the primary election the first week of August. I left them up until November.

Ideally, you would take them back down after the primary election and then put them back up a month or so out from the general election to produce a visual impact or move them around from location to location, but due to the extreme amount of work necessary to do this, most campaigns forsake this strategy. In lieu of this, I usually saved a couple of excellent locations for the final wave of name ID and put them out at the same time as the yard sign blitz.

Before erecting any signs, make sure to determine your local sign ordinances. Each governmental entity in your district regulates when signs can be put up. These can differ from community to community, so make sure to check with them prior to putting up any signs to avoid confusion and unnecessary work.

Organization

Setting up large campaign signs is a job requiring strength and means (i.e., a pickup truck, post driver, and tools). Willing men, whether they are in high school, college, young, working, or retired, make excellent chairmen for the large sign project. Ask several able-bodied individuals to take on this responsibility and you'll be amazed at the results.

Method

Choose locations strategically. Usually funds are tight and only a limited number of large signs are available. You want to make sure they are used to your best advantage. Get a large county or city map and plot the best locations for large signs on the map to ensure that the area is covered adequately. Ideally, the locations will be owned by people you know. If not, find out who owns the land near the locations you have selected by looking on a plat map, asking neighbors, or going up to the house in person. Contact them directly or through a volunteer in some way and ask for their permission to place your sign on their property. Do not assume someone's support and put up a sign without permission. Nothing will get a candidate on the wrong side of an influential voter more than one who puts up a sign without a property owner's permission. Instruct your volunteers to always check with the owner before placing a sign.

Locations can also be found by talking with your precinct captains or political party members from your area who have helped other candidates. Past candidates are also good resources for sign locations.

Once locations are secured, determine the boundaries of the highway right-of-way. In Missouri, the right-of-way is marked by a small steel post topped with a little orange sign. All private signs have to be behind that invisible line or they might be removed by the state highway department. I know from personal experience. During my first campaign, my brother-in-law volunteered to head up the large sign project. He was a real blessing. He found excellent locations throughout the two counties that comprised my district and secured permission from landowners. He recruited captains to help erect them and got the signs out in a timely manner. They went up all across the area and looked fantastic. Unfortunately, we received numerous reports just two days later that the signs were gone. Many had disappeared without a trace!

My brother-in-law called the state highway department on the tip that someone had seen a state highway truck stopped in the area near one of my signs. Sure enough! Highway department officials had discovered all my signs on the highway right-of-way and had pulled them up per their policy. Thankfully, they were still in the dumpster at the local highway maintenance shed. My wonderful brother-in-law promptly went over and retrieved them. They were still in good condition. He talked with the highway officials to verify the exact policy that needed to be followed and put the signs up again. This time they were erected in the correct location and were left undisturbed until it was time to take them back down. To prevent a similar fate, always verify right-of-way policies.

Determine if the sign is more visible running parallel to the highway or perpendicular. If you only have a limited number of large signs, you may want to put a one-sided sign parallel to the road and at a great enough distance from the road so people can read it. Certainly, this is the best approach at "T" intersections.

If you have enough signs, it is common to put two back to back and place them perpendicular to the road so people can see them as they approach the area from both directions. Some candidates get their signs printed on both sides to make this easier. However, be cautious. Sometimes these double-sided signs can look distorted when the sun shines through them, making them hard to read. Two separate signs back to back will not do this.

Most large signs require steel posts as anchors. Ask local farmers or farm supply business owners if they would be willing to loan you some posts as an in-kind contribution to your campaign. Many are more than willing to do so. After positioning the sign, drive the steel posts into the ground far enough that the sign will withstand winds. Punch holes in the sign with a screwdriver and thread the plastic anchor ties through the holes and around the steel post to secure them. Don't scrimp on the anchor ties. Too many large signs start to sag or buckle with the months of weather if they aren't securely fastened. Use four ties for each post to ensure they stand tall until the end.

If you follow these suggestions, you'll be sure to leave a "big" impression for your campaign.

Promotional materials

Once you have designed and ordered your signs, you are ready to consider other avenues to convey your message. Campaign materials are effective ways to raise awareness of your campaign, spread your name ID, and build grassroots support for your campaign. These can include bumper strips, static-cling window stickers, magnetic signs, refrigerator magnets, lapel stickers, pencils, emery boards, or other related items. Too often candidates get carried away ordering too many of these novelty items and overextend their budget, but a few are good to have and can help spread name ID.

Bumper strips, window stickers, or magnetic signs are especially effective at spreading your name ID. People recognize the bumper strip or window sticker as a personal endorsement for you by the car owner. If they know that person, they especially will take note of their support. This is a far better form of advertising than a generic advertisement in a newspaper. People care what other people think and will be drawn to support you if a friend of theirs supports you.

FIGURE 6.6 Example of bumper strip

One car driving around for six months displaying your name is worth a plethora of yard signs. Encourage supporters to use bumper strips throughout the campaign, but keep yard signs locked up until three or four weeks out.

In my first campaign I ordered smaller 9" x 3" bumper strips. (By the way, they used to be called "bumper *stickers*." Now they are referred to as "bumper *strips*." The old name conjured up negative memories of trying to remove the old-fashioned, very sticky campaign items from cars and having a difficult time. This discouraged people from putting them on their cars so candidates started referring to them as "bumper strips." This helped boost use. The companies have improved the formulas also, so they are less sticky. An alternative way to use them is to tape the bumper strip to the middle of the rear window. This is a popular method if the vehicle owner prefers not to place it on his or her bumper.) Later I ordered larger ones, which were 11½" x 4." The smaller ones were nice because I could send them in the mail to supporters who requested them. Here is what they looked like:

In addition, I ordered round lapel stickers that were used in parades. During my third campaign when I had extra funds, I added refrigerator magnets that I distributed when going door to door. I often visit with people who say they are still using the magnets in their homes even after several years of my being out of office. The magnets work and serve as a perpetual reminder of your candidacy. Below are pictures of them:

FIGURE 6.7 Example of lapel sticker

FIGURE 6.8 Example of refrigerator magnet

Some candidates have also found success with distributing a little printed notepad with their name on it. While this shouldn't be a priority item such as bumper strips, it could be an effective tool to increase name ID if you have extra funds.

All in all, compare the cost of the campaign item with the potential benefit in increased name ID. Make sure you have enough money for your primary means of conveying your message (direct mail pieces, newspaper advertising, etc.) during the final days of the campaign and, if you have secured enough funds for these activities and still have money left over, you might want to buy a few of these additional items to test their effectiveness and to bring home your message.

Campaign DVD

America is a visual society. While many people do not take the time to read the newspaper, they will turn on the television to watch the news or view a DVD. Realizing this, candidates are turning to creative means of spreading their message via producing and distributing videotapes or DVDs.

S. J. Guzzetta, in his book *The Campaign Manual*, recommends candidates consider making a campaign DVD to increase your name ID and improve your favorability rating (how favorably the electorate views you). He shares, "Today over 70 percent of all households have a DVD player. For a few thousand dollars you could produce and distribute 1,000 DVD's throughout your district."[1]

Give them out to supporters and ask them to help circulate them. If in a primary race against candidates from your own party, send the DVDs to households or parts of your district that typically vote heavily for your party. Later redirect sending the DVDs to undecided voters in the general election campaign. Send the DVDs with a letter introducing the DVD and ask them to view it and pass it on to their friends and neighbors. Many people will take the time to view it, especially if you are in a closely contested race. If they like what they see, they will pass it on.

To produce a DVD, consider these tips based on *The Campaign Manual*:[2]

1. Recruit a friend with videotape experience to assist in this project or hire a video company.
2. Develop a script highlighting your basic message: who you are, why you are running, and what you are going to do if elected. The introduction should include references to your education, professional background, and community involvement.
3. Decide the presentation format. The two basic formats are: an announcer sharing the message while pictures of the candidate play in the background; and the candidate sharing the basic messages. In the announcer format, the candidate usually only speaks at the end by looking directly in the camera and asking for their vote. In the second format, the candidate talks the entire time while the video changes based on the issues being discussed.

4. If you decide to speak the entire time, choose a comfortable setting with adequate lighting. Pay attention to the audio so your words are clearly heard. Wear a lapel microphone if needed. Introduce yourself by looking in the camera and speaking in a conversational tone. Pretend you are speaking with a close friend as you look into the camera lens and share from your heart.

5. Obtain adequate footage of your family with you in a casual setting, such as interacting outdoors, and include references to them in your talk.

6. Also, generate footage of yourself in various settings reflective of your message. If you are talking about the need for better roads, then take shots of you beside a road in poor condition visiting with area citizens about the problems. If you are speaking about high taxes, take video of yourself visiting with a family who is budgeting and trying to pay bills sitting at their kitchen table with the calculator and checkbook. If you are speaking about education, videotape yourself walking down a school hallway visiting with a teacher while students walk to their lockers. Think about capturing your messages through the viewer's perspective.

7. Conclude the tape with a personal appeal into the camera restating why you are running and asking for their vote.

8. Keep the tape fairly short. Do not exceed thirty minutes. The shorter, the better.

9. Hire a commercial video company to reproduce the tape, and then begin distribution.

DVDs might not be in everyone's budget, but they can be considered as a possible tool in your campaign toolbox. Be creative. Think of new ways to convey your message. No matter what campaign materials you choose, be consistent with the colors, logo, and theme, and your message will be heard and remembered.

CHAPTER 7

PRESENTING YOUR MESSAGE THROUGH PRINTED MATERIALS

N
ow that you have your basic campaign promotional materials and signs designed and purchased, you are ready to start presenting your message through the written word. Printed materials enable voters to learn about who you are, why you are running, and what you hope to accomplish if elected. They impart the knowledge necessary to change minds and win hearts. Hosea 4:6 says, "My people are destroyed for lack of knowledge" (KJV). Campaigns can also be destroyed for lack of knowledge among the voters. That is why it is vital that they be provided with accurate, timely information.

This chapter will explain how to do that through the production of printed materials such a pushcards and direct mail. It all starts with quality photographs.

Pictures

The old proverb "A picture is worth a thousand words" is true. Many people will not read the words on a campaign piece or newspaper article, but they will look at the picture and get an impression from it about you and your candidacy. In the seconds they glance at the picture in your newspaper ad, they will determine if you are someone who is interested in the things they are interested in and whether or not you look like someone worthy of the office you are seeking.

Every candidate needs a professional "mug shot" photo. Utilize a studio or professional photographer for this all-important picture. Now isn't the time to cut corners as this will be the hallmark photo used in your campaign. It will appear on campaign literature and be used by the media to talk about your candidacy. Look pleasant, but professional. You will also want to get a professional family portrait. These two photos will be the only studio shots you will need.

In addition, set aside time to obtain several good, action photos. Take a day early in the campaign to have your picture taken in casual settings representative of your messages. Decide what photos would capture the essence of who you are and what you want to convey. Secure a qualified photographer to take the pictures. Unfortunately, too many candidates ask a family friend to take snapshots, only to discover after a day of shooting that the photos are too dark or blurred to use, and the entire day will have to be set up again. Change clothes between settings so you don't look like you took all the pictures in one day. Take plenty of photos. Later in the campaign when you need to develop an ad or response piece in a hurry, you will have several pictures ready to go.

In my first campaign, I was running on the messages of better health care, quality education, and protecting families. In addition, I sent direct mail pieces highlighting my background in agriculture, my support of 2nd Amendment rights, and my pro-life views. For these, I arranged to have pictures taken of me in the following settings: a doctor's office holding my young nephew and visiting with my family doctor (health care); the front of a classroom while I spoke to a group of students (education); looking at a student's work at his desk (education); in a field of corn at harvest time in front of a parked combine talking with my father and looking at an ear of corn (agriculture); with an area gun store owner as I aimed a shotgun at a target (pro-gun); and with children and an area police chief (tough on crime/family safety). These pieces were highly effective in introducing me to the voters. Just by looking at the pictures, they could see who I was and what issues I would be working on if elected, even if they didn't read the text.

Additional good pictures can also be secured by having someone take unscripted photos of you at a public event as you interact with people. This can be done by using an economical, high-quality digital camera. It is a good idea for the campaign to purchase one early on and keep it handy throughout the campaign. Some of these action shots will turn out great and can be uploaded and easily used in campaign pieces or last minute response ads.

After you have secured quality photos for your campaign, you are ready to use them to convey your message.

Pushcard

The first piece you will want to print is a pushcard. A pushcard is the piece of literature you hand to voters during your campaign, whether going door to door or at public events such as parades. The goal of the pushcard is to provide a forum for sharing information about:

- who you are;
- why you are running; and
- what you are going to do if elected to office.

Basic information included in most pushcards includes:

- A professional photograph of yourself and your family;
- Your logo;
- A quote by you saying what you believe and asking for their vote;
- Your background information (education, professional, community involvement);
- Your plan of action; and

- Required campaign iden-
tification information to
comply with campaign
laws, such as *Paid for by
Citizens for John Doe, Nancy
Banes, Treasurer.*

Candidates differ as to what
form of pushcard they like best.
The traditional pushcard is an 8½"
x 3½" brochure on card stock with
printing on the front and back
but it could also be in various
other forms such as a tri-fold
glossy-paper brochure, a business
card detailing your message, or
a door hanger which can easily
be left when the candidate goes
door to door. Pushcards can be
simple and cost-efficient, utilizing
only a few colors with basic black
type or full-color depending upon
your personal preference and
budget. Examples of several types
of pushcards are listed in Appendix
C in the back of this book.

**VOTE FOR
BARBARA WALTERS**

BARBARA WALTERS has been a resident of Harrisonville for 20 years. She is a widow, mother of three adult children and has five grandchildren. A Registered Nurse, Diabetic Educator and longtime employee of Cass Medical Center.

BARBARA WALTERS is committed to

- QUALITY Government
- QUALITY Leadership
- QUALITY Service
- QUALITY Living
  for a
- QUALITY City

"I am knowledgeable, devoted to helping others and committed to bringing quality growth to Harrisonville. People, community and my faith are important to me. My experience as a homemaker, registered nurse, educator and involved citizen, I believe, makes me the qualified person to represent WARD ONE. I would appreciate your vote. Thank you."

Barbara Walters

Paid for by candidate

FIGURE 7.1 Example of one-sided
pushcard

I used a simple 8½" x 3½" white card with black print and my
logo colors of blue and red in key areas of the card. It worked well.
I could put them in my pockets before walking down the street and
easily pull one out when I met a voter. It also could be placed in the
crevice between the door and the doorframe if the person was not
home or rolled up and slipped into the hole in a screen door handle.
Since it was stiff, it held its place and didn't blow away as easily as
more flimsy brochures would have.

FIGURE 7.2 Example of campaign business card

Keep in mind that people are busy and don't have much time to read a lot of information. If you keep your pushcard simple and easy to read, there is a greater chance that your message will get through before the card hits "file 13."

Good pictures help ensure that it will at least be glanced at before being "filed." Choose your professional photo for the front and another one of your family or an action shot of you for the back of your pushcard. If you develop a brochure, you can use more photos.

Get bids from several local printers before ordering. Some of the printers might help you with the layout of your design. You can hire outside printers, but keeping the business "in district" makes good sense.

Order plenty of these, as they will be the staple of your campaign. Usually you will get a more economical price the more you buy, so it doesn't cost that much more to buy a few thousand extra during the first printing. I ordered five thousand for my first campaign and ten thousand when I ran for re-election. I had some left over, but the cost wasn't prohibitive. These leftovers can be used for last minute get-out-the-vote efforts, so don't be afraid to order plenty.

Direct mail

The campaign plan questionnaire in Chapter 1 asked you to list the types of direct mail pieces you planned to use. It also included a chart where you could list the type of direct mail piece, the print date, quantity, drop date, and target audience. This section will provide more information about this important strategic tactic of your campaign.

A direct mail piece is what its name implies: a piece of campaign mail sent directly to the voter. It could be in the form of a letter, a brochure, an insert in the newspaper, a large card, or a tabloid. Direct mail pieces are often one of the most important ways of conveying your message and one of the most expensive. Postage costs a great deal, even with bulk rates, so a candidate often has to limit the number of households receiving the pieces. Specific groups of voters are targeted with specific messages in order to get the most "bang for the buck."

Objectives of direct mail include increasing name ID through a general information piece; persuading voters to support you through targeted messages to targeted groups; raising funds; clarifying misinformation sent out by the opponent; and/or getting supporters out to vote during the final days of the campaign.

In Chapter 4 you identified groups of voters that you wanted to target with secondary messages. They might be senior citizens, the pro-life community, union households, gun owners, families with young children, or businesses, for example. These people are voters you've identified who might be supportive of your message and can be won to your side. These groups will form the basis of the first direct mail pieces to be produced. You will also probably want to send out a general direct mail piece to undecided voters and plan on sending a get-out-the-vote card to supportive voters just prior to the election. It is not unusual to produce six to eight different direct mail pieces, but is not always financially possible. Your budget will determine how many different pieces can be produced and sent. Ideally, however, you will make your plan and then try to raise the funds necessary to implement your plan.

Later in the book we will explain how to obtain the names and addresses of the individuals you want to target. In the meantime, you can begin preparing the direct mail pieces that send specific messages to specific sets of voters. Most commonly, these messages are conveyed with cards.

Direct mail cards

During my first campaign, I printed and sent out direct mail cards on the following topics:

- Crime
- Agriculture
- Taxes
- Health Care
- Gun Ownership
- Pro-Life
- GOTV postcard

The first six cards were sent to targeted voters with a targeted message. The final get-out-the-vote card was sent district-wide to voters who were most likely supportive of my candidacy. Appendix D has several examples of direct mail cards to give you some ideas for your campaign. You will want your pieces to reflect the issues important to you and your area, which were determined early on in your campaign.

Direct mail pieces should be eye-catching. Obtain and use excellent photographs. Use professional graphics. Use full color, if you have the funds. Make them look sharp and it will increase the likelihood of them being read.

Direct mail pieces can come in various forms. While some candidates send out an "I'm-asking-for-your-vote" letter in a regular envelope or a slick, colored tri-fold brochure telling about their candidacy, most candidates utilize the sending of oversized cards. This is the method of direct mail my campaigns have used. The reasons I prefer the oversized cards include:

- They are cheaper to print than colored brochures;
- They will not get lost in the stack of mail because they are larger than the average sized envelope;
- People have to glance at them as they go through their stack of mail; and
- The pictures, graphics, and your logo make another impression for your campaign, which helps people remember you on election day.

Card sizes can be approximately 5½" x 11" or 8½" x 11." I also used some smaller ones that were 5½" x 8½." They should be printed on a stiff card stock.

I used black and white print with my primary campaign color (royal blue) as the color of the heading and boxes around the text. This helps create uniformity with your campaign. Your yard signs, big signs, campaign literature, and direct mail pieces should all have the same color scheme.

Specialized direct mail pieces can sometimes use a different color card stock. For instance, direct mail cards were sent to gun owners in the area on a hunter orange card with black text.

Take time when you design the direct mail pieces. Utilize a talented volunteer or employ a professional, if needed. These pieces may be the final impression you leave with voters before they go to the polls. Make sure the pieces look sharp, reflect your message, and remain true to who you are.

Get bids from local and national printers before each print job. There can be a large difference in pricing between various companies. Don't just consider cost, however, in your final decision. Consider quality and the potential impact your campaign can make by using a local printer. If the price difference is negligible and quality is

Paid for by Vicky Hartzler for State Representative Committee
Loretta Filer, Treasurer
Street Address
Harrisonville, MO 64701

Bulk Rate
U.S. Postage
PAID
Permit #5
Harrisonville, MO

Nothing is More Important than *Life*

Vicky Hartzler — *Pro-Life* And Proud Of It

**Vicky Hartzler is a Pro-Life
State Representative.**

Vicky Hartzler is deeply committed to the
sanctity of human life and is fighting for the
protection of the unborn child.

In fact, Vicky's pro-life position has gained
her the **endorsement of *Missouri Right to Life*** in
this important race for state representative.

Like ***Missouri Right to Life***, Representative
Vicky Hartzler believes we should protect the life of
a child at all stages of development.

Vicky Hartzler.
The Right Vision.
The Right Values.

**On Election Day this year, there's more than a 'choice' at
stake...there's *life*. Reelect Pro-Life Representative Vicky Hartzler.**

FIGURE 7.3 Example of direct mail card with pro-life theme

acceptable, go with the local printer. It's another way you can reach
out to local voters.

Allow enough lead time with the printer to ensure the pieces are
ready to go when needed. Printers often require a three- to four-week
lead time. Get the copy to the printer on time if you hope to drop
the piece in the mail according to your plan.

Schedule the various direct mail pieces to "drop" at a staggered rate. Alternate the messages. Ideally, your last piece should arrive in the mail the day before election day. The number of direct mail pieces in your budget will determine how soon to start sending them out. If you raised enough money for a deluxe plan of ten to twelve pieces, you could start sending them four weeks out from Election Day, dropping a piece every four days during the first week, every three days the next week, every two days the week before the election, and one every day during the final week.

If you have enough money for six to eight pieces, you will want to start the week before the election and send them every other day.

If you are sending only a couple pieces, then you would want to wait until the last week and try to drop them so they will be in voters' mailboxes on either Wednesday or Thursday and the other on either the Saturday or Monday before election day. A literature drop to targeted neighborhoods over the weekend prior to the election can help supplement the limited number of direct mail pieces being utilized.

Managing the arrival time is sometimes difficult to achieve because direct mail pieces are sent via bulk mail and their delivery times can vary depending upon the workload of the local post office. The best thing to do is to meet with the post office officials ahead of time and discuss the projects. Get their advice on how they should be processed and delivered to them to ensure timely delivery. Most of the time they will be happy to work with you and will do their best to ensure the pieces are delivered on time. If you haven't obtained a bulk rate number yet, you will need to do so if you are going to mail them yourself. Also, confirm the exact size dimensions which need to be adhered to in order to receive the lowest possible rate on the cards. If the cards are even a half inch too large, extra fees can be assessed.

Candidates can utilize a mail house to address and send the direct mail pieces or they can partner with volunteers to get them out. If you are running short of manpower, you might be better off employing a mail house to both print and send out the mail—especially if you have a mailing of over five thousand pieces. Visit with other candidates, your state political party, local printers, or local elected officials to get their recommendations for reliable mail houses.

If, however, you have plenty of volunteers, label and send out the pieces as a campaign team. Involving volunteers saves money and generates enthusiasm for your candidacy; plus it is fun. To hold a mail drop party you will need to have gathered all the supplies (direct mail pieces, mailing labels, post office tubs, refreshments such as water and a light snack, trash sacks for the label backs), lined up a group of volunteers, and secured a location for the party, such as an office conference room or a home. Someone who is familiar with the postal regulations regarding bulk mail needs to head up the sorting activities to ensure your campaign receives the cheapest rate possible.

It is important that you, the candidate, participate in at least part of the activity. It is a good way to show that you are a partner with the volunteers, and it gives you an opportunity to thank them in person for their support, friendship, and help. You will be amazed at how quickly several thousand pieces of direct mail can be labeled and ready to mail with a group of enthusiastic supporters.

Letters

Letters are another form of direct mail utilized in campaigns. They can be mailed through a variety of means, depending upon a candidate's budget and volunteer base. Hand addressing the envelope and sending it first class ensures the greatest chance the letter will get opened. However, funding restraints and a limited number of volunteers often preclude personalization except for special events such as exclusive fundraisers.

An alternate method uses window envelopes. These work well if the letter is printed from a database that includes the individual address of the voter. Utilizing envelopes with a window saves time and money by avoiding the labeling process. Volunteers only need to fold the letter, stuff the envelope, and seal the flap.

If you purchase preprinted envelopes with your return address in the corner, avoid preprinting the postal indicia in the stamp corner. It is far more personalized to receive a letter with a precanceled bulk rate stamp or with a meter stamp using a bulk rate permit, than one that is preprinted on the envelope.

Consider these ideas when sending letters to voters.

Tabloids

Tabloids are another option that more and more candidates are using to convey their message. Tabloids are a mini-newspaper with exclusive "news" about you and your candidacy. Articles can be written highlighting your qualifications, sharing family information, featuring your experience and background, outlining your stands on campaign issues, and showing your participation in the various activities from the campaign. Tabloids can also be used to feature endorsements from area leaders.

There are three types of tabloids according to S. J. Guzetta in his book *The Campaign Manual :*[1] general, issue-oriented, and comparative. General tabloids are sent to a wide range of voters. Issue-oriented tabloids are sent to undecided voters as determined by your phone campaign. The purpose of issue-oriented tabloids is to inform and persuade voters that you are the best candidate to represent them. Comparative tabloids can be used in a close race. They compare the qualifications and stands on issues between the two candidates and are intended to sway voters near election day.

When designing the tabloid, avoid overcrowding the paper. Use plenty of white space. Feature a large number of quality photographs. Every page should have at least two photos. Remember that some people will read it cover to cover, but others will only glance at the pictures. Make sure the pictures convey your message.

Tabloids can be stuffed into your local newspaper for a price or sent out in bulk mail. Once again, your budget will dictate your options, but keep tabloids in mind as another possible tool to use in your campaign message toolbox.

No matter which direct mail pieces you use, they all carry your message directly into the households of your voters. Take time to design them effectively, and you will see results on election day.

CHAPTER 8

PRESENTING YOUR MESSAGE THROUGH EARNED AND PAID MEDIA

Ideally, in a campaign every candidate would like to meet every voter in his or her district. Realistically, this is not possible. You can maximize your time by focusing on events where the most voters will be and going door to door every day but still fall far short of the desired mark. Because of this, candidates have to rely on other means to convey their message. Direct mail is one way to reach the voters. Another way is through the media.

There are two types of media a candidate can use to spread his or her message: earned media and paid media. Both are important parts of a well-rounded, strategic campaign. Earned media entails media coverage the candidate did not have to pay for, such as newspaper articles, letters to the editors, and news releases on radio or television. Paid media includes traditional forms of advertising in newspapers, and on cable, television, and radio stations.

A well-organized campaign will include strategies for utilizing both earned and paid media. To maximize this opportunity, you need to develop good relations with the media in your area.

Earned media

Mark Twain once advised, "Never argue with someone who buys ink by the barrel." His statement provides insight into the sometimes tenuous relationship between candidates and the press. The candidate needs good press but does not control what is printed in the end. The reporter may have a different philosophical viewpoint that clouds his or her writing, and sometimes newspapers get caught up in the race to be the one to "break the news," not realizing or caring that the "news" they generate can "break" a family.

Ultimately, reporters and editors are people, too. They live in your town and are human. They come with their own viewpoints just like you, but most are professionals who feel an obligation to get factual information out to the public. They see it as a privilege to serve as guardians of the truth and we should thank them, ultimately, for their work and the free speech our country enjoys. Treat them fairly and most will treat you fairly. Provide accurate information to them and be available. You can experience a positive relationship with them. Be prudent in the words you choose to speak, but assume and expect the best.

Early on in your candidacy it is wise to meet with area media one on one. Stop by the office of your local newspapers or radio station and introduce yourself to the editors and reporters. While you are there, ask for an ad sheet that lists the prices for advertisements. Get their fax numbers, contact information for the editor and reporters including e-mail addresses, and schedule deadlines for all their papers. You might want to make an appointment ahead of time if their schedules are hectic.

When you go, take your campaign photograph with you and a press release you have written about yourself and your candidacy. Many papers will print or broadcast your initial release and subsequent releases you provide throughout your candidacy. Elections are big news and so your campaign's activities are newsworthy to them. Provide them with releases about your campaign issues as you roll them out—events you are hosting, fundraising or community proceedings you are participating in, and/or your reactions to your opponents' activities or comments on a news event.

Press releases

Press releases are not hard to write. The words "FOR IMMEDIATE RELEASE" should be written at the top left in capital letters followed by the date of the release and the contact name(s) and phone number(s) in case the reporter wants to follow up on the release. The contact person could be you or a campaign spokesman. The release is headlined by your press release title in bold letters. The beginning of your release should cite the city where the news is originating followed by a hyphen and then the beginning of your text.

Remember that news is written in a different format from a story or school report you may have written in the past. News stories follow an "inverted pyramid" model. Rather than the story leading up to a final conclusion or surprise ending, news stories highlight the important information up front with the rest of the release providing extra details about the main point. The first sentence should tell the who, what, when, where, and why of the article. Further paragraphs just expand on the first sentence theme.

The reason press releases are written in this format is because news reports are confined by limited space or air time. Reporters often crop extraneous material from press releases. You want to ensure that the most important point of your press release is featured, so it is listed first. Keep the press release short—no longer than one page and include at least one quote from you, the candidate. You want your name to appear in the newspaper to increase your name ID and so people will relate the activity with your candidacy.

The end of the press release is designated with the number -30- centered at the bottom of the page with hyphens on either side.

Below is a sample press release written in the correct format:

Sample Press Release

FOR IMMEDIATE RELEASE

April 17, 2007

CONTACT: John Doe (area code-123-4567)

**Candidate Doe to Host Neighborhood Forum
to Discuss Crime-Fighting Initiatives**

Anytown, MO.–John Doe, candidate for County Sheriff, will visit with neighborhood families and unveil his plans to combat crime in our community on Monday, May 1, 2007, at 7:00 P.M. in the community hall at 123 Hawthorn Lane, Anytown.

This neighborhood has been plagued with crime in recent years. One home, at 456 Johnson Drive, was condemned as a meth house last week. John Doe believes this scourge must stop. "It is time for our community to take a stand against crime. The blight of drugs is hurting our children, our families, and our community. I want to visit with the families of this area to hear their concerns. I also want to share with them my plan of action to address these problems."

All community members are invited to attend.

-30-

FIGURE 8.1 Example of press release

After the neighborhood forum, candidate John Doe should follow up with a subsequent press release telling about the forum and concisely describing the initiatives that were unveiled, with quotes from John Doe and quality photos of the candidate participating in the event. Fax or e-mail the press release to the papers in plenty of time prior to the paper deadlines to ensure you are covered in a timely manner.

Newspapers may not run either release, but they might. If they do, it provides free press for you and your candidacy. In addition, it lets the news editor and reporter know what you are doing and what you believe, which can be helpful if they endorse candidates prior to the election. If you are doing and planning great things but they don't know about it, how can they make an accurate assessment of your efficacy as a candidate?

Take the time to send regular press releases to area media throughout the campaign.

Interview tips

In the course of the campaign, you may have the opportunity to be interviewed by a reporter about an issue or your candidacy. This doesn't have to be stressful. It should be a pleasant conversation about your candidacy between professionals. To increase the likelihood of a positive interview, take into account these tips:

All interviews

- Consider ahead of time what points you want to make and how you want to make them. If a reporter calls and wants to ask you about your reaction to comments your opponent has made, consider calling him back after you've taken a few minutes to prepare. You don't have to talk with him right then. He will visit with you in a half hour or so. Say, "I'd be happy to talk with you about this in about a half hour. Can I call you back then?" In the meantime, think about what points you want to make and then stick to them during the interview. Many times a reporter will ask the same question several different ways, trying to get you to say something different or controversial. Keep to the point. Just keep rephrasing your original point and then you don't have to worry about a side comment appearing on the front page the next day.

- Keep your answer brief. Proverbs 10:19 says, "When words are many, sin is not absent, but he who holds his tongue is wise." Likewise, Proverbs 17:28 explains, "Even a fool is thought wise if he keeps silent, and discerning if he holds his tongue." Many a person has gotten tripped up when rambling on about a subject. The more you talk, the more opportunities you create to be misquoted.

- If you don't have an answer, say so. You can always get back with a reporter on your answer. Say, "I don't have the information on that at this moment and will need to get back with you on that." And make sure you do. This establishes your credibility with him or her.

- Don't say, "No comment." That makes you appear as if you are hiding something. If you don't want to comment because you don't have the information you need, then you can reply as above. If you don't want to comment because it is an unrelated topic or a trap question such as the cliché example "So, do you really beat your wife?" then divert the question back to your main points, "I'm a family man who's been married for thirty years. I care about my family and the families of our community. That's the reason I'm running. I'm running to protect our families, strengthen our schools, and improve our roads for the good of community." Ignore the set up. Get right back on your main points and repeat them again and again.

- Don't repeat the reporter's words. Reporters will often use a technique to get a good quote by trying to put words in your mouth. They will ask a question hoping that you will quote it back to them using their words. For example, a reporter may say, "So do you think your opponent was being belligerent or rude when he responded to you like that at the forum?" He or she wants you to say, "Yes, I thought it was rude that he did such and such." Even if you try to minimize his negative words by adding positive ones, you can still be in trouble. If you say, "It was rude, but I didn't let it bother me. I'm running a positive campaign and look forward to our next meeting," you have just left yourself open to seeing this blaring headline: "Candidate Calls Opponent Rude," with all your nice comments left out of the article.

Watch for this reporter technique. Be ready for it and don't fall into the trap. You don't have to address their topic in the way they present it. Say what you want to say and be quiet. Heed the words of this saying: "Silence is often misinterpreted, but never misquoted."

- Use "Off the Record" with discretion. It is okay to ask that a comment be made "off the record," but you need to ensure that the reporter understands this and agrees to it before proceeding. A reporter who is a professional should abide by this wish and won't violate your trust. However, this request should not be overused.

- Take your time. Remain poised during the interview. If a reporter asks a difficult question, feel free to pause and think through your answer. There's no rush or need to look like a polished commentator. The most important thing is for the right words to be relayed to the readers.

Television interviews

If you are interviewed on camera for television, consider these additional tips:

- Dress conservatively. Wild patterns and tweeds will "move" on the camera and look tacky. Wear solid, dark colors such as navy, gray, burgundy, or black. You can add color with a scarf or pin or tie. Avoid reflective jewelry. Have hair arranged neatly off your face. Wear a jacket or blouse that lends itself to easy attachment of a lapel microphone where the cord can easily be hidden.

- Look at the interviewer; not the camera. Keep your eyes on the interviewer and respond to questions by looking as natural as possible. Smile, if appropriate, or look serious if the topic warrants it. Overall, look pleasant.

- Keep good posture. If standing, keep hands loose at your sides. Use gestures, if appropriate, but don't overdo it. If sitting, keep hands resting comfortably on your legs and sit up straight toward the front of the chair. Avoid sitting back in your chair and resting your elbows on the arms of the chair. Generally, it's not a good idea to cross your legs. It looks too casual. If you are a woman, keep your legs side by side with your ankles crossed under the chair.

- Know what you want to say and say it over and over! This is especially true in television as most reports only include a brief sound bite from your interview. You want the clip to feature your main point, not some side comment!

One year I was being interviewed by CBS News when I was a spokesperson for the Coalition to Protect Marriage in Missouri. I went to a satellite video production studio to tape the interview. The news reporter asked his questions over the telephone. I had to respond as if he was there and I was visiting with him in person. The interview took over twenty minutes to tape. When the report ran, I was on camera approximately fifteen seconds. I had visited with my eighty-seven-year-old grandmother earlier in the day and mentioned I was going to be on the national news that night. She wanted to watch and asked what time the show was going to be on. Later that evening she called to say, "I almost missed it! You were only on there a few seconds!" I had to smile. Such is the case most of the time with television interviews, so determine your *most important point* and repeat it over and over during the interview. This will increase the likelihood that your message will be heard once the editing is done.

Letters to the editors

Letters to the editors can be effective ways to convey information about you and the issues important to your race. Early in the campaign you should identify individuals who might be willing to write a letter to the editor for your campaign. These volunteers should be good writers with credibility in the community. Throughout the campaign these individuals can write about various issues important to voters during your election and mention your position on these topics. They should avoid sounding like a campaign ad, however, or many newspaper editors will decline to publish them. In the event of an attack from your opponent's campaign, your friend can write a rebuttal to the newspaper and be far more effective than if you, the candidate, responded.

Always follow the rules outlined by the newspaper for submitting the letter and pay close attention to the timeframes outlined by the paper. The most carefully crafted letter will remain ineffective if it misses the deadline. Utilize the letter to the editor opportunity as another means of reaching the voters.

Paid media

Newspaper advertising

Newspaper advertising is a popular way to get out your message. Newspapers go throughout your district and reach a wide group of people. In some ways they are similar to the orders given in Bible times by Mordecai, which were "written in the script of every province and the language of each people and also to the Jews in their own script and language," which were sealed and "sent by mounted couriers, who rode fast horses especially bred for the king" to ensure everyone received the news (Est. 8:9–10). Newspapers today provide information to the households throughout your district.

If you live in an area with small, local newspapers, you need to have a visible presence in newspapers during the last three weeks of your campaign. If you live in a metropolitan area, this may not be cost-effective. Contact every newspaper in your area and ask for their pricing guidelines for various sizes of advertising. Ask them for their circulation numbers to determine which papers to hit if funding does not allow you to be in every paper. Use your budget to determine how many ads and in what sizes can be placed in the newspapers. Ideally, you will want to place an ad in every weekly newspaper in your district for the three weeks prior to the election. Similarly, you will want to place an ad in every daily newspaper on the top two distribution days during the week. The final issue should highlight two or three ads of different sizes and shapes, creating a crescendo effect for your campaign. Remember that you want your campaign to build momentum throughout the campaign, culminating in a final surge of support on election day.

The layout of the advertisement makes a difference. Work with the newspaper to design your ad if you don't already have one prepared. Many times they will provide this service free as part of the advertising cost, but you need to have an idea what you want before talking with them.

Now is the time to use excellent pictures. People who peruse a newspaper often stop and look at the pictures. They skip the text. Your ad should feature at least one picture of you, two are better. The picture should capture the essence of your message. It should convey who you are and what you have to bring to the office you are seeking. A general rule of thumb is for the ad space to be divided with a ratio of two-thirds pictures and one-third text.

Use your logo in your ad. People should recognize your campaign by the logo by now. Seeing your logo while looking at a newspaper inside their houses will reinforce the yard sign impact they are seeing outside.

Feature endorsements you have secured. This could be in the form of quotes from community leaders or just a listing of individuals or organizations that have endorsed you. Endorsements can be used effectively in a contrast ad or direct mail piece as well, because endorsements do say something about the candidates. For this reason, don't seek an endorsement from any group you wouldn't be proud to list alongside your name.

Make the ad visible by using a lot of black ink or white space. Black can be added by choosing a bold border, using large letters, or creating a "reverse" ad (black background with white letters). Your name should be the blackest part of the ad so people remember your

FIGURE 8.2 Sample newspaper ad

name and associate the ad with your candidacy. White space reduces the clutter of ads. The reader will be able to pick out your ad if you leave plenty of white space around pictures or text.

Consider the maxim "less is more." Sometimes impact can be achieved by using only a few words in a large space rather than a lot of text. People are busy and often won't take the time to read a lot of text. Can you say your message in a few words or with a winning combination of effective pictures, good logo, and few words? If you can, you've probably designed a good ad.

I used quarter page ads during most of my campaigns. The last week of the campaign I supplemented the quarter page ads with a bumper strip size ad which was different than the customary box or rectangle shaped ads. In general, ads below a quarter page get lost among the regular ads in the newspaper. If you can afford quarter, half, third, or full-page ads, the advertisement will probably be seen. Think "outside the box" of traditional newspaper advertising and you will achieve greater results.

Radio and television advertising

If your area has access to other forms of media, you will want to investigate the costs of utilizing them. Other common forms of advertising include radio ads, television spots, and cable television ads or promos. Enlist a volunteer to contact the stations and find out the following information:

1. *Pricing for a thirty-second or sixty-second spot*—Ad prices are determined by the time of day the ad is run. You can lock in the time when your ad will play (preferably during the news or prime time, if television, and drive time, if radio) or pay for the ad to be run in ROS time. ROS time is the "run of the station" time which allows the station to run the ad whenever they want. You lose control over when your ad will run if you buy ROS time, but it is usually cheaper this way.

If you have cable in your community, find out the rate for political advertising on the local channel as well as popular channels such as the Family Channel, CNN, and ESPN. Sometimes the rates for cable advertising are more reasonable than you think.

2. *The numbers and demographics of the station*—Radio and television stations collect demographic information about their audiences. This is used for advertising purposes. The stations can often tell you the ages, genders, economic status, and philosophical preferences of the people who typically listen to their stations at various times of the day. They also should have an idea of how many people listen or watch their television programs. This information can be helpful to you as you budget your funds and target your audience.

3. *How much they will assist you in developing your ad*—Sometimes the station will record the spot and provide assistance in writing it. Others require you to have the ad completely ready to be aired.

4. *Whether or not your opponent has bought air time*—Radio and television stations are subject to federal law and are regulated by the Federal Communications Commission (FCC). Current law requires political ads to be sold at the lowest commercial rates. It also stipulates your political ads have the right to be matched by your opponent. They have to give equal air time to your opponent if he or she has the money to buy it. This regulation also gives *you* the right to find out what air times your opponent has purchased so you can match his or her schedule. Ask a volunteer to call daily and inquire if your opponent has purchased air time. This will help determine your opponent's game plan and if you need to communicate through this medium, as well.

After you have gathered this information, you can decide if purchasing radio or television ads is a cost-effective way to get your message across to the electorate. Radio ads may be reasonable and targeted to a specific community in your district and thus a viable option for your campaign. Most local candidates cannot afford television ads. In addition, television often wastes money because the audience is too broad for your particular race. It isn't cost effective.

This is especially true in urban areas where an expensive television or radio ad for a county office might be broadcast over a ten-county region, wasting precious campaign dollars. However, if the ad is on a rural radio station, it might only broadcast to a two-county region that matches your constituency. A careful analysis will ensure that money is wisely spent.

Radio and television message tips

Once your campaign has gathered the cost information and the decision has been made to move forward with radio or television advertising, consider these tips recommended by Chris Benjamin:[1]

Radio

- Thirty-second spots are good for name ID, but you will need a sixty-second spot in order to get out a message.
- Ads can be recorded at the station. If you use an outside vendor, it will cost more.
- Purchase ads for only Monday–Friday runs except the Saturday and Sunday immediately before election day.
- Run ads only in the morning on election day.
- Follow this plan if your campaign has plenty of money: Four weeks out, begin running four spots per day during drive time. Two weeks out, run eight spots per day. One week out, run ten to twelve spots a day. For a more modest budget, run ads closer to the election during drive time spots.
- Fourteen to sixteen spots a day are considered the "saturation point" if you are running two different ads in rotation during the same week.
- Verify that the stations run the ads. Have a volunteer listen for them and let you know. If they neglect to run your ad as purchased, ask for a free run time to compensate.
- Pursue earned media by sending in a radio version of the press release electronically. This is called a "radio actuality."

A candidate digitally records the short, fifteen-second spot using a microphone attached to his computer and sends it via e-mail to the station. The station might run your comments as part of its news and give you free press.

Television

- Use your demographics to determine the best times of day to run TV commercials. For example, if you are running in a rural area, your ads might want to be placed in the 5:00–6:00 P.M. news slot, on early morning shows, and possibly a farm show. If you want your message to reach women, you might consider running it during late morning or late afternoon TV talk shows that appeal to women, in addition to the news hours. If you want to reach senior citizens, consider running the ads during game shows or other programs the station has identified are popular with them.
- Use a professional vendor to produce the ads.
- TV is the best medium to increase name ID, get the message out, and change polling.
- Run each ad for three days before changing.

Both

- The candidate's voice must be on television and radio advertisements somewhere per the Federal Communications Commission regulations. Check with them prior to production to ensure compliance.

Another option to explore is advertising on cable. Some local candidates have successfully utilized their cable's local channel to convey a visual message to the electorate. In his book *How to Run for Local Office,* former mayor of Westland, Michigan, Robert Thomas, describes how he used the local cable channel to promote his candidacy for as little as five dollars for an hour of air time.[2] He set up an interview in his home in front of a fireplace, answering questions about his race and the issues that were important to him. He chose the local Teacher of the Year to do the interviewing and ran the program between two o'clock and three o'clock *in the morning* on the local cable network a few days before the election. It was a tremendous hit and came as a total surprise to his opponent. People were watching at that hour of day and spread the word about Robert and his candidacy. Maybe it would work for you, also.

Check with your local provider to determine usage and if cable advertising is worthwhile. Ask what programs are most popular and what the demographic makeup is for each channel. Running two to four spots per day per selected cable channel for two weeks will help convey your message, unleashing another powerful weapon from your advertising arsenal.

Consider all avenues for getting out your message and don't be afraid of the media. They are an important resource for conveying your message and, like Mordecai's couriers, can enable your message to be heard throughout the land.

CHAPTER 9

PRESENTING YOUR MESSAGE THROUGH THE INTERNET

Today's candidates enjoy both the challenges and the unlimited potential of a new avenue to convey their messages and garner support: the Internet. While candidates in the past relied on newspaper ads and direct mail pieces to win elections, today's candidates are faced with a new reality: many people get the information from the Internet and, if they want to get elected, they need to be a part of it or lose out to a more computer-savvy opponent.

In an article in *Campaigns and Elections* magazine, Waldo Jaquith credits much of the success of the Democratic Party in the 2006 election cycle to the use of the Internet. Jaquith relates the traditional methods used, then says, "Simultaneously, the party and its candidates embraced the netroots' model and became smarter about how they use the Internet by using blogs to get the message out, focusing on accumulating many small donations from individuals who often lived outside candidates' districts and learning to function within the non-hierarchical structure of the Internet."[1]

The use of the Web has made a difference in past elections and promises even greater potential in the future. According to Internet World Stats, over 69.9 percent of the United States population uses the Internet.[2] More and more people are using the Web to access information and share ideas with others. Young voters are growing up surfing the Web daily, blogging, text messaging their friends, researching topics, downloading files, and establishing their opinions from the Web. They expect to find out about candidates the same way.

Campaigns that utilize the Internet are winning elections, and you can, too. It starts with developing a good Web site.

Web sites

Web sites provide a place for voters to find out more about the candidate's background, to see a picture of him or her, to learn about his or her views on issues of importance, to contribute, or to sign up to volunteer. Smart candidates will take the time to learn more about how to utilize this important tool or at least hire someone who does.

The basic steps to set up a Web site include the following:

1. Register your domain name. The domain name is the main content of a Web site address prior to the .com. Keep the name fairly short, easy to type, and one that makes sense to voters. Most candidates use their name, if possible, such as www.johndoe.com. Some use their campaign name: www.johndoeforsheriff.com. Choose a name that people can remember and use easily, and then register the domain name on a registry such as register.com or godaddy.com.

2. Choose a Web hosting company to host the site for you. There is a huge variety of Web hosting companies to choose from. Most of them also provide domain name registration services, and prices range from somewhere in the neighborhood of $2 per month for basic Web hosting to substantially higher for full-featured sites. Christian Web hosting sites like www.axletreemedia.com are popular options, but other sites can be accessed through search engines like Google and Yahoo.

3. Decide what information you want to put on your Web site. The homepage should act as the "front door" for your campaign, showing what information can be found on the Web site and providing a way to access it at a click of the mouse. Basic information included on candidate homepages often includes:

- the candidate's photo;
- campaign logo;
- the basic message(s) of the campaign;
- upcoming events;
- candidate background;
- family photos; and/or
- links for: Make a Contribution, Get Involved, Contact Us, Issues, and Newsroom.

In order to take contributions online, you need to set up a payment system account with PayPal or a credit card service company. If you don't want to pursue an online system, the Web site link should, at a minimum, contain a contribution sheet with the campaign address so people can print it off to send contributions to you via mail.

The Get Involved link provides voters with an opportunity to volunteer with your campaign. This can be done through a printable form or through an online form. A printable form allows volunteers to complete the form at home, then mail it to your campaign headquarters. An online form is filled out on the computer and sent to headquarters via a click of the mouse. This online method enables your campaign to receive the information in electronic form, eliminating the need for data entry. Most campaigns will want to utilize both formats in order to attract the greatest number of volunteers.

The Newsroom link often lists news articles that have been printed about you or your campaign.

The Contact Us page can either be a direct link to your e-mail address or go to a page that lists your campaign's address, phone number, and e-mail address link.

4. Compile the information for your Web site. This involves writing the text and choosing the photographs and graphics that will share your message.

5. Create the Web site. Putting together a modern, user-friendly Web site can be a daunting task if you have not created one before. If you plan to feature a blog, user comments area, streaming video/audio, or payment processing on your site, the level of complexity can increase to the point where it requires a large amount of time to build and maintain.

    Most candidates hire a Web designer to put their Web site together or enlist the services of a campaign volunteer who does Web design for a living. During the process you'll want to meet with the Web designer and specify what you want and meet with him or her regularly to watch how the site's development is progressing.

    If you choose to create a site yourself, you can buy or download some of the popular Web design tools. NVU (http://nvu.com) is a popular site design tool and is free for the asking. Adobe Fireworks can be purchased for a reasonable price and is also very popular.

6. Launch! Once you have your Web site developed, you are ready to launch. Use this opportunity to send out a press release. E-mail all your friends and invite them to visit your Web site. Ask them to send the e-mail to their friends. Use feedback to fix any beginning glitches so that it will run smoothly throughout the rest of the campaign.

7. Update your Web site regularly. Manning the site is a great opportunity for a tech-savvy volunteer. Ask him or her to weekly post new articles, new photos, and comments from voters about your candidacy. Try using a weekly poll to keep people coming back to your site to see the posted poll results.

Send an e-mail out to your database linking them to your Web site so they can click and see the results. Hopefully, each time they come back they will not only see the poll results but will also learn something new about you and your candidacy.

8. Sell your site. People have to know about your site in order to benefit from its messages. Include your Web site address on all your direct mail pieces, signs, pushcards, and advertisements. Don't miss an opportunity to let people know about your Web site.

Take the time to make your Web site look professional and reflect your candidacy. Your Web site can help shape opinion about you, garner financial support, recruit volunteers, and put you over the top on election day.

Blogging

A blog is a Web log. It's a free place where people can go online, read your comments, and post their responses. Blogs have the power to spread your message quickly, generate buzz about your campaign, and get media attention. Increasingly, journalists are reading campaign blogs to get ideas for their stories. By taking advantage of this new medium for your message, you can increase the impact of your campaign.

Blogs can be a part of your Web site or a stand-alone place on the Internet. They are usually centered around one general topic and linked to other blogs. By linking your blog to other like-minded sites, you can increase the likelihood of your thoughts being read. This is called connecting to the blogosphere (a "spaghetti network of sites and content"[3]).

Your Web designer can integrate a blog into your Web site for you. If you want to develop a stand-alone blog, it can be created rather easily according to Stuart Shepard in his article "Now Entering the Blogosphere."[4] The steps involved are:

1. Go to a popular blog development site such as http://blogger.com, http://wordpress.com, or http://typepad.com. Create a Google account if you don't have one, or sign in if you do.
2. Enter a title and the URL (Web) address of your blog.
3. Choose a design template for your blog.
4. Decide whether or not you want to allow comments from the readers. If so, choose that option.
5. Log in to http://blogspot.com. Click on New Post. Enter a title and type.

Blogs are something friends can do for you. They can set up a blog that talks about your campaign and facilitate the blog postings. They can also filter the outside comments prior to posting to ensure that the integrity of your site is preserved.

The potential for spreading information about your campaign (good and bad) through blogging is huge. Consider adding this tool to your campaign toolbox.

E-mail

While a blog is an open-ended site, which people may or may not access, e-mails are a way of disseminating information in a specific, targeted way. The impact of e-mails has a way of multiplying as receivers forward them on to their friends who forward them on to their friends, etc. This exponential factor of communication can deliver your message to multiple households at basically no cost, making it a very powerful tool of your campaign.

Of all the Internet tools, e-mails probably provide the greatest opportunity for local candidates. While voters in many parts of the U.S. are still not used to searching out the Web page of a candidate running for county assessor or the local school board, they will read e-mails about those candidacies that arrive in their inbox. Take time to develop this tool first, and then proceed with other Internet options if you have the resources.

There are many way to use e-mails in a campaign. They can be in the form of a weekly campaign update e-mail to supporters or a press release e-mail sent to the media and copied to everyone you know. They can be used to generate campaign funds or to react to campaign controversies which arise, enabling you to get out information in a timely fashion.

Start collecting e-mail addresses early. Include the e-mail address line as an option on all your volunteer sign-up sheets. Ask friends and campaign team members to share e-mail addresses of likely supporters with you. Hopefully, your e-mail list will grow and grow throughout the campaign and afterward.

If possible, develop e-mail subgroups along with a large, general group listing. Subgroups might be based on gender, interests (pro-guns or pro-life, for example), church, organizations, or political party. By developing detailed e-mail lists, you can send targeted e-mails to particular groups, generating the biggest impact for your candidacy.

A word of caution: Just as your positive campaign message can spread rapidly via e-mail, so can misinformation, so be cautious with your words. Don't disseminate anything that is not verified or doesn't glorify God. Whatever you put out can be used against you, so use caution. If in doubt; don't. You can't take back words once you click the send button and you can't control where the words will travel. As Psalm 141:3 says, "Set a guard over my mouth, O LORD; keep watch over the door of my lips." Keep watch over what is sent through your campaign's use of the Internet to ensure integrity and peace of mind.

Text messaging

While e-mails are usually sent to a computer, a text message is sent to an individual's cell phone. Text messages are obviously shorter than e-mail messages and contain less "rich" content (pictures, videos, etc.) due to the constraints of their environment (a cell phone vs.

a computer), but they can be invaluable for sending information to large numbers of people and reaching them no matter where they are or what time of day it is.

Text messages sent to a cell phone are typically known as "SMS messages." You can send text messages to individual cell phones directly using your own cell phone, but a more likely use for SMS messaging would be to send a "mass mailing" to all of your supporters' cell phones at the same time. This is known as "bulk SMS messaging." To do this, you can sign up at one of the popular bulk SMS messaging sites such as http://smseverywhere.com and http://bulksms.com.

Online videos

Short videos you can watch over the Internet are called online videos. Video Web sites like YouTube have emerged as a powerful medium for spreading messages to the masses. According to the article "Moving Pictures Move People," over a hundred million clips were viewed daily at YouTube in July 2006 and 65,000 new videos were uploaded every 24 hours.[5]

Candidacies have fallen over these videos. In 2006, U.S. Senator George Allen was caught on video making a derogatory remark about his opponent's campaign worker. That video was spread via YouTube and, as they say, the rest is history. He lost narrowly on election day and his video is still remains online for the world to see.

Conversely, candidates have won utilizing this medium. Mark Funkhouser ran successfully for mayor of Kansas City, Missouri, in the spring of 2007 without securing a typical campaign team. Instead, he relied heavily on the Internet, setting up a Web site, blog, and link to his spot on MySpace. Most interestingly, his Web site featured several videos that conveyed his campaign messages, showed testimonials of supporters, and shared creative, humorous videos produced by supporters. The Internet buzz he created through these mediums helped push him over the top on election day defeating a longtime respected politician who ran a more traditional campaign.

Producing a Web video is easier and cheaper than you think according to Stuart Shepard, managing editor of Focus on the Family's daily e-mail update *Citizen-Link*.[6] If you want to produce a Web video, all you need is a video camera, which can connect to your computer, and a broadband connection. Video editing software helps you make a more professional-looking video but isn't necessary. Your computer may have come with movie making software, so check to see what's on your computer before buying additional programs.

Below are the steps to creating a Web video:

1. Develop your script. Decide what message you want to send. Consider telling your basic message: who you are, why you are running for office, and what you hope to accomplish, if elected.

2. Choose your setting wisely. Going outdoors or sitting by the fire gives a more friendly setting to share your message. Include family members and pets.

3. Consider the lighting. Indirect outdoor lighting looks nice.

4. Wear a lapel mike to ensure high-quality audio.

5. Don't zoom in and out while recording.

6. Keep it short. Try keeping it less than 120 seconds. Say what you want to say and quit.

7. Record at a resolution of 320 x 240 and fifteen frames per second for optimal posting.

8. During editing, avoid "jump cuts" between scenes. Use a "cutaway" shot in between or dissolve from one shot to the next.

9. Upload your video to your Web site or a site such as YouTube. You can upload a video directly to your site for viewing, but be aware that the required bandwidth might involve an extra cost with your Web hosting company. If that turns out to be the case, another option is to upload your video to YouTube or another video hosting site and link to it from your site.

This has the advantage of making your video accessible to more viewers and shifts the bandwidth cost burden to another site.

Podcasting

Podcasts are digital audio files that are distributed over the Internet for playback on personal computers and portable media players such as iPods. A podcast can be used to deliver your message in a manner similar to a radio broadcast. Recordings of speeches and personal messages from you, the candidate, are examples of things you could make available to download from your Web site as podcasts.

To make a podcast, follow these basic steps:

1. Make an audio recording of your message or speech in a digital sound file so it can be played on a computer. This can be done by hooking up a laptop computer loaded with the right software with the sound system where you are speaking. Common software packages that create such source files are Audacity and Adobe Audition. Operating them is similar to operating a tape recorder.
2. Encode your speech as an MP3 file so it can be downloaded easily from the Internet by the user. The recording software you are using should be able to convert your recording to an MP3 file without requiring you to install additional software.
3. Upload your recording to your Web site and create a link to it, or send it to your Web designer and have him or her integrate it into your Web site.
4. Send the message to the radio stations in your area, as well. They may play parts of your podcast as a news story.

You are now ready to enter the Cyber World and start sharing your message. No matter what methods you use, the possibilities for using the Internet are limitless. Hopefully, you will have a computer-savvy volunteer (or son or daughter) who can head up the development and management of these projects if you are not familiar with the process. But even if you have to pay someone to help you in these areas, it is worth the effort in today's high-tech world. It's the new way to convey your message.

CHAPTER 10

TARGETING THE VOTERS

Targeting voters was a political term new to me previous to my first campaign. The term conjures up images of an archer sighting his arrow on the bull's-eye of the target and carefully releasing the arrow so it hits dead center with a resounding ping. In the campaign world, it involves identifying those individuals most likely to vote for you and focusing your energies on securing their votes.

While it would be nice to chat for hours and send volumes of information to every person in your area, the limited resources of time, money, and personal energy usually prevent that. A campaign only lasts for a limited amount of time and you, as the candidate, (unless you are truly Superman or Superwoman) cannot physically get to know the life history of every person you are going to represent; thus, the need to "target."

Targeting doesn't limit your "heart" for everyone in your district or your desire to serve all. It just employs the wisdom of focusing your time, energies, and efforts on the strategies that will enable you to win and, thus, serve all after the election.

Absalom targeted his voters. In verse two of 2 Samuel 15, we see he didn't waste his time on those who were not from Israel, i.e., who couldn't "vote" for him. As people approached, Absalom would

ask, "What town are you from?" If they said they were from one of
the tribes of Israel, he continued the conversation and presented his
"campaign message" to them.

Targeting takes on various forms, depending upon the method
being used to meet the public. In going door to door, it involves
identifying the registered voters and going to their doors with your
literature. In attending large gatherings such as service organization's
fundraising dinners, grand openings of businesses, or community
gatherings, targeting means attending those functions in your campaign area where the largest number of voters will be located. In
direct mail, it means producing message pieces for a target audience
and sending the mailing only to that group.

Obtain good voter information

Targeting begins with obtaining lists of registered voters. A wealth
of important voter information can be obtained from your local
election authority such as:

- Precincts in your district and corresponding maps of your
  district;
- Election polling sites;
- Registered voters;
- Registered voters' addresses;
- Registered voters' ages and genders;
- Households of more than one registered voter;
- Voter history (which elections voters voted in, not how they
  voted);
- Number of registered voters in each precinct;
- Number of people who actually voted from each precinct for
  a given election;
- The percentage of people who voted in each precinct;
- The percentage of people who voted in a given election;
- Vote totals for various candidates in past elections;

- People who voted by absentee ballot; and
- In some states, political affiliations of voters.

Obtain a copy of this information on disc if you have access to a computer and possess the skills to manipulate and print out walk lists and labels from your headquarters. If you can't, ask the election authority to print out what you need. They will charge only a nominal fee since voter history is considered free public information. Another option is to ask your political party, which might have similar lists to share with candidates.

You will want to use this information in a variety of ways. Since your time and funds are limited, you will want to use your time wisely in the campaign and focus your efforts on people who actually vote and who will be most likely to vote in your election. For instance, if you are running for city council, you can sort the information by voter history to obtain a list of people who typically vote in elections where there are city council races and only go door to door at their houses. Not everyone votes in every election. Some people only vote in the presidential general elections. If you have time, it would be nice to try to get everyone out to vote for you, but most of the time you don't. Using your list, you can target frequent voters that show a likelihood of voting in your election.

Another way you can use this information is to determine the households with more than one frequent voter. If you are going door to door and only have a few evenings left to campaign or want to do a last minute get-out-the-vote literature drop, you might want to target the multi-voter households compared to ones that don't often vote or have only one voter living in the household.

Direct mail pieces can be targeted to certain ages or genders by using this list. In addition, precincts that contain a large percentage of people who actually vote in your type of election can be targeted.

Absentee ballot information can be used to target individuals with your campaign literature just prior to the time absentee voting begins.

The information obtained free from your local election authority can help you run a smart, focused campaign with tremendous results. Get a copy of it and start using it to your advantage.

Targeting door to door

Analyze your district to target precincts. This is not hard but does take some time. This would be a good project for a detail-oriented volunteer. In this analysis, you are going to:

- Identify the precincts most favorable to candidates from your political party (your base precincts);
- Find precincts with the greatest number of split-ticket voters (your swing precincts); and
- Determine areas of high and low voter turnout.

This information is instrumental to your targeting efforts. It allows you to prioritize the order of your door-to-door efforts so as to ensure maximum exposure with the voters most likely to support you or ones who could be persuaded most easily to vote for you. Generally, if you are a Republican, you will want to prioritize your door-to-door schedule from precincts most Republican to least Republican and, if you are a Democrat, vice versa. But the listing should also take into account the caveats of the number of split-ticket voters and the raw numbers of registered voters who actually cast ballots on election day. These factors can change the final order of precinct door-to-door priority.

Step One: Determine basic political loyalty of precincts

To determine the basic party loyalty of precincts, you will need to obtain election results from key races in the past. You can get a basic idea by looking at one race, but two or three are better.

If you choose to analyze only one past race, consider looking at a candidate whose race reveals the base of support for a candidate from your party—one where people voted for the candidate just because of his or her political affiliation. A good example would be a statewide candidate who received little attention in the election and whose vote results are probably reflective more of party loyalty than personal conviction, such as a state treasurer's race.

List the raw numbers of votes your party's candidate received along with the number of votes the opponent received. Determine the percentage of votes your party's candidate received by dividing the number of votes your candidate received by the total number of votes cast in that precinct for all candidates.

By looking at the percentages of support for a candidate in a base election, you can make an initial door-to-door schedule by ranking the precincts most favorable to candidates from your political party to those least favorable.

Here is an example of an analysis for Suzie Smart, State Treasurer candidate.

Precinct Number	Number of Votes for Suzie	Number of Votes for Opponent	Total Number of Votes Cast	Percentage for Suzie	Precinct Priority
1	184	101	285	64%	1
2	303	412	715	42%	3
3	67	97	164	40%	4
4	437	489	926	47%	2

FIGURE 10.1 Example of voting analysis for Suzie Smart, state treasurer candidate from your political party

If you have time, analyze several races of unknown statewide candidates or unpopular local candidates to get a more complete picture of precinct voting loyalty by political party. Determine the percentage of votes the candidates from your party received, then record the percentages on the form, add them up, and divide them by the number of races you reviewed to get the average. The precinct order would be determined from looking at the averages and ranking them from highest to lowest.

Precinct Number	Percentage for Suzie	Percentage for Candidate 2	Percentage for Candidate 3	Average Percentage	Precinct Priority by Political Loyalty
1	64%	57%	62%	61%	1
2	42%	45%	38%	41%	4
3	40%	54%	53%	49%	2
4	47%	49%	45%	47%	3

FIGURE 10.2 Example of voting analysis to determine precinct priority by analyzing three races

By analyzing and averaging several elections, we got a better picture of the political allegiance of the precincts. If you are limited on time, the basic calculation from these examples may be the only precinct analysis you want to do. In my first race for state representative, this was the only analysis we did and it proved to be a good tool in helping me to prioritize my time going door to door. However, if you want to get a more complete understanding of the voting patterns in your district, you might also want to determine the potential number and precinct percentage of split-ticket voters.

Step Two: Determine split ticket potential by precinct

Split-ticket voters are sometimes called independent voters or swing voters. They are the individuals who will cross party lines to vote for a candidate of their choice—ones who are not tied to voting due to a strong political allegiance. These individuals often determine the outcome of an election and are highly sought after by all candidates. By analyzing past voting results, you can determine the areas of your district with the largest number of individuals who might cross party lines to vote for you (or your opponent). These areas are called swing precincts. When going door to door, candidates are wise who target not only precincts that typically vote for candidates of their political party, but also swing precincts.

Compare the election results from a "base" race and a "high" race of the same election year to determine the number and percentage of independent or split-ticket voters. (It is important to ensure the analysis is from the same type election, as voter turnout differs in presidential election years.) The base race would be one like the State Treasurer example above. The high race would be another candidate in that same election from your political party who was well known and won in your district by a large percentage. This could be a presidential candidate or popular local candidate from your party. Record the percentage of votes this candidate received in each precinct. This is the potential high number of votes you could receive. To determine the percentage of independent voters in each precinct, do a simple two-step calculation:

1. Take the number of voters who voted for the popular candidate from your party and subtract the number of voters who voted for the base candidate. This gives you the raw number of split-ticket voters from that election.

2. Take the raw number of split-ticket voters and divide it by the total number of votes cast in that precinct for the high race candidate. This gives you the percentage of potential independent voters from that precinct. Rank your precincts accordingly.

Here's an example of what an analysis for independent voters might look like.

Precinct Number	Number of Votes for Suzie	Number of Votes for Popular Candidate from Same Party	Total Votes Cast in Popular Candi-date's Race	Raw Number of Split-Ticket Voters	Percentage of Split-Ticket Voters	Precinct Priority
1	184	267	439	83	19%	2
2	303	387	572	84	14%	4
3	67	145	285	78	27%	1
4	437	603	1015	166	16%	3

FIGURE 10.3 Example of voting analysis for swing precincts.

"Swing" precincts are the ones with a higher than average percentage of people who cross party lines to vote. To find the average of the precincts, divide the total of the percentages by the number of precincts. In the above illustration, the average percentage of split-ticket voters is 19 percent.

From this analysis, you can see that Precinct 3 has a tremendously high number of independent voters (27 percent), which is 8 percent higher than the district average. It is the only true 'swing' *precinct*. Precinct 3 should be considered for door to door inclusion even if it would not have been prioritized high based on its past support of candidates from your political party.

Step Three: Look at raw numbers of voters

The third piece of election results information you might want to look at is the raw number of registered voters who voted during the high election in a precinct. Sometimes there are very small precincts with a high percentage of voters who are favorable to candidates from your party, but their small numbers might lower their priority rating. It makes more sense to spend time going door to door in areas that may not historically be as favorable but can deliver more total votes.

Step Four: Putting it all together

Now you are ready to determine your door-to-door target based on your analyses. Your campaign team will prove invaluable in this important discussion. Put all three pieces of information side by side to determine your final precinct priority. Also, consider such additional factors as where the candidates live, explosive issues in one area that might work for or against your candidacy, or physical setting of the precinct. Precincts in predominately rural or urban areas may be difficult to reach through door-to-door efforts and, thus, affect their final door-to-door priority ranking.

A sample final analysis based on the above calculations might look like this:

Precinct Number	Precinct Priority by Political Loyalty	Precinct Priority by Split-Ticket Voters	Raw Number of Registered Voters who Voted	Additional Factors	FINAL Precinct Order
1	1	2	439		1
2	4	4	572	Candidate Lives Here	3
3	2	1	285	Very Rural Area	4
4	3	3	1015		2

FIGURE 10.4 Example of final precinct priority ordering after considering all factors

In the final sample analysis, Precinct 1 was chosen as the number 1 priority due to its historical voting pattern of supporting candidates from your same political party and the high ranking of split-ticket voters.

Precinct 4 was selected as the second precinct of your door-to-door focus due to the potential large number of voters living in that precinct who actually vote and the very rural nature of Precinct 3, which would make it hard to go door to door despite its historical support of candidates of your political party and its dominance as a swing district. No doubt Precinct 3 will want to be a focus of your direct mail and get-out-the-vote efforts but will not rank high on your door-to-door schedule.

Precinct 2 was chosen as the third precinct on your door-to-door schedule because you live in this precinct. Even though it historically does not vote for candidates of your party or contain a high number of split-ticket voters, it is hoped that your personal relationships with your neighbors will help pull additional votes your way and reward your efforts to meet them.

Step Five: Use the analysis as a tool, not as a predictor of your destiny

These calculations are meant to only give you a guide in your door-to-door efforts. They are not meant to give a false sense of security if past election results have been positive or cause discouragement if past results have not been so favorable.

One of the realities of my first race, which made it even more of a leap of faith for me to say, "Yes" to the call to run, was the fact that my area had been represented by someone of the opposite political party for the entire history of its existence except for a short stint right after the Civil War and one two-year term in the early 1970s. People told me it was "impossible to win" for someone who aligned with my chosen party's affiliation.

When I analyzed the precincts for political tendencies, there was no one area that was strongly aligned with my party. Conversely, there were areas which were very supportive to the opposite party. This could have been very discouraging, and would have been, had I not known that God had called me to run and the campaign was in His hands. Win or lose, I would press forward. I was to do my part. The results were in His hands.

A political advisor suggested I just write off those precincts most favorable for my opponent's party. I wasn't so ready to do this. I did agree to put them last on my door-to-door schedule, but I wanted to go into the "lion's den" and let God work. My thinking was, *Of course they will continue to vote the way they always have if they are never presented with a good alternative. They will continue to vote a straight party ticket unless shown that candidates of my party were worthy of their support.*

When I did campaign in those typically unsupportive precincts, the response was encouraging. I did meet several people loyal to the opposite political party when going door to door, but I met more people who were appreciative of my visit—interested people who listened to my presentation and responded positively. My area is growing and I soon discovered the new people moving in were very open-minded and did not hold a strong allegiance with any party. They were more independent than anything and agreed with me on my positions. There is a strong possibility that people will vote for the person who expends the effort to come to their doors. I'm glad I took the time to go. While I did lose the four precincts that first election most typically aligned with the opposite political party, I only lost them narrowly. I won the rest. In the next two campaigns, I won them all.

I had a friend who ran for state representative who was advised to not waste his time campaigning in a certain area because of its historical voting pattern of only 38 percent for candidates from his party. He made it his goal to achieve 43 percent of the vote there, however, and worked hard campaigning in that area despite the overwhelming odds against gaining its support. When the votes were tallied on election day, my friend received 45 percent of the vote from that area—enough to help gain a total of 53 percent of the vote that put him over the top in a very tight election.

Don't ever write off anyone. True, it is wise to target and expend your limited resources and energies on those most likely to vote for you; however, you can gain great ground by believing and acting upon the belief that everyone is reachable. Proceed with the belief, "They will like me. They will want to hear and will support my message." Don't run and hide. Run to win.

Target households within each precinct. Now that you have determined your door-to-door schedule, you are ready to target specific *households* within each precinct. You will want to use the list of registered voters to develop your door-to-door strategy. Going to unregistered households is depicted as a waste of time by most political strategists.

To be candid, I struggled with this advice during my initial campaign. First of all, I didn't believe the list of registered voters I obtained was current and, secondly, our state had recently implemented a new form of registering voters: the mail-in postcard. After following the political advice and skipping several houses on the street due to their names not being on the list but later discovering the persons who resided there were registered households, I determined to make it my goal to go to every house in the towns in my district. This took a lot more effort but gave me peace of mind that I didn't skip anyone. In addition, I decided to try to register those who weren't registered. Who better to provide the service of registering them to vote than the one who is asking to work for them as their representative in government? Wouldn't they remember you on election day if they had registered and exercised their right to vote due to your assistance?

My strategy involved looking at my list before approaching a household. If that house was not on the list, I assumed the residents were unregistered and acted accordingly. After I'd shared some information about myself and my campaign I'd add, "Does anyone in your household need to update their voter registration? I have a voter registration card here which is very easy to fill out and pop in the mail." Depending upon the response, I would add, "How many would you like?" or "I always carry them with me because so many people I meet have moved or changed their names or whatever and need to update their information." This approach helped individuals feel comfortable taking a card to update their information. I avoided saying, "So many people I meet are unregistered" or "My list shows you as being unregistered."

I don't know how many people registered to vote and voted for me as a result of my stopping at their house, but I'm glad I was able to do it. Even if they didn't vote or did vote and chose my opponent, it was good for me to have the chance to meet them. I would later serve them, too. In addition, every person you visit with knows other people, and talks. While they may not have voted, telling a family member that a candidate stopped by who was genuinely interested in helping and serving can be worth five or ten times the number of votes you can obtain by buying advertising.

During my second and third campaigns, I didn't have the luxury of 100 percent of my time being devoted to campaigning like my first campaign when I was able to campaign during the summer and during the fall after my school board granted me a one-year leave of absence from teaching. My subsequent campaigns occurred while I was working for the people as their state representative. My time was limited due to my responsibilities. I had to narrow my target so I did go door to door to only those listed as registered voters.

My advice, however, to beginning candidates is: if you have time, go to every house. Try to register those who aren't registered. Meet, visit with, and get ideas from as many people you will be representing as possible. If your time is limited, target only those who can vote to give you the job.

Print out a list of registered voters from each precinct by street in ascending order. This is your "walk list" that enables you to go up and down the street and know who the registered voters are. You can put the list on your clipboard and as you approach the house, see whom you will be talking with. The registered voter list will have the voter's name, gender, and date of birth. In addition, you will see how many registered voters live at that address. This is important. You will want to make a special effort to gain their support as this household could represent multiple votes if they have several older children or family members living at home.

Make note if they have a college or military-aged child listed at their address. This might be a good opportunity to discuss whether or not they need an absentee ballot application if the family seems favorable to you. Always carry a few applications with you so you can aid in the absentee ballot process should a family member be out of town.

Spend your time visiting with the targeted voters of your district and you, like Absalom, can maximize your time and increase the likelihood of success with your campaign.

Targeting direct mail

Targeting also is critical when deciding whom to send your message to. Most campaigns send information to voters prior to the election, detailing positions on issues. Direct mail pieces represent a targeted message sent to a targeted group with the aim of providing them with the information they need so they will want to support and vote for you. Directing messages to targeted groups of voters is more effective than sending out a generic campaign piece to everyone. People have to have a reason to care about who is elected. They will stop and read a direct mail piece if it contains information about an issue they care about, whether that be health care costs, the quality of education, or gun issues.

What groups of individuals in your area would appreciate hearing your views on issues? What groups would be supportive of your stands and could be encouraged to get out and vote for you? Which groups did you choose as targets when discussing issues in Chapter 4? Examples of typical groups of individuals who are often targeted include: senior citizens, gun owners, pro-life supporters, church members, union members, farmers, business owners, women, and young families with children.

But once you've identified your target populations, how do you reach them? Where do you get the lists containing the names, addresses, and phone numbers of the individuals in these groups? This is the million-dollar question. Obtaining good lists is one of the most critical aspects of a campaign and can be worth political gold for those who have them. Larger campaigns purchase lists from political consulting companies. This is impractical for most local candidates due to the cost. They have to secure lists elsewhere.

Most political parties have invested time and financial resources over the years to develop targeted lists for the candidates in their party. Contact them to see what resources they might be able to provide for you. If they have accurate, timely, detailed lists you can use, great. If not, you will have to develop your own.

This would be an excellent project for someone who wants to volunteer. It involves obtaining available lists or possibly developing your own. It also involves entering the information into a computer so your campaign can print mailing labels for your direct mail pieces. These endeavors can consume many hours, but pay big dividends in the end.

Lists can be derived from your voter registration information, be obtained, and/or be developed. Each of these will be discussed below.

1. Utilize the information on your voter registration list. You can use this information to print out mailing labels for senior citizens

or people in their thirties who might be parents of small children or young people, because you can sort the list by date of birth. This is helpful if you have targeted a specific age group with your mailings. Another use of the voter registration list would be to sort by voter history and send a general mailing about your candidacy to voters most likely to vote in your election.

In addition, with the absentee voting information, you can print out mailing labels for people who typically vote absentee and send them a special letter.

2. Obtain helpful lists. Explore several avenues to locate lists.

- Ask current elected officials in your party if they would be willing to share their lists of targeted voters with you. Many times they will.

- Contact the organizations who endorse you. Sometimes they will share their membership lists with you.

- Obtain names of business owners by asking your city halls for their business license list or requesting a membership list from area Chambers of Commerce.

- Obtain names and addresses of farmers through your county assessor's offices. Ask them to provide the names and addresses of taxpayers who claim livestock or farm machinery on their personal property tax statement.

- Ask volunteers to consider sharing their church directories with the campaign.

Once secured, check the names against the voter registration file. If you are going to send a fundraising letter, it might be all right to send a letter to a business owner who lives outside your district. If, however, you want to send a direct mail piece trying to get him or her to vote for you, you have wasted your money. Therefore, cross reference the names with your voter registration list before entering the names, addresses, phone numbers, and e-mail addresses, if available, into a computer database that can later generate mailing labels or e-mail directories for your campaign. Volunteers can help cross reference and enter this data from home and send it to the campaign headquarters via e-mail.

Names and addresses of like-minded individuals can serve as a target for fundraising letters, volunteer solicitation letters, or direct mail pieces.

3. Developing lists. More sophisticated campaigns are able to develop their own target lists through phone banking. This requires a lot of dedicated volunteers and a good deal of time, but it provides the best way to target voters in your district.

Phone banks are manned by volunteers. Steps to developing your own target lists are explained below:

How to phone bank for targeted information

Obtain a voter registration list with phone numbers. This is usually obtained from your state political party. If one is not easily available for your area, you will have to obtain a voter registration list from your local election authority and have volunteers look up phone numbers for you. This is a project volunteers can do at home. It takes a good deal of time but allows older volunteers or moms who work from home to contribute to your campaign's efforts. After the phone numbers are looked up, you are ready to call them.

Find a location with several phone lines to use. Real estate, insurance, and mortgage companies might be good locations with multiple phone lines, or individuals with calling plans can meet at someone's house and call using their cell phones.

Line up volunteers to call in one-hour shifts from 6:00 P.M. to 9:00 P.M. in the early months of your campaign. Include a fifteen-minute training session prior to each shift.

Develop a script such as:

Sample Voter ID Phone Script

"Hello, Mrs. Jones?" (Always verify who you are talking to so you'll know later if the information you obtain matches up with the name and address on your list.)

"This is Karen and we're conducting a short election survey tonight and wondered if we could ask you a couple of questions? It will only take about three minutes."

If "No," then say, "Thank you anyway," and go to the next person.

If "Yes," then say, "Thank you. I am going to read you a list of five issues. Please tell me the one you are most concerned about:

        _____Quality schools;

        _____ Restoring moral values to our society;

        _____ Improving the economy;

        _____ Reining in the drug problem; or

        _____ Generating more jobs.

"Are you, or someone in your household, a gun owner?"

"Do you consider yourself pro-choice or pro-life?"

"If the election were held today, would you vote for John Smith or Suzie Meldon?"

"Thank you very much. This concludes the survey. Have a good evening."

FIGURE 10.5 Sample voter ID phone script.

The script should ask identifying questions that are important to you and your campaign. This could be to target pro-life voters, or gun owners, or those concerned about education. You should know the issues that are important to your campaign from the beginning. By phoning the voters in your district, you find like-minded voters who can later be targeted for get-out-the-vote efforts.

The survey also identifies "undecided" voters and those who have already decided to vote for your opponent. This information is crucial to your campaign. You know who is NOT going to vote for you. You should not expend any more resources on them—no more phone calls; no direct mail pieces sent to their houses.

The undecided group can be targeted with a follow-up letter or flier sent to their homes. Another phone call can be made to their houses later to determine if they have made their decisions. You can further divide the list until election day by repeatedly calling the undecideds. At that point, you will know who is supporting you and can concentrate on your get-out-the-vote efforts (see Chapter 16 for more on getting out the vote).

Record the answers on a sheet of paper or the registered voter list. Make columns at the end of the lines for the response options. Volunteers can indicate the status of the call (i.e., AM = Answering machine, • = Talked with voter, NA = No answer, etc.) and circle the appropriate responses to the questions. A sample record sheet for the above phone script might look like this:

Voter Name	Address	Phone No.	Status?	Quality Schools	Moral Values	Eco-nomy	Drug Problem	Jobs	John Smith	Suzie Meldon	Unde-cided
Al Black	123 E. 31st	123-4567	AM	QS	MV	E	DP	J	JS	SM	UN
Juan Gon-zales	456 W. 32nd	234-5678	•	QS	MV	Ⓔ	DP	J	⒥Ⓢ	SM	UN

FIGURE 10.6 Example of voter ID record sheet

Have a volunteer enter the information into your database. If you have obtained your voter registration list from your election authority in a spreadsheet format on a compact disc, it will be easy to add a few more fields beside their names to record the new information. This information can later be sorted and mailing labels can be printed for everyone who indicated they were a gun owner, for example.

You may not get through your entire voter registration list the first campaign, but if you are successful, you can continue to build on it year after year, which will help develop an accurate profile of your district. You will not only know the names of the people in your district, but also what they are concerned about. This will not only serve you well in campaigns but, most importantly, it will also make you a better representative of the people.

After you have defined and generated lists containing the names and addresses of individuals in your targeted groups, you are ready to send your targeted direct-mail pieces you developed in Chapter 7. These are most often sent out in the final two weeks of a campaign. With the information you have obtained, you will be more effective in your efforts.

Take the time to target your message, and you will stand a greater chance of hitting your mark on election day.

CHAPTER 11

GO MEET THE PEOPLE—DOOR TO DOOR

For people to vote for you, they have to know you. Who are you? Why are you running? Conveying the answers to those questions can be accomplished via campaign materials, direct mail, and the Internet, but the best method is meeting them face to face. If a person has met you and had an opportunity to look you in the eye and shake your hand, he or she will have a good feel for what you are like and if he/she wants to vote for you. More times than not, voters will choose to side with the candidate whom they have met over someone they have just read or heard about.

Absalom went to where the people were—the side of the highly traveled road into the city. In addition, he got up early to do this. He was committed and anxious to meet them. A good candidate will be, also.

While it will serve you on election day to meet the public by garnering their votes; just as important is the benefit *you* will obtain by meeting *them*. You will be working for them. They are your bosses. You are their employee—a public servant. You need to meet them, visit with them, hear their ideas, and glean from their expertise. After a campaign season of meeting and visiting with the people in your area, you will know your district, township, ward, or state. You will understand what the people are concerned about, what their needs are—and what they don't need. You will be in a better position to represent them and make decisions on their behalf.

In addition, you will know whom to call on when you need more information or insight on a given topic. Most people can only be an expert in a few areas. Yet, as an elected official, you have to make important decisions on a wide range of topics. What can you use as a basis to make this decision? Where can you turn? Certainly, you can read information or search the Internet, but one of the most important things to do is to talk to the people in your district who are experts in this area. They will have a good grasp of the topic and be able to give wise counsel on how best to proceed. In addition, you represent them and have the opportunity of incorporating their ideas and expertise into the development of good policy. That is how representative government is supposed to work. But you have to know whom to call or talk to in order for this to work. That only happens when you have met and know the people of your area.

So how do you meet the people? One of the most effective ways to meet the people of your district is to go to them by visiting their neighborhoods, walking down their streets, going to their homes and knocking on their doors. This takes time and energy, but there's nothing like it to get a feel for the people you will represent. You come to know their interests, their lifestyles, their ages, their challenges, and their concerns.

Some of this information is discovered through conversations you have with them while standing on their front porch. But a lot of it is learned by observing the sights and sounds of the world around them. You see potholed streets and crumbling roads. You hear the sounds of children playing and see the challenges of parents. You learn what's of interest to the people of your district by reading the bumper stickers on the cars/trucks parked in their driveways. You notice handicap ramps going to front doors and meet heroic people who are overcoming physical challenges while living at home. You get to meet retired experts from many fields who can become a wealth of support and knowledge to help you do the best job possible for the people of your district. Bottom line: you develop friendships.

Also, they get to meet you, the candidate. It's an informal job interview. You want them to hire you. By going to their homes, you give them an opportunity to meet you in person and assess whether or not this is someone they want representing them. When they go to the polls on election day to "hire" that representative, they are more likely to hire you if they've met and visited with you, and if you made a good impression, especially if they never got to meet the other "job candidate" and only heard about him through ads or fliers received in the mail.

Going door to door can be the single most important aspect of campaigning. Elections are often won on this one strategy. I had a friend who ran for state representative and who was up against a well-funded candidate. My friend committed to an aggressive door-to-door effort and won despite being outspent $100,000 to $40,000. He attributes his victory to his door-to-door efforts. Going to meet people at their homes can make the difference in your campaign, as well.

Start early in your campaign going door to door. It always takes longer to get around your district than you think. If you have time to visit each household twice, that is even better. Candidates should devote at least two hours a day to going door to door, but more is preferable. Set a schedule and stick to it for campaigning. In addition, remember the door-to-door basics.

Door-to-door essentials

Have a humble attitude. Absalom was the son of the king. He was held in a place of honor by his subjects and afforded the respect demanded by the office. However, Absalom did something very unusual during his campaign. Second Samuel 15:5 reveals what he did. "Also, whenever anyone approached him to bow down before him, Absalom would reach out his hand, take hold of him and kiss him." Absalom might have been the first politician to shake hands and kiss babies! And, it worked. "Absalom behaved in this way toward all the Israelites who came to the king asking for justice, and so he stole the hearts of the men of Israel" (2 Sam 15:6). Eventually, he led a coup and became the king of Israel for a time.

Why was he able to "steal the hearts of the men of Israel"? Because he connected with the voters through his outwardly humble demeanor. Absalom refused to let people bow down to him or honor him. He rejected public praise. People respect that. Conversely, they are turned off by candidates or politicians who act like they are important and should be treated likewise.

Unfortunately, Absalom's actions were not genuine and only covered up an impure heart. There are too many politicians today who put on a similar act during the campaign season. As Christians, we should strive to be genuinely humble and allow God to raise us up if He desires. One way to do that is to keep a proper perspective of who you will be visiting when going door to door.

You are going to the door of your potential future employer. You are the one who is honored that this person would take time out of his or her busy personal lives to visit with you, not vice versa. Keep this reality in mind, and it will enable you to keep a humble attitude.

Print out a good walk list of registered, frequent voters as was discussed in Chapter 10. Take the voter registration list you obtained from your local election authority and sort it by voters who have a voting history of voting in similar-type elections as yours (i.e., if you are running for city council and your election is in April, determine the voters who have voted in April elections over the past two April election cycles. If you are running for sheriff in a primary election in August, determine which voters typically vote in August elections). Then sort these voters by street address in ascending order so you can go door to door targeting registered voters who typically will vote in your election.

If time is of the essence, you might also determine the households with more than one likely voter and only stop there. You can maximize your potential vote if you focus on stopping at a house where there are three or four registered voters who usually vote in your type of election rather than stopping where there might be only one vote. Time will determine the level of refinement of your walk list.

Go meet the voters. With pushcard printed and walk list in hand, you're ready to go door to door. The first step is to gather the following items:

- A list of registered voters listed in a walk list format;
- A clipboard to help you manage the list;
- A couple of pieces of blank paper for notes;
- Empty voter registration cards;
- A couple of pens or pencils;
- A couple of strong rubber bands;
- Sunscreen;
- Plenty of water and a snack if going to be gone long;
- Hand sanitizer;
- Comb;
- (If a woman) Powder and hairspray (to freshen your look);
- Map of the community and a bright colored marker;
- Your pushcards; and
- A few campaign volunteer cards.

Once you've gathered your supplies and picked the neighborhood to target, drive to the area. I usually parked at the halfway point of a given street block and walked down one side and then back up the next then back around to my car. That is preferable to crossing the street all the time and saves steps. You can also park at the end of the street, but I liked being closer to my car in case I needed extra supplies or a drink of water, which meant I tried to park halfway down the street most of the time.

Load up your pushcards in your pockets or under your clipboard. Add a few voter registration cards and sheets of blank paper. Rubber bands come in handy to manage your clipboard. Wrapping the rubber band around the top of your clipboard in an X pattern allows you to keep your pencil under it with less chance of losing it. Putting another rubber band around the bottom of the board keeps the walk list from blowing in the wind.

If it is sunny, you might consider using sunscreen. If you neglect this item, you may be the lobster candidate by the end of the day!

Now that you're "loaded," you're ready to meet your voters. Look at the list and familiarize yourself with the names. Head for the first door. As you approach, make a mental note of the surroundings so you can get to know them before you even meet them. Watch for clues, such as children's toys in the yard, bumper strips on vehicles parked in the driveway, or types of statues or decorations in the yard. These clues often indicate the age, family type, hobbies, and philosophies of the residents, which help you know which topics to focus on when you visit with them.

If you are wearing sunglasses, remove them before knocking. I can't stress this enough! Too many candidates wear dark sunglasses while talking with voters. They have forgotten that "Your eye is the lamp of your body. When your eyes are good, your whole body also is full of light. But when they are bad, your body also is full of darkness" (Luke 11:34). People instinctively know this. They don't want to meet a "shady politician." They want to see your eyes so they can discern your heart.

Be prepared to share your message. You need to have thought through ahead of time what you want to say. You need to:

1. Introduce yourself;
2. State why you are at their door;
3. Articulate succinctly why they should vote for you; and
4. Ask for their vote.

My introductory "speech" was something like this: "Hi, I'm Vicky Hartzler, and I'm running to be your next state representative. I'm a teacher at Belton High School and my husband and I farm south of Harrisonville. I'm running for office because I believe there's a need for ordinary people with morals and values and who have been living with the laws, to get involved. I have some information I'd like to give you about myself (as I hand them the pushcard) and I'd like to ask for your vote."

You can gauge their reaction and follow up with a question if they seem open to it. Some possible questions include:

"What would you like to see done to improve things at the state (county, city)?"

"Does anyone in your household need to update their voter registration card? I always carry them in case I meet someone who's moved or had a name change. How many would you like?"

"Do you have any questions?"

"Can I count on your support?"

"May I place a yard sign in your yard closer to the election? My volunteers will place the sign and come pick it up after the election."

"Would you be interested in volunteering with the campaign? Here's a card that lists some opportunities where you could make a difference."

If they express concerns, share ideas, or want a yard sign, make a note of it beside their names on the voter registration sheet or a separate piece of paper. There are several things you can do with this information. You can review it periodically and develop a mental political picture of your area, which will serve you well in the future as you serve them in elected office. Volunteers can develop a yard sign list for later use.

You can write a follow-up "glad to have met you" card telling the voter you appreciated the opportunity to visit with them about their concerns. If you are genuinely interested in and supportive of their ideas, you could add a statement pledging to take their concerns with you to office, if elected.

You can also use your notes to strengthen your database after the election. Volunteers or staff could take your notes and develop lists of people who are concerned about certain projects or issues. When those issues come up for discussion or vote in your elected office, you could write or call them, stating that you remembered they were concerned about this and thought they might want to know you were doing your best to represent their ideas. After the vote or decision is made, a follow-up letter to your constituents explaining how their concern was addressed will be met with appreciation.

Try to take opportunities during the door-to-door visit to verify whom you are talking to. Many times the voter registration walk list provided by your election authority or political party will be wrong. Our society is so mobile that it is hard to maintain an accurate list of registered voters. There are several ways to verify their names.

You can open the conversation by saying the person's name. Look at the sheet before going to the door or as you ring the doorbell. "Mrs. Jones?" If she nods, then go right ahead with your speech, "I'm John Doe and I'm running to be your next county sheriff . . ."

If she says, "No," or looks confused and looks at your clipboard, you'll need to adjust your speech. Make sure and tell her who you are and why you're on her doorstep first thing. Most will assume you're trying to sell something or taking a survey and will be wary. "I'm John Doe, and I'm running to be your next county sheriff. I'm visiting with voters in this area and got this list (pointing at your clipboard) from the county (election board, etc.) and it must be out-of-date. I'm sorry. The list says this is the Jones household. What is the correct listing? Great. Thank you. I just wanted to meet you and let you know a little about myself. I'm a police officer . . . (and continue your speech)."

Remember that residents may be embarrassed if they aren't registered to vote. Don't put them on the spot by asking, "Are you registered to vote?" Just give them the opportunity to "update" their voter registration information with the county and tell them how glad you are to meet them.

If they seem favorable toward you and they live at a great location, ask if it would be okay to place a yard sign in their yard. Save these spots for corners of intersections or homes on highly traveled streets. Use your resources wisely.

Also, having a few volunteer cards on hand will enable you to share about opportunities to make a difference with your campaign, should they seem interested.

Regardless of the outcome of the visit, always thank them for their time and ask for their votes. "Thank you very much. I'd appreciate your vote in November."

Many times, voters will not be home. Leave your pushcard in their doors with a personal note on it. I spent evenings writing out those notes ahead of time and took two kinds of notes with me: ones without writing for people I would find at home and ones with my "Sorry I missed you. I'd appreciate your vote. Vicky" note written across the front. You can write the note while standing on the front porch, but it takes time. Make sure and write the note in a visible, colored pen so they know you really wrote it and didn't just have it printed to look that way. The personal touch will make a difference.

Another option is to print "Sorry I Missed You" door hangers. They can save time and provide an alternative if the budget allows.

FIGURE 11.1 Example of "Sorry I Missed You" door hanger

After leaving a home, make a note on your voter identification sheet if the residents were home or gone. If they agreed to allow a yard sign to be in the yard, write "YS" beside their names. If they were concerned about an issue, make note of it. At the end of the day, it is fun to go back and count how many doors you went to and to record how many people were home and how many cards you left. This becomes helpful later in the campaign when you can show you earned their votes by sharing that "I've spent the past four months meeting the people of this district and have personally knocked on over 5,000 doors. It would be my honor to work for you as your state representative, county treasurer, etc."

Utilize your street map and colored marker by marking the streets you've covered when you go back to your car. That way you can visualize where you've gone and the amount of ground still needed to be covered. If you keep doing this day after day, you'll be amazed at the distance you will cover, how many wonderful families you'll be able to meet, the things you will learn, and the memorable experiences you will have.

Door-to-door precautions

Drink plenty of water throughout the day. You can get dehydrated before you realize it. I remember one day when it was in the upper 90s with typical Missouri humidity and I was spending a July day going door to door. I usually started out about ten o'clock in the morning and went until about five thirty in the evening. It was about three thirty in the afternoon and I had pushed it hard. I went up to a door, rang the doorbell, and wiped the sweat from my forehead as I waited. I was looking at their rosebush when I noticed it started to sway a little . . . and there wasn't a breeze. I felt weak as the door opened and a kind man and little girl stared out at me. I said my usual speech, although I think it was a little slower than usual. Initially, they just stared at me. Then, with concern in his eyes, the man said, "Would you like a glass of water or like to come inside in the air conditioning for a few minutes?" My first reaction was to try to remain looking strong, but I realized I probably *did* need to cool down, so agreed to the glass of water and said I'd just sit down on the front step a minute, "if I might." He said, "Sure!" and rushed to get me a glass of ice water. That water never tasted so good. I had become dehydrated and overheated.

I gave myself permission to sit there a few minutes and chatted with the man and little girl who came out to join me on the step. It turned out I used to teach school with his wife. He was very supportive of my candidacy and glad to help me out on a hot day. I realized it was probably time to call it a day and, after recuperating and thanking them, walked back to my car and went home for a nice cool shower and needed rest.

Be wise in all aspects of your candidacy, including taking care of yourself. Remember all those things your mother taught you: eat right, drink plenty of water, and get enough rest. Stretch out your muscles before embarking on door-to-door exercise. This will reduce the chances of sore or strained muscles.

I learned to carry some hand sanitizer in my car after coming down with several colds during my first two campaigns. You shake a lot of hands while campaigning. It's also easy to get less sleep, which translates into getting run down and more susceptible to germs that you encounter. A friend advised me to pick up some hand sanitizer and use it frequently. I did, and it helped save my health.

I also utilized Sunday as a day of rest and chose not to go door to door on this day. I spent that day honoring the Lord at church, then at home recuperating and reenergizing for the upcoming week.

Use caution in approaching children. In today's world, children are trained to not speak to strangers, and parents are rightly concerned about adults approaching their children. So even though it is totally innocent, consider skipping a house if small children are playing in the yard. This is especially true for male candidates. The man of God should be above reproach, so avoid any circumstance which could cause alarm or accusation.

Think safety. Safety was my main concern when considering the idea of going door to door. As a woman, I wasn't sure about the safety of walking up to households and knocking on strangers' doors by myself. Also, I'd never done anything like that and was nervous about meeting people. Would they like me? Would I get doors slammed in my face? I was worried, needed courage, and was looking for solutions to my dilemma. What should I do?

For starters, the Lord reminded me to look to His Word for the answers to my concerns. It was He who had called me to run, and it was He who would be faithful to enable me to fulfill His call. He did and I'm so grateful for His goodness. Some things I learned:

Pray without ceasing! Start each day with prayer, asking for guidance as to where to go, for safety, and for favor. Ask Him to use you to minister to the people you are going to meet. Remember that the reason God may have called you to run for office may not be to serve as an elected official; it may be to provide the opportunity through a campaign to meet someone who is hurting and who needs to hear the message of God's love.

Jesus sent out His disciples. He may be sending you—not to Africa to be a missionary—but to your community's front doors. If you do nothing else during your campaign, you can pray for your neighbors as you walk along their streets. You might make not just a difference in election day outcomes; you just might also impact your area for eternity.

Here are some of the Scriptures that were meaningful to me during campaigns:

"Righteousness goes before him and prepares the way for his steps."

—Psalm 85:13

"With your help I can advance against a troop; with my God I can scale a wall . . . It is God who arms me with strength and makes my way perfect . . . You broaden the path beneath me, so that my ankles do not turn."

—Psalm 18:29,32,36

"I will instruct you and teach you in the way you should go; I will counsel you and watch over you."

—Psalm 32:8

"Commit your way to the LORD; trust in him and he will do this: He will make your righteousness shine like the dawn, the justice of your cause like the noonday sun."

—Psalm 37:5–6

"If you make the Most High your dwelling—even the LORD, who is my refuge—then no harm will befall you, no disaster will come near your tent. For he will command his angels concerning you to guard you in all your ways; they will lift you up in their hands, so that you will not strike your foot against a stone."

—Psalm 91:9–12

"Commit to the LORD whatever you do, and your plans will succeed."

—Proverbs 16:3

"May the favor of the LORD our God rest upon us; establish the work of our hands for us—yes, establish the work of our hands."

—Psalm 90:17

God will give you wisdom for each detail of how to proceed if you seek Him and listen to Him.

Consider going door to door with others. This option can be helpful for your campaign, also. If you have a person who is from that community who is willing to go door to door with you, it can help open doors for your campaign.

In my first campaign, I had a couple of people who volunteered to go with me door to door in their neighborhoods. They would walk with me and when the door opened, they would speak first. "Hi, Jane. This is my friend, Vicky Hartzler, and she is running for state representative, and I wanted her to meet some of my neighbors, so we're just going around this afternoon visiting. Vicky, I'd like you to meet Jane Smith. . . ." It was fun to go with someone else and gave me more credibility with voters.

Sometimes family members are willing to go with you door to door. This can be effective, plus provide some memorable campaign moments. I had a friend running for state senate who went door to door in a typically liberal part of his district with his wife and five-year-old daughter. My friend is a conservative, but he wanted to meet all the residents of the area he hoped to serve. An older lady opened the door at one house and promptly asked, "What are your thoughts on guns?"

Before my friend could give a discreet answer, his little girl piped up proudly, "My Daddy just LOVES guns! He has a whole cabinetful at home and if ever a bad guy breaks into our house, my Daddy is going to get his gun and blow his head off!"

Judging from the horrified look on the woman's face, my friend realized he had probably just lost the woman's vote but kept his sense of humor, "Well, you probably don't have any more questions for me, do you?"

The woman mustered a wan smile and agreed. I doubt if ever the woman or my friends will forget this campaign moment!

I know several candidates who have older children who go door to door with their spouses and children. They divide up the street and the wife and a couple of kids go down one side and the candidate and the other children cover the other side of the street. This method works as well, although most people want to meet the candidate. A spouse and family members are the second best option. Volunteers are third. You can make contact with more households with volunteer teams, but your impact isn't as great. However, in large districts or due to a tight timeframe, this may be your best option. Certainly, this method is safer for the candidate rather than going alone.

Use wisdom when approaching a house. If you choose to go door to door by yourself, make sure you pray, asking for safety beforehand and while you are going door to door. Ask the Holy Spirit to give you discernment and wisdom about which houses you should approach. Ask Him to reveal to you if there is something amiss about a house and impress upon you to skip going there. Be aware of your surroundings, the presence of people in the neighborhood who may be within earshot, and possible avenues for escape, if needed. Stand away from the front door a little when it opens. Never go inside a house unless you're sure it's safe. Take a cell phone with you. Most of all, ask God for safety and for favor. He is big and He is able to take care of you.

Beware of dogs. Most communities require them to be confined to a fenced area, but occasionally some will escape. One day I was walking through a neighborhood going from house to house, and all the neighborhood dogs started barking at this stranger who was invading their neighborhood. The farther I went down the street, the more upset the neighborhood dogs became. I passed one house, and as I was walking toward the next house, I looked over to see three very angry dogs run around the back corner of the house and viciously jump up on the fence. I remember thinking, *Boy, I'm sure glad they're behind the fence!* I went on up the street and doubled back to return to my car and finish leaving my pushcard in the doors of the homes on the opposite side of the street. As I came again to the house of the vicious dogs, I remember hearing the angry howl of dogs. I turned to look at the direction of the commotion and was horrified to see the fence gate give way as they forcefully jumped against it. They came at me with all they had. All I had was my clipboard! I stuck it out in front of me and yelled, "Down!" They bared their teeth and barked viciously. I quickly glanced around to see if there was anyone who could help, but the neighborhood was quiet. It was up to me and God. I breathed a prayer for protection as I slowly started backing toward my car, keeping the clipboard between me and the dogs. One tried to circle around me and I swung my clipboard at him, hitting him on the nose. He retreated. I quickly recovered for the other two and kept saying "Down!" I'd heard that if you don't run, stand your ground, and speak forcefully, you'll have less chance of getting attacked, so I kept backing slowly to my car. I got the door unlocked, quickly got inside, shut the door, and breathed a prayer of thanks! Whew! God is faithful.

Dogs aside, I had a great experience going door to door and continue to enjoy doing it. Most people you meet are very friendly and appreciate the fact that someone running for office has taken the time and effort to come meet them at their home. They recognize hard work and dedication and can discern a candidate who sincerely wants to meet and serve them.

I was pleasantly surprised (and grateful!) by what a positive experience it was. God gave me favor and enabled me to meet so many wonderful people. He also kept me safe. God is good and He will bless you efforts, too, if you are committed to Him.

CHAPTER 12

GO MEET THE PEOPLE—EVENTS AND PARADES

Going door to door is only one way to meet the voters of your area. It is a good way, but you will want to meet your potential "bosses" through other means also, while constantly evaluating the best use of your time.

Absalom "would get up early and stand by the side of the road leading to the city gate." As people passed, he visited with them. You need to do the same.

Common methods of meeting voters include attending large gatherings of people, holding public meetings, and participating in parades. These forums provide the opportunity to meet as many people as possible in the short timeframe of a campaign.

Events

Before you can attend an event, you have to know about it. You have to be aware of what's going on in your community and familiar with the leaders, organizations, and their activities. If you haven't subscribed to the local newspapers yet, now is the time to do it. Read it from cover to cover. Familiarize yourself with the businesses in town. Learn the issues being discussed by the city council. Acquaint yourself with the service organizations and their activities. Read about the sports, the youth, the schools, and the senior citizen activities. Peruse the want ads. What jobs are being sought after? What are the trends in home sales? Is the economy good or bad? What are the issues with the youth in the community? What are the churches in the community and their pastors' names? All of this can be gleaned by a serious study of the area newspapers.

One important feature to note is the advertisements section announcing an organization or church's Fish Fry, Bar-B-Q, or Taco Dinner. You also will notice announcements about large banquets or events like a Business Expo, community festivals, a new business's open house event at an area mall, auctions, 5K runs, and sporting events. These are all opportunities to meet a large number of people.

Don't feel like you have to attend them all, however. Use wisdom and remember your primary objective: to meet registered voters in your area. If there is going to be a large public event in your district, think about how many attending will actually be registered voters from your district. I once attended an auction hoping to connect with voters in my area, only to discover that almost everyone I met was from a nearby community or visiting from out of town. I finally left and went door to door that afternoon, realizing I was better able to target my voters that way than through the large public auction.

Also consider the appropriateness of attending the event. Football is huge in my community with standing room only crowds every weekend. When I first ran, someone suggested I go and hand out my literature at the game. I wore my name badge and went to the game with some handouts, but quickly discerned that people were there for the game and it would appear that I was grandstanding if I actively campaigned there. So I just sat down and enjoyed the game wearing my name badge. I enjoyed the evening, and several voters recognized my candidacy without my appearing inappropriate.

Some tips to remember:

1. Wear a name badge. A state representative friend advised I devise one when I first ran for office. He said, "You'll feel awkward wearing it at first, but then you'll get used to it. People will know who you are and understand why you are approaching them. It helps." It was good advice.

The name badge can be simple. All it needs is your name and the words, "Candidate for _____." I made one on my computer by typing "Vicky Hartzler, Candidate for State Representative, District 124," and cutting it to fit into a plastic name holder I'd saved from a conference. Other than church on Sundays, I wore it everywhere. It is especially important to wear when you go door to door or attend events. People recognize who you are without your having to say you're running for such and such office. They'll see the name tag and get the idea.

2. Meet the people using discretion. I learned there was a political term for this: working the room. I don't like that connotation as it implies a cynical motive of strategically hunting down people with the sole aim of getting votes. Unfortunately, this may be too true with many candidates. It doesn't have to be for you.

The best way to prevent that is to remember *why* you are running. Is it because you need money through a job? To get power? To beat the other guy? To get back at somebody who has done something in office you don't like? To stroke your ego by becoming famous?

Or are you running for office because the Lord has called you to *serve* and wants to provide you an avenue for helping others, pointing them to Him, or impacting your culture? If He has, then meeting the people provides an opportunity to meet those you want to serve and *minister to*. If you approach events with this attitude, you'll have more success, because people can discern whether a person is just meeting them because he needs their votes. Instead, pray ahead of time and ask God to not only give you favor, but also to allow you to meet people whom you can learn from or minister to. It will make all the difference.

But how do you meet the people? Get there early so you can visit with people before the event begins. Start with the organizers of the event. Introduce yourself to the people putting on the event, whether they are at the registration table, working in the kitchen, or serving as emcee for the event. This is common courtesy as they are the sponsors of the event. Discern how comfortable they are at having you there. Ask them if it's okay if you meet some of the people who've come to their event. If they act uncomfortable, you should respect that and only eat, smile, and leave. If they welcome you, you have more leeway to meet others at their event.

If you know people, walk up to them, smile, and shake their hands. Ask them about their work and families. Listen to see what important things you can learn that would help you better represent them. If they ask about your campaign, be positive! Tell them it's going great and mention some of the things you have been doing. Don't complain or downgrade your opponent. Stay upbeat about what exciting things are going on with your campaign. Tell them you appreciate their support, or ask for their help if they seem favorable.

Don't spend too much time on any one group, as you will not get to meet very many people if you spend all your time in one place. Yet, don't always be looking for the next person. Too many candidates get into this "I've got to meet everyone" mode and spend much of their time looking over the shoulder of the person they are talking to. This is not only rude; it makes the person feel like a number. One of the best compliments I have heard about an elected official is, "When he talks to me, I feel like he really cares and listens. He wasn't always looking for the next voter." Use your time wisely, but don't forget to focus on the people you meet. Listen and learn.

If you don't know people, approach them and wait for them to look at you. Smile and quickly introduce yourself. You might say something like, "Hi. I'm Vicky Hartzler and I'm running for state representative. I'm out meeting the people of this area today and just wanted to introduce myself to you. What are your names?" Be considerate of their time. Most will politely listen for a minute, but you'll want to excuse yourself fairly quickly so they can return to their former conversation unless they act interested and ask you questions.

3. Remember names. Oh, for the gift of remembering names! Every person I've met, whether a candidate or not, has wanted to be able to do a better job of remembering names. And no wonder—the ability to remember a person's name is one of the most positive things you can do for another. It conveys *value* when you remember someone's name. It bridges philosophical divides. It lays groundwork for friendships. It garners support.

There is no magic bullet for this, but any memory device you can think of should be diligently pursued, as remembering names is so important. It not only will help your candidacy, it will also open up doors for service through the relationships that are forged through the beginning stage of remembering a person's name.

Here are a few tips for helping to remember names:

(a) Visualize the name. Approximately 65 percent of people are visual learners.[1] That means they remember things by *seeing* them. They recall items by picturing the word or item in their heads before speaking. For instance, when answering a question on a test, they visualize their page of notes or "see" the blackboard where they learned the concept being tested. Then, after recalling the information through seeing, they go ahead and answer the question. Most people don't realize they are doing it, but this is the process that is going on nonetheless.

Only small percentages (30 percent) of people are auditory learners who recall information by *hearing* it.[2] These people can more easily remember names because most of the time in introductions people are *told* the name of the new person. They later see the person again, want to recall his or her name and do so by *hearing* the name in their head. Lucky people.

For the vast majority of us who remember through sight, name tags are a blessing! We can more easily remember someone's name during introductions when we can look at the name tag during the introduction. That enables us to have a visual reminder of the name, which can be more easily recalled later.

If there are no name tags, you will have to picture the name in your head while you are hearing it. Some people picture a person's name written on his or her forehead as they look at them. Others try to write down the names as soon as possible or ask for a business card, if appropriate. If someone gives you a card, write on the back where you met him or her and some information which will help you recall the person in the future. Notes might say something like "Habitat for Humanity Banquet. Wife, Carol. Wants better roads." Review these cards when you get home before filing them. Files can be developed for each community. Prior to the next event in that community, you can improve your chances of remembering names by getting out the file and reviewing the names of people you've met. Articles from newspapers can also be clipped and placed in the community file. Pictures are great for this purpose. They list significant people in the community with their names under the picture. If you have the picture filed away, it can be a great resource for remembering names prior to the next event.

(b) Say the person's name. Try to use his or her name in a conversation in the next few minutes after being introduced. "You're right, Nathan. Taxes are too high. That's one reason I'm running." Or "What do you think the government should do, Nathan?" By practicing using his name, you are imprinting his name and increasing the likelihood that you'll be able to recall it at a later date.

(c) Associate the person's name. As you are being introduced, try to associate the name with something or someone to help you remember him or her in the future. For instance, try to remember another person you know with the same name and find something similar about the two. If you know a Carol with blond hair and the woman being introduced to you is blond and her name is Carol, you can think about the association for an instant and this will help.

Usually, the associations aren't that obvious, but many times you can think of something helpful to associate with that person.

(d) Practice the person's name. If you have a chance later, mentally practice the names of the people you've met. A banquet or formal meal allows time for this. Try to rehearse the names of the people you've met as you see them across the room.

(e) Be prepared for mistakes. It takes courage and wisdom to step out and use people's names. Sometimes we are going to fail. Thankfully, most people are gracious and understanding in that they, too, struggle (and have failed) in using people's names.

One particularly embarrassing incident occurred a couple of years after I had been elected state representative. I was invited to come to a Ducks Unlimited banquet and give the opening prayer. I arrived on time and visited with some of the individuals attending and the organizers of the event. One of the organizers came up, shook my hand, and thanked me for being there. He looked familiar and I knew I'd met him during one of my campaigns. I assumed he was Mike, who had called and invited me to come. I soon discovered he was the Master of Ceremonies. He welcomed everyone and, after a nice introduction, invited me to come up on stage to say the prayer. I smiled and strode confidently to the podium while members of the audience gave supporting nods and smiles. I felt good. I arrived at the microphone, smiled at the audience, and said, "Thanks, Mike, for those kind words. Now, if you will all bow your heads . . . " and proceeded to bless the event and food.

When I had returned to my seat, my husband leaned over and said, "His name is *Jim*."

Needless to say, I was horrified and humbled and had to pray for grace and favor again. Whenever I try to do things on my own, I fall flat. I must rely on God to help me. Sometimes that is through your spouse or another person. If in doubt, ask others. They may know the person's name and help you avoid an embarrassing incident.

Thankfully, *Jim* is a very gracious person and didn't hold it against me. He continues to be friendly when I meet him, and believe me, I remember his name now!

I hope you don't have too many "Mike" incidents, but some are bound to happen. Just apologize, if appropriate, and go on. Everyone can relate. Just make a note and try to do better next time.

(f) Pray! Most of all, pray and ask God to help you remember names. Although I don't find "the gift of name recall" listed as a gift of the Spirit, the Bible does promise in John 14:26, "But the Counselor, the Holy Spirit, whom the Father will send in my name, will teach you all things and will remind you of everything I have said to you." We can ask the Father to teach us *all things,* and that includes teaching us the names of the people we are called to serve. We can also ask Him to *remind us* of names, information, and incidents. We can do all things through Christ which gives us strength. (Phil. 4:13). What is impossible with man is possible with God (Luke 18:27).

Press conferences/public forums

Candidates often host public forums to give voters an opportunity to share their ideas, hear their plan of action, or to meet a fellow office holder who is endorsing their candidacy. These provide wonderful opportunities for free press, but make a less than stellar impression if only a handful of people show up.

Typically, these events are advertised through sending out a press release and putting up fliers around town announcing the event. Additional ways to increase awareness and increase attendance include conducting a "no knock drop," sending out postcards telling about the event, or calling voters in the target area.

A no knock drop entails dropping literature at people's front doors the night before (if a morning event) or morning of the event (if an evening event), inviting them to come. This lets people know about the event and conveys energy about your campaign.

A postcard is a good way to show that a fellow officeholder endorses your candidacy. A picture should be taken of you with the officeholder. This picture should be the focus of the postcard announcing that he or she will be in town at your event to talk about your candidacy. Voters will remember the endorsement even if they don't get to attend the forum.

Phone calls announcing the event can be made by volunteers to voters in the area, also. These contacts increase your name ID along with giving voters a personal invitation to the forum.

Try employing one of these methods to increase the number of people you get to meet through your public forum or press conference.

Parades

The story of the first politician, Absalom, tells that "In the course of time, Absalom provided himself with a chariot and horses and with fifty men to run ahead of him." This not only served the purpose of making him look kingly, but it also may have been the first political parade!

Parades have been around since biblical times at least. They are certainly a part of the American tradition. They are the focus of celebrations in every small town and community in the United States. Parades serve as an occasion to honor hometown heroes or celebrate the winning sports team. They also provide an opportunity for candidates to become known to the people in the area. It is a chance for you to reach many of the voters with your message of who you are, why you are running, and what you have to offer the citizens of the area, while creating a buzz about your campaign.

This is accomplished by carefully planning ways to incorporate your message into your parade entry with creativity and fanfare. Consider these ideas before your next parade.

1. Involve several people in your entry. It's easy and fairly common for a candidate to rent or borrow someone's convertible, show up at a

parade, and ride in the back waving at the crowd. This used to be the norm and brought an expected collective yawn from the bystanders. The reaction: "Oh, another political candidate."

Absalom went beyond that and today's candidates should, also. He not only provided himself with a Bible-times convertible (chariot and horses). He also provided fifty men to run ahead of him.

It may be hard to find fifty people willing to run ahead of you, but try to find as many willing to walk as possible. One candidate I know secured ninety people to walk with him during the first parade of the campaign. The large showing not only energized the candidate's supporters, but also sent shock waves through the opponent's camp. They were playing catch up from that point forward.

Having supporters walk with you in the parade not only makes for an impressive visual entry but also demonstrates a large endorsement for your candidacy. It broadens your support by increasing the likelihood that people will know people walking with you and, if they know and respect them, they will think, "Well, if Sally and Bob know John Doe and they are supporting him, he must be a good person. I think I'll vote for him, too."

Try to find people from the same community as the parade to walk with you. Also, consider involving people who represent all ages and demographics of your district. You will reach more people. If you only have young people or retired individuals walking with you, you miss speaking to large parts of your population. Invite retired couples, young families, teenagers, professionals, men, women, everyone to participate. Every person who walks with you helps broaden your base of support and increase the likelihood of your winning on election day.

2. Walk or ride? There are many options for parade entries. During the years, I've seen a lot of variations. Here are just some examples:

- A convertible with the candidate in the back waving.
- A vintage tractor pulling a wagon loaded with hay with volunteers riding in the back.

FIGURE 12.1 Example of positive parade entry

- An antique car with the candidate inside waving out the window.
- A pickup truck with candidate standing and waving with volunteers sitting along sides and on tailgate.
- Candidate walking with family, pulling a red wagon filled with literature and candy for distribution.
- Candidate and family walking with a dog dressed in a campaign T-shirt.

Each candidate will differ in his/her preferences and each parade will demand variations to meet the needs of that particular event. However, overall, I preferred to walk in the parades rather than ride and would highly recommend it. Walking and being one of the people better reflected who I was. Walking conveys the idea that you are not afraid of work. If you crisscross the street shaking hands, smiling, and looking people in the eyes, it will show that you are a dedicated, enthusiastic, hard worker.

Usually, our parade entry started with a couple of teenagers holding my campaign banner. Then I walked behind that waving and sometimes running over to the side and shaking hands of people along the parade route. A patriotically-decorated pickup truck followed me, usually driven by my husband. Volunteers rode in the back, waving, and children threw candy to bystanders if it was allowed. Other volunteers walked along the side of the pickup truck and behind it carrying my yard signs. Others walked beside or behind the truck handing out my literature or sticking campaign stickers onto the shirts of young parade-goers along the route.

Be creative and involve others to gain support.

3. Get your message across. This can be done several ways. One way is to distribute literature or "freebies" from your campaign as you proceed along the parade route. You can hand out your pushcard or brochure. You can also hand out stickers featuring your name or campaign logo. Stickers are a big hit with children and usually are worn all day throughout the festival so you get a lot of advertising bang for your buck. One word of advice regarding stickers: They come on a roll. We found it worked best to remove the sticker from the roll and actually stick it on the person's shirt or hand it to him/her ready to stick on rather than tearing off the sticker with the backing attached and handing it to him/her. Applying it directly reduced the amount of trash left along the parade route plus increased the likelihood of the sticker actually being worn.

Balloons featuring your logo are carried by children or tied to strollers and continue to get your name out there without your being there. Helium balloons can be tricky, however, in trying to carry them along the parade route and distributing them in that the wind can tangle them and cause problems. Carrying and distributing balloons might be something you might consider for later in the day, if you want to use them.

I would think twice about handing out bumper strips in a parade. Bumper strips are expensive, and too many times people take them and, if they don't throw it away, they never put it on their cars. You want to ensure that the more expensive campaign items get distributed to those who will actually put them on their cars. You can better reach these people by giving them to your volunteers or having them on a table at a fair booth.

Another way to get your message out in a parade is with banners or posters. I developed the theme "Vicky cares about . . . " during my first campaign. It corresponded with the red heart that was drawn around the first four letters of my last name (Hart) on my logo. My pushcard highlighted areas I cared about and then listed qualifications under each of the following categories: Vicky cares about Education; Vicky cares about Senior Citizens; Vicky cares about Agriculture. I carried this theme through my parades, also. Posters were made telling different things I cared about and appropriate volunteers carried them. The "Vicky cares about Families" sign was carried by a young couple pushing a stroller with their cute baby daughter inside. The "Vicky cares about Agriculture" sign was carried by an area farmer wearing a farm cap. The "Vicky cares about Education" sign was carried by some school children. The "Vicky cares about Senior Citizens" sign was carried by an older couple riding in the back of the pickup truck.

All volunteers wore my campaign T-shirts with my yard sign color and logo on it.

FIGURE 12.2 Example of parade reflecting campaign theme

4. Get their attention. Parades are full of visual candy. Your entry will be competing against marching bands, funny clowns, Shriner mini cars, decorated floats, regal horses, and beautiful event queens and their courts. Believe it or not, many people won't care that much about the political entries. You have to do something to get their attention.

Throwing candy to the children along the parade route is a popular idea in my area. However, it must be done correctly and "legally." Some parade organizers do not allow the distribution of candy because it can be dangerous. Children have been hurt and even run over on rare occasions in parades across the country when the candy wasn't thrown far enough and it landed in the street and a child excitedly ran out to retrieve it and a parade vehicle driver didn't see him.

Make sure you have candy throwers who can throw well enough to reach the sidewalk. Check the parade rules beforehand to make sure it is acceptable to throw candy before proceeding. Remind any driver in your entry to watch out for children along the route.

If the parade does not allow the distribution of candy, think of other creative ways to make your parade entry stand out. One year we tried blowing bubbles. Several children volunteered for the task and got in the back of the pickup. Each had a bottle of bubbles and a couple of the older ones used big bubble maker wands to make long, big bubbles. It started out great! The breeze caught the bubbles and blew them across the crowd. The children along the route "oohed" and "ahhed" and had fun running in the yards and trying to pop them.

However, by the end of the parade route, the bubble brigade was pooped! They were blown out, plus they were having a hard time standing. The bubbles had dripped, popped, and spilled onto the floor of the pickup bed, making it a giant slick mess! The children's clothes were soaked in bubble concentrate. Their arms and faces were slimy, but they had had fun. One positive thing: it was easy to clean up!

We learned that if you are going to use bubbles, to try to devise or use a bubble machine of some kind. Maybe the children could have just waved flags or banners or something else or made music on fifes and drums. Think creatively and you'll come up with a winning idea.

Another candidate I know distributes campaign Frisbees along the route. Wisely, he does not throw them into the crowd. He walks along and hands them out. They are very popular and serve the function of both getting out his message and getting attention during the parade.

5. Follow the rules. Most parades are organized by hardworking volunteers. They are giving of their time to create something special for their community. They have spent time thinking through the rules for the parade to ensure safety and to make it the best parade possible. Be respectful of that. Take time to find out what the rules are and follow them.

Most parades have a lineup time. It can be up to one and a half hours prior to the beginning of the parade. With all you have to do, it's tempting to want to arrive near the beginning of the parade and ignore the suggested lineup time. Resist this temptation. You can ask your volunteers to arrive at a later time or your driver could arrive earlier than you if you have somewhere else to be, but someone from the campaign should arrive on time.

Pay the required entrance fee, if required. Some parades request a small fee. Some ask that a fee be paid only by political entries. Pay it on time without questions. You are supporting the community you hope to serve.

If you follow the rules, it will be remembered by the organizers and talked about positively in the community. The reverse is true, also.

One hot July day, I was waiting for the 4th of July parade to start at the listed 11:00 A.M. hour. I'd been there since 9:30 A.M. and had been placed in line by the organizers at the number three position. The 11:00 hour finally came. The marching band started, followed by the first fire truck. Just then a longtime elected official wheeled in. His wife was driving. She stopped for the person directing lineup, said some words and then, with a wave of the hand, she pulled the convertible forward and wheeled around, nosing in line behind the fire truck. The parade director motioned briefly at her to stop, but it was too late. They were gone, moving down the parade route waving and smiling.

The organizer walked over to me when I headed out and apologized. "I'm sorry about their cutting in line. I told them they needed to go to the back of the line, but she told me, "But my husband's a *senator*, and senators *always* go ahead of *candidates!*"

I was approached by an organizer in another parade. This parade asks for a donation fee from political candidates. I had sent mine in with my registration. The volunteer ran up to me and said, "Thank you for paying the parade fee. We really appreciate it. Some of the other candidates and office holders ignored it and yet still showed up and got in the parade. We could hardly stop them, but we wanted you to know we appreciate your support. Thank you."

In both these cases, I felt bad for the parade organizers and ashamed of my fellow political candidates or office holders. This high and mighty attitude is what gives politicians a bad name. Don't become one of them. Not only is following the rules the right thing to do, but it is also smart public relations. I have no doubt that these incidents (both good and bad) were probably shared in coffee shops across the community weeks after the event.

Wherever and however you meet the people, remember that you are always sending a message of who you are. Make sure it is the right message. Remember also to have fun. Parades, large events, and door to door should be enjoyable. Look forward to meeting the new people. Involve friends and family and don't take yourself or the specific event too seriously. Remember that God is in control and He is the one who is going to give you favor and place you in office, if it's His will. You are to do your part, but victory is in His hands. Keep your focus on others and what you can do for them, and the desired end result will fall into place.

CHAPTER 13

FUNDRAISING

When you talk with candidates, you often hear something like this: "I want to run for office, but I don't want to have to raise money!" The idea of fundraising is often met with groans and a range of feelings from mild trepidation to full-fledged loathing. Many candidates would rather give a speech than ask someone for money and that is saying a lot since most people are scared to get up and talk in front of people.

But fundraising is an essential part of your campaign. You need funds to be able to do what you need to do—mailings, yard signs, advertising, and handouts all cost money. Your campaign has to invest resources in order to see returns on election day. Because of its importance, fundraising activities consume 80–90 percent of a candidate's time during the first few months of any campaign.[1]

The only other option to fundraising is to fund your campaign yourself. Some candidates with financial resources can do so; however, their campaigns are often unsuccessful. Why? Because the people of that district have been denied the opportunity to invest a part of themselves into the candidacy. They see the self-funded candidate as someone who is trying to "buy" his or her office—a "lone ranger" out on his personal mission—someone who is out to implement his or her own agenda rather than "one of them."

You can provide the people of your district with an opportunity to partner with you in your efforts to bring better government to them through not only giving their time, but also giving of their financial resources. In order to do this with a pure heart, you need to, again, evaluate your own motives and reflect upon your own track record for giving.

Luke 6:38 says, "Give, and it will be given to you. A good measure, pressed down, shaken together and running over, will be poured into your lap. For with the measure you use, it will be measured to you."

Have you been a giver? Have you been obedient to what God has called you to do in the past regarding the investment of His resources? If you have, you have a wonderful promise from God that resources will be given back to you when you need them.

Philippians 4:19 promises, "And my God will meet all your needs according to his glorious riches in Christ Jesus." God enables whom He calls. He will make a way if the idea of running for office is from Him. Trust Him. He is faithful.

Yet, asking for money can still be hard to do. Many feel awkward approaching friends, colleagues, and strangers and asking them for money. Here is one of the keys: You are not asking for money. You are asking them to invest in your candidacy. You are asking them to partner with you in bringing good government to your area. They should not give money to *you*. They will want to give money to *what you are working toward that impacts them*.

There's a big difference between asking, "Would you give me $25?" and "Can I count on you to partner with me for better government by investing $25 in our campaign?"

This difference in approach shouldn't be something you do strategically. It should be something you believe. Embrace the "partner concept" and "team approach" and not only will your candidacy succeed; your public service will also succeed.

1 Corinthians 12:27 lays the foundation for this concept, "Now you are the body of Christ, and each one of you is a part of it." Not every Christian can leave his or her work and family to serve in public office. It's physically not possible, any more than it is for every Christian in America to be the pastor of a church. Numerically and philosophically, it would not be a wise plan. God needs people in every walk of life to be salt and light. You need some of your fellow Christians to be teachers and others to share Christ as they work alongside colleagues on the assembly line. You need honest Christians handling the money in your bank and caring brothers and sisters in Christ in the medical profession. Likewise, they need you to help be a voice for righteousness in state, local, or federal government. You are just one part of a team that God is putting together to help bring positive change to our world through public service. Recognize and embrace your part, yet keep things in perspective. The others need you, but you also need them.

We all need each other and have a vested interest in seeing that all succeed in the calling God has given them. First Timothy 5:18b says, "The worker deserves his wages." You are committing your time, energy, and finances to run for office. Others will welcome the opportunity to partner with you if asked.

Sources of financial support

Where do you go for financial support for your campaign? To your partners. Make a list of those individuals and groups who support you and have a vested interest in the success of your campaign. Depending upon your campaign platform, they might include:

- Family and friends who personally care about you and want to support you
- Businesses
- Church members
- Gun owners
- Labor unions

- Farmers and agri-businesses
- Elected officials
- Political Action Committees (PACs)

Political Action Committees can be controversial sources of funding for campaigns. Some candidates feel so negatively about them that they make a campaign decision to not accept any monies from PACs. I know some candidates for state representative who have made this pledge and been successful in being elected, although fundraising was more difficult than it would have been otherwise.

PACs can provide a great deal of money to campaigns for state or federal office. Occasionally, they will give to local campaigns, as well.

PACs are entities established according to law by like-minded groups of individuals with the sole purpose of helping candidates who support their beliefs get elected. Often an organization based on a trade or occupation will form a PAC. Examples include: teachers' unions, farm organizations, labor unions, and trial lawyers. Businesses often form PACs and give their employees an opportunity to contribute. These PACs could be telecommunication companies or healthcare businesses or insurance agencies.

While PACs are often viewed as evil by both the media and the public, in reality, the funds in a PAC come from hundreds of individuals who care about the issues affecting their industry. The money comes from $1 or $2 or $10 or $25 contributions from the paychecks of hardworking men and women. Many live in your district. They give advice to those in leadership and often have a say in which candidates receive these funds.

The problem candidates have run into is when they start catering their message to meet the desires of the PACs rather than sharing who they are and what they want to accomplish with the PACs and asking for their support only if they agree with their positions. There's a big difference in establishing your platform and having a PAC come alongside you to support you because it agrees with the leadership you are going to provide—and developing your message to suit the PACs and pursuing them to garner help.

Another excellent source of funds is people who often give to political campaigns. Cathy Allen in her article "How to Ask For Money" in *Campaigns and Elections* magazine says, "The same 10 percent of contributors fund 90 percent of all campaigns."[2] That's a stunning number. You can locate these people by securing copies of past election reports from your local or state election official. If running in a countywide race or city election, obtain copies of past campaign finance reports from candidates who ran in similar races. This is a public record available to all candidates. See who gave money to them. Consider adding those individuals to your list of people to contact to increase the likelihood of a positive response.

Ethics

In all of your fundraising activities, consider the following ethical guidelines:

1. Know your state's campaign laws and follow them. There are no good excuses for taking money inappropriately. It is your responsibility and the responsibility of your treasurer to find out what the current guidelines are for lawfully receiving and disbursing campaign funds. These laws can change yearly, so it is good to check periodically with your state's ethics commission or other entity that regulates political funding. They can provide you with copies of the latest laws and regulations and answer questions you may have. It is always better to ask a "dumb question" than to find out later that you have violated campaign finance law.

2. Correct mistakes promptly. Even with your best intentions, sometimes mistakes happen.

I know one candidate who had read the laws and thought she knew the campaign-finance regulations. She understood that no campaign was supposed to accept cash over $100. Everything over $100 had to be accepted with a check only. The candidate was visiting with a local business owner one day and the owner pulled out his wallet and brought out a $100 bill and handed it to the candidate, saying it was "for your campaign." The candidate was appreciative. The candidate made a photocopy of it (as she always did of all checks before depositing them to maintain a good record of receipts), gave it to the treasurer, who then deposited it and included the contribution on the next campaign finance report in accordance with state law.

Later, the candidate and treasurer were surprised and horrified to receive a letter in the mail from the state regulatory agency stating that the campaign had accepted a campaign contribution "inappropriately" and that it should "make amends immediately"! The state law was being interpreted by the regulatory agency as meaning the candidate could accept cash contributions *up to $100* and anything *$100 or above* had to be received via check. They had missed it by $1!

The candidate had to call the contributor and explain the mistake and arrange to meet him to give him back the funds via a campaign check for $100. He then was asked to contribute $100 again, but this time by check. The business owner was willing to do this, although he said, "No other candidate has ever asked me to do this and I have given cash before." To the candidate's naïve surprise and disappointment, it became apparent that not all candidates act ethically. No doubt others took the cash and never reported it at all.

While you cannot control the actions and decisions of others, you can help set the standard by complying with the laws and doing what is right to the best of your ability. You may make a mistake due to the complexity of campaign finance laws, but if a mistake is discovered, take immediate steps to correct the situation to the best of your ability. If someone questions you about the mistake, acknowledge it and tell him or her what steps were taken to correct the situation. This can prevent a small incident from becoming a political disaster.

3. Watch the percentages of PAC versus local money given to your campaign. You don't want to have your campaign almost entirely funded by PACs. No more than 40 percent of your campaign funds should come from PACs, in my opinion. The rest needs to come from

people in your area. If you get too high a percentage from PACs, you can be criticized by your opponent and look like you are bought by "outside interests." In addition, a low percentage of local money suggests that you have a low level of support among local voters. This is not good. Local individuals are the ones who will vote for you, not PACs.

When a person invests in your campaign, he or she is invested in your success and will be more likely to get out to work and vote for you. It may take more effort to raise $250 through ten $25 contributions than from writing a letter to a PAC and receiving a check for $250, but the impact on election day will be worth the effort.

4. Check out the source of funding before accepting a check. Who contributes to your campaign says a lot about you. By public law, contributions over a certain amount are public record. Others, including your opponent, can find out who has given to your campaign. This can be good if they are individuals, businesses, and reputable PACs. However, if you accept money from an disreputable entity, its image can reflect badly on you.

If you aren't familiar with a PAC or an individual, find out more about the entity or person before depositing the check. This can be done by a volunteer asking discreet questions, surfing the Internet, or calling the donor. If the check is from a PAC, you can ask it where the money comes from (individual employee donations or company contribution) and what it stands for. If you have doubts or questions, send back the check. You can write a note of appreciation, but say that your campaign has a policy of only accepting funds from individuals or organizations that you know, so you will not be able to accept the contribution at this time. It might be a little awkward, but it is better than accepting a contribution from an entity only to see your name linked with it in blaring headlines a few weeks down the road!

5. Avoid the "desire to get rich." First Timothy 6:9–10 says, "People who want to get rich fall into temptation and a trap and into many foolish and harmful desires that plunge men into ruin and destruction. For the love of money is a root of all evil. Some

people, eager for money, have wandered from the faith and pierced themselves with many griefs."

This Scripture could have been written about so many politicians. We see their faces and hear their stories on the television on an all-too-often basis. They have wandered away from the truth and pierced themselves with many griefs. Most of the people started out just like you and me. They were ordinary citizens who had a heart for public service and wanted to make a difference. They were championed by their local voters as upstanding citizens and leaders in the community. Then something happened along the way. They wanted to be elected or stay in office so badly that they put aside traditional wisdom and integrity regarding fundraising in favor of shady deals. It became easier and easier to overlook customary practices, because the end justified the means. The amount of money raised would enable them to mount an aggressive campaign or stay in office so they could help people. It got easier and easier to do until the truth was clouded and conscience seared, so a second thought was no longer given to the "new ways" of fundraising.

The slippery slope to destruction starts with a small act of impropriety. You may be confronted with such an "opportunity" during your campaign. Your true character will be revealed for all to see.

During one of my campaigns for re-election, I remember one evening when my husband came home from work with $250 in cash that a big supporter had given to him to pass on to me for my campaign. This individual had already given me a check for the legal limit of $250 for that election and couldn't legally give me any more. The supporter had told my husband to just give me the money in my husband's name (which could legally be done because my husband hadn't given me $250 during that campaign cycle) to get around the campaign laws.

While technically, it could be done, I knew in my gut that it was not ethical. On paper, we could legally say that it was a contribution from my husband, but inside I would always know it was from the supporter. It felt shady to do it that way, and I decided not to be a part of it. Although it was difficult and awkward, I had to give it back and explain why. I made an appointment with the supporter and gave back the money. It wasn't easy, but it was the right thing to do.

I believe God is going to bless you if you do the right thing. He will provide the needed funds to enable you to do what He has called you to do. In addition, He may use you to set the example for others in your community and be a witness for integrity. Don't be fooled by the idea of "needing the money." What you need most is God's blessing and empowerment. The rest will come and you can sleep soundly at night if you keep your moral compass in tune. Let your goal be that of Paul when he collected an offering for the distressed church in Jerusalem. In 2 Corinthians 8:20–21 he says, "We want to avoid any criticism of the way we administer this liberal gift. For we are taking pains to do what is right, not only in the eyes of the Lord but also in the eyes of men." Take pains to do the right thing and God will honor your efforts.

Methods of fundraising

So how do you raise funds ethically? After you have considered who might financially partner with your campaign, how do you contact them and ask them to help? Which steps should be taken to see that your efforts are successful? Below are some ideas to help you meet your financial goals:

1. Pray! Seek God and ask Him that His hand of favor be upon you. You are embarking on a mission similar to the ones Ezra and Nehemiah took in the Old Testament. Ezra was returning to Jerusalem with the goal of rebuilding the temple. Nehemiah was returning to Jerusalem to rebuild its walls. Both needed God's favor and intervention in order to meet the financial, safety, and leadership needs of their endeavors. They had to go to others and ask for their assistance in carrying out their missions. These men of God give us good examples of how to seek God and find success.

Nehemiah fasted and prayed before the God of heaven saying, "Give your servant success today by granting him favor in the presence of this man [the king]" (Neh. 1:11). Ezra "devoted himself to the study and observance of the Law of the LORD, and to teaching its decrees and laws in Israel" (Ezra 7:10).

The Lord honored these men and provided them with favor and the financial resources they needed to accomplish their tasks. Ezra 7:6b says, "The king had granted him everything he asked, for the hand of the LORD his God was on him." Nehemiah says, "And because the gracious hand of my God was upon me, the king granted my requests" (Neh. 2:8b).

Ask God for His favor and for His gracious hand to be upon you. This paves the way to open the hearts of others to want to partner with your campaign more than any "sales technique" others may recommend.

2. Ask! This sounds obvious, but it is the often neglected reality in fundraising. People are not going to contribute to your campaign unless they are asked. Occasionally someone will come up and hand you a check, but most of the time people need and expect to be asked. You've got to take the initiative to seek them out and invite them to partner with your campaign.

When you ask, it is important to consider the terminology you use. Avoid terms like "give" and "donation." When someone "gives" a "donation," it implies that the motivation should be charity—the desire to take something you've earned the hard way and give it away to someone less fortunate. You don't expect to get anything back other than a good feeling.

Conversely, you want people to "invest" in your campaign by "contributing." This approach implies that they have a vested interest in what you are doing and are needed to contribute a part of themselves into the achievement of mutual goals. They are not giving something away, never to think about it again. They are investing a contribution that will keep them engaged in the campaign throughout the election process and beyond. They will get something back for their investment and will welcome the opportunity to improve their lives, their businesses, or their country by partnering with you.

In addition, their partnership will translate into votes. S. J. Guzetta, in his book *The Campaign Manual*, illustrates this point. "Remember, every contributor, no matter how small the amount given, impacts seven people, on the average, to vote for the candidate."[3]

Be persistent and bold in your asking. In the parable of the man asking for the loaves of bread to feed his visitors, Jesus laid out the value of being persistent and bold in asking (Luke 11:5–8). He was relating the guideline for prayer, but the example also demonstrates the reality of human nature. People will often give to a friend who is bold and persistent and gives them a reason to give, so don't be afraid. "Ask and it will be given to you" (Luke 11:9). Typical ways of asking are through a letter and in person.

Make a list of individuals and entities you think will support you. Send them a well-written letter telling about what you are doing and why they should support you. Use the same theme as was developed in Chapter 4—know your audience; state the problem; and provide your solutions to the problem.

Other tips include:

- Keep the letter to one page in length, if possible, but two can be acceptable. Use short paragraphs made up of only a couple of sentences. Add an extra space between the paragraphs for easy reading. Personalize the letter so that it sounds like it comes from your heart and not from a canned campaign speech. Give them a reason to invest their money in your campaign and give them the opportunity. Ask them to partner with you.
- Give them several monetary options. Start with the higher amount and list downward so they read the highest figure first. Stating the large amount first implants an expectation in their minds similar to an auctioneer saying a desired amount first before starting the bids at a lower amount. This method has been used for centuries. Jesus even used it as He shared the parable of sowing and reaping. In Matthew 13:8 and 23, Jesus tells the crowd that the good soil "produced a crop—a hundred,

sixty or thirty times what was sown." He wanted them to hear the largest potential return first, motivating them to work hard to be "good soil" for God's message. We can share the largest expectation, also, for contributions to our work.

Here are a couple of excerpts from fundraising letters that "close" the sale.

Closing Example 1—Team Approach:

> "Would you join my Good Government Team? Your contribution of $250, $200, $150, or $100 would be appreciated. I need to raise a tremendous amount of money to get out our good government message. Will you help?
>
> Please consider joining the team and sending your support by July 1. Working together we can keep our communities going strong."

FIGURE 13.1 Example of closing example—team approach

Closing Example 2—Financial Need Approach:

> "To win this campaign it will take a tremendous investment of money. Campaign advisors have given us estimates of anywhere from $16,000 to $30,000. This figure seems like quite a challenge! I hope, as a friend, you will consider helping us.
>
> Presently we are ordering yard signs and large signs for along major roads. They are costly. By making a generous contribution of $250 you will enable us to order fifty yard signs. An investment of $100 will enable us to buy 8 large signs; $50 will purchase ten yard signs to reach all of the voters of this district; $41 will buy a roll of stamps. Will you invest in our efforts in one of these ways? I look forward to hearing from you and want to thank you, in advance, for your partnership."

FIGURE 13.2 Example of closing example—financial need approach

- Send out several different types of fundraising letters targeted at the various groups you hope to partner with. Your theme and appeal can be adjusted according to the audience to whom you are writing. The more personalized the letter, the greater your chance of receiving a contribution.

- Enclose a contribution envelope with your letter. The easier you make contributing, the greater likelihood you will get funds. It is well worth the money to print up contribution envelopes. They should have your campaign address printed on the front and a form for writing required campaign contribution information on the back flap of the envelope. This ensures you have the necessary information to comply with your state campaign laws without your treasurer having to call everyone prior to sending in the forms. It is important for your campaign records to compile the names, addresses, phone numbers, places of employment, and contribution amounts for each person who invests in your campaign. Get this information up front, and it will save time and energy later. It is not necessary to stamp the return envelope. This can be a costly gamble. It usually increases the return percentage, but most campaigns do not provide the stamp, as they simply cannot afford it.

Below is a sample contribution envelope with printed form:

FIGURE 13.3 Example of envelope front

Envelope Flap:

Back of Envelope:

Glue adhesive for the envelope flap here

NAME_____

ADDRESS_____

CITY _____ STATE____ ZIP CODE____

HOME PHONE_____ WORK PHONE_____

E-MAIL_____ SPOUSE'S NAME_____

OCCUPATION (If self-employed)_____

EMPLOYER (If not self-employed)_____

DO YOU HAVE A CONTRACT WITH THE STATE IN EXCESS OF $500?

Yes_____No____

❏ YES, I want to be a member of the "250 Club" for John.

❏ YES, I want to be a member of the "100 Club" for John.

Please make checks payable to:

John Doe for County Sheriff

State Law stipulates that:

• Each individual (i.e. husband, wife, child) can give up to $250 to a State Representative candidate during each election cycle (primary and general elections). An individual must be at least 14 years of age to contribute.

• A name, address, employer of occupation, must be listed with a contribution in excess of $25. CONTRIBUTIONS CONNOT BE ACCEPTED UNLESS THE INFORMATION IS PRESENT WITH THE CONTRIBUTION.

• A business may also contribute up to $250 per election.

Paid for by John Doe for Country Sheriff, Susie Smith, Treasurer

FIGURE 13.4 Example of envelope—back and flap

• Follow up letters with a phone call. People have good intentions, but often life takes over and letters get set aside. A follow-up phone call from you can be just the prompt they need to go ahead and fill out the check and get it in the mail.

The conversation could go like this:

Phone Script For Fundraising

"Hello, Sam? This is John Doe. As you know, I am running for County Sheriff and recently sent you a letter outlining my goals for the Sheriff's office and asking for your partnership in this effort. Did you receive my letter?"

If "No," then you can offer to send another one. Proceed with telling him what you hope to accomplish in office and ask him to partner with you.

If "Yes," then proceed, "Great. As you know, this campaign is going to require a lot of people partnering with me to help bring good government to our area. Would you like to be a part of the Good Government Team by contributing $250?"

If he says, "Yes," thank him.

If not, give him various options in reducing amounts until he finds an amount he is comfortable with.

No matter what the response, thank him for his time and ask him for his support. You can also sign him up to volunteer while you are visiting with him. Perhaps he would like to be a Yard Sign Captain as well as make a contribution or make phone calls in lieu of dollars if the budget is tight.

FIGURE 13.5 Sample phone script for fundraising

Use this opportunity to share your ideas, impart your vision, and invite participation. You will be pleased with the results.

3. Establish a "100 Club" (or "250 Club" or "500 Club" or "50 Club"). I heard this idea when I first ran for office. I had gone to the state capitol to visit with current state representatives about the challenges and nuances of campaigning. I was a neophyte and needed their help. Some of the best ideas for fundraising and campaigning come from others who have been there. Proverbs 15:22 advises, "Plans fail for lack of counsel, but with many advisers they succeed." The truth in the proverb is evident in every area of campaigning, and fundraising ideas are no exception. Ask around and find out what creative methods have worked for other candidates.

When I was visiting with one state representative, he said, "I raised $1,000 every day for ten days by starting a "100 Club." I determined to find ten people every day for ten days who would contribute $100 to my campaign and wouldn't come home until I'd met my goal." He ended up raising all the money he needed in a short amount of time early in the campaign so he could spend the rest of his time meeting the voters.

The "100 Club" idea starts with creating a list of individuals whom you think might give you $100. Make sure and look at the names of people who have given to political campaigns in the past from your area. Your goal might be to find a hundred people who will give you $100. The "250 or 500 Club" would be similar. The amount you ask for is partly determined by your past research that shows how much money the person has given in the past. This gives you an idea of not only his or her propensity to give to like-minded candidates, but also the financial resources available for such purposes. Do the research ahead of time to help determine which clubs people might be interested in joining. The individuals on this list don't receive a general fundraising letter. Instead, you call them and make an appointment to go see them.

When you arrive, tell them about your candidacy (who you are, why you are running, and why it matters to them), then ask them for their advice in the area of expertise they are familiar with. The appointment is about more than securing funds for your campaign. It's about increasing your knowledge about an important subject and establishing a valuable resource that will serve you well when elected.

After getting their input, then you can approach the idea of your "100 Club" and ask them if they would like to partner with your campaign by joining. Explain to them the financial needs of the campaign and how they can help make the important initiatives happen. You will be amazed how many people will join after meeting with you. They appreciate someone taking the time to call and make an appointment and coming to seek input and share their vision for good government.

When I first ran for office, I made appointments and visited with family friends, community leaders, small business owners, longtime party supporters, and leading farmers in the area. It was a very positive experience. If you enjoy people, you will enjoy visiting with them and learning from them, no matter the financial outcome.

Be prepared for some of them to say "No." I don't know any candidate who receives a 100 percent positive response to fundraising strategies. Some people don't have the funds available to give or aren't used to contributing to political campaigns. That doesn't mean they don't like you or won't support you by casting a vote for you on election day. It also doesn't mean that they won't contribute to your campaign at a later date.

I remember visiting with one prominent attorney in town during my first campaign. During the appointment we enjoyed discussing current laws that needed to be revised and issues of importance to our community. When I presented him with the opportunity to join my "100 Club," he politely declined, saying he never gave to political campaigns. Although I was disappointed, I certainly respected his position and thanked him for his time, telling him I looked forward to visiting with him again in the future and possibly calling upon his expertise on legal matters should I be elected. To my amazement, I received a check for $100 from him in the mail a few weeks before the election. I can only assume he'd had a change of heart, for which I was grateful. I'm sure I never would have received that contribution or had the opportunity to partner with him had I not taken the time to go visit him and ask for his support.

Visiting with people personally not only generates funds, but also serves as a smart tactical move to garner support. By targeting key community leaders and seeking their advice and input, you are not only building support for your candidacy; you are also helping neutralize possible future opposition. It is hard to give money to an opponent or oppose someone who has humbly come to ask for advice and support. Even if people disagree with you or normally adhere to another political philosophy, they will probably not openly oppose you. Sometimes it pays not only to find people who will work *for* you; but also to recruit key people who will not work *against* you. Either way, you win.

4. Host a golf tournament. Golf tournaments have the potential to raise a large amount of money. A common goal may be $5,000, but some candidates and current office holders running for re-election have held golf tournaments and raised as much as $25,000, $30,000, and more! Bringing in this much money does not come easily, however. Organizing and hosting a golf tournament takes a tremendous amount of time and dedication by the candidate and volunteers committed to making it a success. This is not a one-person operation. It can be carried out with positive results if you get together a group of volunteers who understand golf and want to take this project on.

Necessary steps include:

- Securing a time, date, and favorable location for the tournament;
- Creating a flier;
- Developing a list of potential golfers and sending out the flier to them;
- Following up with phone calls to the golfers to secure their entry and entry fees;
- Obtaining giveaways such as a free golf towel or visor to every golfer;
- Securing donations for prizes;
- Working out details for refreshments prior to, during, and after the tourney;
- Calling and asking supporters to sponsor a hole;
- Creating signage for the hole sponsors;
- Lining up volunteers to help run the event; and
- Writing thank you notes to all participants and volunteers after the event.

During the golf tournament, campaigns often employ different fundraising tactics, such as the selling of mulligans or the sponsorship of putting, hole-in-one, and nearest-to-the-pin contests at various holes. These can be additional sources of revenue for your event.

The golf professional at the golf course can often give good advice and assistance. Don't be afraid to ask for help and seek out honorary and working chairmen for the event. The more people involved, the better.

For all the weeks of work, golf tournaments can be very beneficial for your campaign. They can not only bring in a significant amount of needed funds, but also involve people in your campaign who normally wouldn't have been involved. Election day's results will reflect that difference.

5. Try creative "fun-raising" ideas. Traditionally, candidates have raised funds through letters, phone calls, personal visits, and an event such as a Bar-B-Q or picnic. These are excellent avenues for securing the funding your campaign needs, but don't be afraid to brainstorm with your campaign team to see what other creative ideas come forth. Allow a volunteer to organize and head up the event. He or she will amaze you with the results.

Some creative fundraising ideas I have heard about include:

- Pie and chili suppers;
- Campaign bingo;
- Birthday events; and
- Selling yard signs or campaign items.

Pie and chili suppers are easy to carry out because they only require finding a few people to bring a pot of chili and a few others to bring pies. No advance tickets need to be sold. A calling committee invites friends and follows up on any invitations that are sent out. The event is short and fun. People eat and then the candidate shares a few words about the campaign. A hat is passed for contributions. Music is sometimes provided by a friend who plays an instrument.

Drawings for small prizes take place. Money is raised without a lot of effort, and everyone shares an enjoyable evening.

Campaign bingo was invented by a friend of mine who served as a state representative for eight years. A simple supper was organized and people were invited. The main focus of the evening, however, was not the meal and speaker; it was on the bingo after the meal. A campaign card was designed with various candidate or office holders' pictures in each box. Sometimes words or campaign themes were inserted in a box. My state representative friend called the bingo. Attendees enjoyed cheering and groaning for the various people who were called, depending upon their political leanings. Small patriotic prizes or campaign freebies were given away when a person bingo'd. Money was raised by selling the bingo cards, plus a hat was passed in the end after motivating comments by a friend of the candidate.

Birthday events can be successful if the candidate's birthday falls during the campaign season. Invitations can be sent "in secret" to supporters, asking them to come surprise the candidate on his or her birthday. Cake and punch are all that is needed for refreshments. The hat can be passed or contributions can be inserted through a slit in a large "birthday present" to give to the candidate.

Most candidates give away their yard signs. This is common practice and necessary to increase name ID, yet sometimes you can raise funds by selling the yard signs or bumper stickers at a campaign event. People feel like they are getting something for their money, plus contributing to your campaign. Their contribution would probably go to help pay for the yards signs or bumper stickers anyway. By allowing them to "pay" for it directly, some supporters may be more likely to invest in your campaign.

6. Enlist key supporters to raise funds for you. This can take the form of a "Campaign Finance Team" or large ticket events organized by supporters.

A Finance Committee is made up of supporters who pledge to raise a given amount of money for your campaign. Presidential campaigns are using this more and more. In 2004, George W. Bush enlisted "Pioneers" who raised $100,000 each and "Rangers" who raised $200,000 and up. U.S. Senator Hillary Clinton recruited individuals to raise $1,000,000 for her campaign. Obviously, most Finance Team members won't need to raise that much, but you might find ten people who will commit to raise $1,000 for you. Remember that you have not because you ask not. Perhaps there are individuals willing to do this for you. Allow them this opportunity.

Ideally, Finance Team members will be from different professions. They will have different spheres of influence to draw from. Farmers could solicit funds from farmers; teachers from teachers; business owners from fellow business owners, etc. A wide variety of leaders on your Finance Team will allow the greatest exposure of your fundraising efforts.

While some individuals might be willing to raise money for you by asking others or introducing you to key donors in your area, others may want to raise funds for you by hosting a dinner or reception where tickets are $100 or $200 or a similar large amount. If you have a supporter who has contact with such individuals, this may be a good way to raise some needed funds.

In addition, consider enlisting your spouse to help raise funds by writing a letter in his or her own handwriting, telling why he/she is supporting your candidacy and why funds are needed. Run off the handwritten letters and let your spouse personally sign them. This personal approach is very effective.

7. Hold a campaign event. This type of event would be more organized than an informal ice cream social or chili and pie supper, but less costly than a large ticket reception or banquet. The three-way goal of this event would be to raise funds plus generate enthusiasm for your campaign and recruit volunteers.

When I first ran for office, I formed a Kick-Off Committee who helped organize a barbeque dinner for me to kick off my campaign. We charged $25 a ticket. Well-known office holders from a nearby area were invited to be the featured speakers along with comments by me. Tickets were sold ahead of time by committee members who also decorated the tables and planned the menu. It was a big hit with over 200 people participating. We raised money and recruited a winning team who would be my partners throughout my years of public service.

8. Hold a large fundraising reception and banquet. If you have a well-known person who is willing to come to a campaign event for you, you might consider holding a high dollar fundraising banquet. This is usually not feasible for local candidates, but might be an option for candidates running for state representative or state senator.

A host committee is formed to plan and carry out this type of event. Tickets are sold for $100 or $250 or more. Different levels of contributions are offered, depending upon the seating location and opportunity to participate in a private reception before the banquet and/or the chance to have a picture taken with the celebrity. The host committee is made up of individuals who are willing to pay the full amount as well as have their name publicized with the event.

Depending upon your location and candidacy, this type of event may or may not be feasible for you, but it is a popular method of fundraising used every year in the United States to raise thousands of dollars for candidates.

9. Ask again. Many individuals will give more than once to a candidate during a campaign. Don't be afraid to ask them again for a second or third contribution. They are your partners and will be willing to invest further if there is a need. It will be easier for them to give again if they have been kept up to date about the progress of your campaign. This is one reason it is vital to keep the lines of communication flowing between your partners and you. Send out a regular e-mail newsletter updating them on what you have been doing. Develop a simple newsletter that can be sent to supporters. Stop and talk with partners when you see them at church or on the street. Let them know what is going on, and be positive.

No matter which avenues you choose to raise funds, one constant remains: be grateful! It is imperative that you spend adequate time thanking contributors, no matter which method of fundraising you use. Remember that it is a very important trust someone has bestowed on you if he or she invests hard-earned money into your candidacy. Don't take this investment lightly, and don't forget to thank your donors. Write them a letter, send them a card, or call them and thank them. Any recognition on your part of their financial sacrifice will be noted and appreciated and will make giving easier for them the next time.

In summary, the sky is the limit for creative approaches to raising campaign funds. Be original and have fun. Don't stress through the days of campaigning without enjoying the opportunities to make new friends, gain knowledge, improve your skills, and share the love of Christ along the way. While initially the idea of fundraising may have brought trepidation, in the end, it can bring some of the most rewarding memories of the campaign.

CHAPTER 14

IN THE TRENCHES—PART I OFFENSIVE AND DEFENSIVE STRATEGIES

Y ou've developed your campaign plan. You are executing your door-to-door strategy. You are meeting people at events, designing your direct mail pieces, and have raised money. However, you lack one thing: engaging the opposition. Sometimes campaigns can be won without any direct contact. Occasionally conflict can be avoided, but candidates need to remember that the world calls your campaign a *race* for a good reason: your campaign features opponents with differing views, who are competing to win. You are either on track or off track. You are running and exerting effort to reach the goal: a victory on election day. While your heart may be right in desiring to serve, the reality is that in order to get to serve, you have to win. The way you win is by showing the voters the differences between you and your opponent and winning over the voters. People need to know what makes you unique—the preferred contrast between you and your opponent.

Most of us avoid conflict. The idea of facing your opponent in a debate or rebutting a negative comment made by the other camp brings knots to our stomachs, but you need to be mentally and spiritually prepared early on for the reality of campaigning and prayerfully be prepared to get in the trenches and speak the truth in love, when needed, to see your side on to victory.

Pray that God will grant you an easy campaign without much negative conflict. He can protect and keep you from it. It's wonderful when you can win without having to go through the fires you've witnessed from other candidates. Sometimes, though, He allows negative campaigning. These are times of testing and growth where you get to rely upon the Lord more than you've ever done before.

"Consider it pure joy, my brothers, whenever you face trials of many kinds, because you know that the testing of your faith develops perseverance. Perseverance must finish its work so that you may be mature and complete, not lacking anything" (James 1:2–3).

You will grow through any trial that comes your way. Although it is not fun at the time, you can come out the other side a better person by relying on some of God's great promises, such as Isaiah 43:1–3: "Fear not, for I have redeemed you; I have summoned you by name; you are mine. When you pass through the waters, I will be with you; and when you pass through the rivers, they will not sweep over you. When you walk through the fire, you will not be burned; the flames will not set you ablaze. For I am the LORD, your God, the Holy One of Israel, your Savior."

God was gracious in my first campaign. My opponent was also a Christian who served as mayor of one of the towns in our area. He contacted me early on and said he planned to run a positive campaign. Admirably, he was true to his word. We both placed ads in the paper and sent information to voters featuring our qualifications and what we wanted to accomplish. We didn't criticize each other and remained friendly throughout the campaign. He was gracious when I won, congratulating me and remaining professional the entire time. We were able to maintain a positive relationship after the election as we worked on mutual issues for the community and still view each other with respect.

Unfortunately, my next two campaigns weren't as positive. My opponents launched negative attack ads, which made for some challenging days, but God saw me through and He will see you through, as well.

The pattern I experienced with the different campaigns spoke volumes not only about the candidates themselves, but also about the nature of elections in general. When there is an open seat, campaigns tend to focus more on qualifications and what candidates want to do if elected. Once someone is the incumbent, challengers have to walk a fine line between coming off as being negative and giving voters reasons to change the course.

Incumbents have the advantage for several reasons: the nature of being in office has allowed them more opportunities to meet voters as part of the carrying out of their official duties; it is easier for them to raise funds because many organizations and individuals find it easier to invest in a known rather than an unknown; and voters tend to stay committed to people they've voted for in the past unless given a good reason to change. They feel an ownership in those persons, since they initially helped put them in office and would have to admit that they had made a mistake if they'd voted for someone else. So opponents taking on incumbents, like Absalom, must draw distinctions between themselves and their opponents and show voters why they would be a better choice this election. Conveying this message can be done professionally and with character. But you've got to be ready to go into the trenches and engage.

The next two chapters will discuss ways to engage. They will cover offensive and defensive strategies for campaigning, as well as tips on how to successfully navigate public forums and debates. Winning always starts with a good offense.

Offense

Offensive strategies involve the proactive actions and communications your campaign initiates during the months preceding the election. Offensive tactics are done not in response to an action of your opponent, but are something you strategically do or say to get elected. The offensive strategy you want to plan depends upon the type of race you are involved in.

Open seat: If you are running for an open seat, as I was the first time I ran for state representative, you will want to highlight your qualifications and what you will do if elected. You should ignore saying anything about your opponent, as a general rule.

Incumbent: If you are an incumbent, you will want to feature your record and accomplishments since elected to office. You, too, will generally want to ignore the opponent.

Challenger: If you are a challenger taking on an incumbent, like Absalom, your offensive strategy will need to be altered to give people a reason to switch their votes from the incumbent to you. This must be done right, though, with careful planning, prayer, and a series of proactive offensive tactics done in order.

Offensive steps of a challenger

Step One: Increase your name ID. As a general rule, the person with the highest name ID will win. The incumbent has a built-in advantage on this front due to the nature of serving in public office. A challenger must take steps to increase his or her name ID to at least the same level as the incumbent's before talking about the opponent.

S. J. Guzzetta, in his book *The Campaign Manual*, explains the importance of increasing name ID before criticizing your opponent. "As you build your name ID, you are establishing your credentials with the electorate as a viable candidate. Until you have done this, they will not be receptive to positive messages from your candidacy. Of even greater significance, they will not find your criticism of your opponent to be credible. **To go on the attack before doing this is usually counter productive.**"[1]

Name ID is often increased through billboards, bus signs, yard signs, newspaper ads, newspaper articles, door to door, and public events. Early stages of the campaign should focus on these activities. Ignore the incumbent during this stage.

Step Two: Highlight your qualifications and accomplishments. Once people know *who* you are, they will be interested in hearing *what* you will do if elected. Ignore the incumbent at this point, also. Talk about your experience, education, and community leadership. Be positive, proactive, and purposeful. Build your favorability rating as a viable candidate.

Step Three: Work harder than your opponent. One advantage a challenger has over an incumbent is the amount of time he or she potentially has to campaign. The incumbent is often tied up at the capitol or courthouse doing the job, but you may have more time to be going door to door or meeting the public.

This was one way Absalom overcame King David. While King David was in the palace, not ensuring people's grievances were heard and acted upon, Absalom was at the city gate meeting the people and pledging to see that they got justice. This worked to his advantage and gave him the opportunity to win over their hearts.

Take advantage of this time element and make the most of it.

Step Four: Closer to the election, give the voters a reason to change. People do not like change and will tend to vote for the same person they voted for last time unless given a credible reason to change. Now is the time to do that through the Compare and Contrast method. You can compare and contrast your qualifications or stands on issues. This is not negative campaigning. This is letting the voter know how your qualifications or experience differs from the incumbent's.

This can be done through several methods. Depending upon what comparison you want to make, you could send a direct mail piece or run a radio ad contrasting your experience, community involvement and background, education, or stands on issues.

A candidate I know in a local race for mayor contrasted the differences by developing a direct mail piece that showed quotes about the candidates from the city's major newspaper. The piece highlighted the differences in experience and job performance through the newspaper quotes without personally attacking the opponent. It worked. The candidate who sent the contrasting direct mail piece won.

Where can you locate your opponent's stands on issues? The first place to look is his campaign literature. Quotes from newspapers are also a good resource. Another source is published surveys from organizations. Throughout the campaign, candidates are often bombarded with surveys from organizations asking them what their positions are on various issues. These surveys are used to determine endorsements or to provide information to their members. The results of these surveys can be revealing and are fair game to share with others.

For this reason, you should use discretion when deciding whether or not to fill out surveys sent to you. What you say can, and will, be used against you, so only fill out surveys if you want their endorsement, you agree with their tenets and hope to raise money from them, or they are local media doing a story on your race. Otherwise, file the survey so you can use it for future reference of what issues are important to that group, but decline filling it out and sending it back in.

In the meantime, when developing contrast pieces on your opponent, pick whatever separates you as candidates and highlight it.

Step Five: If it is the last month of the campaign and you've built up your name ID and people view you favorably, but you are still behind, then it is time to pray about waging a more direct offensive about your opponent's record or qualifications. If voters still view your opponent more favorably than you, he or she will probably win. It is a challenger's role to let voters know the truth about why you are a better candidate for the job. The incumbent surely won't do it! A few words of caution about initiating an offensive:

Pray about it. Seek out the wisdom and advice of others close to you who are believers and who have had experience in campaigns. If you don't feel peace about doing it, then don't. You are the one who will have to live with your decision, so listen to your heart and

God's voice. Ecclesiastes 3:3 and 7 say there is, "a time to tear down and a time to build," and "a time to be silent and a time to speak." Now is the time to discern. Which time is it?

You can't criticize without a fairly high name ID. Remember, you are only credible as a candidate if people know who you are and see you as a viable alternative. To use football as an example: People wouldn't listen to a little-known high school quarterback if he told a TV reporter that the local NFL team should hire him because he's a better quarterback than the current starter. People would ignore him because they don't know him or see him as viable. Political campaigns are the same way. Make sure you've established yourself as a credible candidate before bringing up negative points about the person currently in office or people will ignore you, also.

Don't engage in personal attacks dealing with the opponent's family members or poor personal decisions unrelated to the office. These can backfire on you—especially in small, local elections. People perceive these ads as cheap shots. Additionally, they are not honoring Christ. Could you look your opponent in the eye if you met him or her on the street after the election? Do everything with a clear conscience and then you can sleep at night, win or lose.

Stick with the facts in the offensive information you share, such as exposing a public record. It is not a negative ad to tell voters that your opponent voted for abortion 85 percent of the time or he or she missed 70 percent of the meetings while in office. This is valid information, which could be of interest to the voters. However, make sure you base the claim on documented proof rather than on rumor or hearsay.

Absalom highlighted David's weakness by targeting David's job performance: "Then Absalom would say to him, 'Look, your claims are valid and proper, but there is no representative of the king to hear you.' And Absalom would add, 'If only I were appointed judge in the land! Then everyone who has a complaint or case could come to me and I would see that he gets justice'" (2 Sam. 15:3,4).

A modern-day ad conveying this message might look like this:

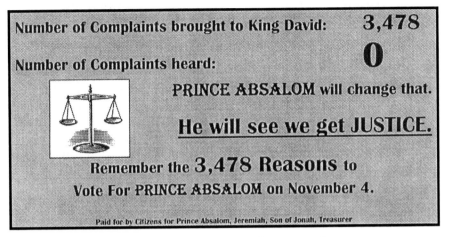

FIGURE 14.1 Example of contrast ad

Use humor, if possible, to draw these distinctions. The pill is easier to swallow if it is coated with a little honey. If you can make your point about the opponent's weakness in a humorous way, it is more palatable to the electorate.

Follow up with a positive ad so voters are left with a positive last impression about you and your candidacy. Say what you would do differently so voters understand that you are not only relaying a problem, but also providing a solution.

Inoculation

Inoculation is the political term for discerning the possible future offensive attacks of your opponent and heading them off at the pass through your actions or words. It is a combination of defensive and offensive strategies.

One of the best ways to inoculate yourself from a future attack is to follow the advice of Proverbs. "If your enemy is hungry, give him food to eat; if he is thirsty, give him water to drink. In doing this, you will heap burning coals on his head, and the LORD will reward you" (Prov. 25:21,22). Pray about what you can do to bless your opponent. Maybe it's taking an extra bottle of water over to her at the next parade and visiting with her. Or maybe it's calling her at the beginning of the campaign and pledging to run a positive campaign or sincerely saying something positive about your opponent when you are in public. Not only will the Lord reward you for these actions, but you can possibly head off future negative attacks. It's hard to launch a brutal personal attack against someone who has been kind and sincere to you.

Another way to inoculate yourself is to discern what attack your opponent may be planning and take proactive steps to defend against it. The first step involves discerning what your opponent is going to do. There are at least three ways to do that.

1. Consider your opponent's past campaign history. Does the candidate usually drop a negative attack piece a few days prior to the election? Is this the usual tactic of the people who are advising the candidate or his/her political party? If there's a pattern of negative campaigning in the past, then you can assume he or she will try similar tactics on you.

2. Study your opponent's campaign reports. Look for clues on what tactics he or she will be employing. How is he spending his money? Has he bought air time at a local radio station? Has he purchased yard signs? Has he prepaid a large amount of money going to a printer, which would indicate direct mail drops? These expenditures give clues to what to expect in the future.

3. Pray for discernment. David sought God and asked Him what his opponent was going to do in the future. God revealed it to Him. First Samuel 23:10–11 shows how David inquired of God: "O LORD, God of Israel, your servant has heard definitely that Saul plans to come to Keilah and destroy the town on account of me. Will the citizens of Keilah surrender me to him? Will Saul come down, as your servant has heard? O LORD, God of Israel, tell your servant." And the LORD said, "He will."

If God answered David's prayer and revealed his opponent's plans to him, He can do it for you, also. John 16:13 promises the Holy Spirit will lead us into all truth and tell us of things to come. "But when he, the Spirit of truth, comes, he will guide you into all truth. He will not speak on his own; he will speak only what he hears, and he will tell you what is yet to come." Do you believe the Holy Spirit "will tell you what is yet to come"? James reminds us, "You do not have, because you do not ask" (James 4:2). So often candidates run around stressed out, worrying what their opponent might throw at them, but don't take the time to seek the One who knows. Consider being wise like David and ask God something like, "Will my opponent send a direct mail piece against me? What topic will it be on?" Perhaps God will show you if you seek and listen.

The four-square analysis of Chapter 4 will also help you determine what messages your opponent might use against you. In that exercise, you thought about what your opponent will want voters to think about your candidacy on election day. A smart candidate will be thinking of ways to inoculate herself against these claims and will be ready should the need arise.

Once you have determined the probable areas of attack, you are ready to formulate a message to inoculate yourself against them. Use the wisdom of Proverbs 21:22 to do this: "A wise man attacks the city of the mighty and pulls down the stronghold in which they trust." Figure out what stronghold (claim, issue, statement) your opponent is trusting in to dismantle your campaign and then preempt the attack. You can pull down the pillars of the argument before he or she has a chance to do damage.

One year my opponent claimed at a public forum that I wanted to dismantle Social Security and would try to do so if re-elected state representative. I pulled down that stronghold in which she was trusting by clarifying at the forum that I had no intention of doing that and didn't have the authority to do so since Social Security was a *federal* issue and I was a *state* representative with no jurisdiction over Social Security. Assuming she might send out a direct mail piece promoting this claim to area senior citizens as a scare tactic, I developed a campaign piece to inoculate myself. The 8½" x 11" page piece was folded in half, making a book-like brochure. It featured pictures of me with area senior citizens bullet-pointing the positive actions I had taken as a state representative to help them. I also specifically addressed the Social Security issue. (A copy of the brochure is in Appendix D). I sent the piece to senior citizens of my district using the date-of-birth information obtained from my voter registration list. Sending this piece inoculated me against her message and preempted any last minute campaign tactics she waged. It worked. Senior citizens didn't buy her claim and her attack was negated.

If you believe you are going to be attacked, take proactive steps to inoculate yourself.

Defense

Despite the best intentions, sound offensive strategies, and steps to inoculate yourself, you may still hear the following words:

"Half of your yard signs have disappeared!"

"You won't believe the piece of campaign literature I just got in the mail and what it says about you!"

"Did you hear the rumor that's being spread?"

Attacks! They are what every candidate dreads and his or her family dreads even more. Possible attacks have to be prepared for realistically, but not feared. If you truly believe that God has called you to run for office, then He is able to protect you and keep you throughout the process and bring you out unscathed on the other side (win or lose).

Keeping this truth in mind, prepare for battle and the possible conflicts in the following ways:

- Understand the possible motivation for political attacks: fear. People fear loss of power, self-esteem, and control, as well as the impacts upon issues they care about. Fear is often displayed as anger and rash, desperate actions. David nearly got killed twice by King Saul because the king was "afraid" of David and burned with anger (1 Sam. 18:6–15,29). Similar emotions may be behind any attacks you receive. In the end, David prevailed and you can, too, with God on your side.

- Understand it is not uncommon for opponents to make up lies if they feel threatened and can't find any sound basis to accuse you. Time and again in the Bible we see this pattern, and it still happens today. Jesus was falsely accused of subverting the nation and opposing payment of taxes to Caesar (Luke 23). Opponents of Stephen secretly persuaded some men to claim they heard Stephen speak words of blasphemy against Moses and God (Acts 6), and Paul was falsely accused of defiling the holy temple (Acts 21). Don't be surprised if your opponents lie about you, also. While you may not be able to prevent the lies, you can lessen their impact by following this saying: "If anyone speaks badly of you, live so that none will believe it."

- Buy extra yard signs and keep them back for last minute replacements. Unfortunately, it is common to need to replace yard signs due to theft or damage. It may not be your opponent's fault at all. Many times enthusiastic supporters take it upon themselves to "help" their candidate by stealing the signs of the opponent. Your opponent may have no knowledge of this, so don't accuse him or her of orchestrating it. You would look foolish—especially if some stranger who is going to vote for you takes it upon himself to help you out in a similar way! Keep extras back for the final days of the campaign so you can replace signs when needed. Prepare your yard sign volunteers for this reality.

If attacked, there are several things to keep in mind as a Christian.

- Pray. Take the situation to the Lord as David did when attacked, "I have done no wrong, yet they are ready to attack me. Arise to help me; look on my plight! See what they spew from their mouths—they spew out swords from their lips, and they say, 'Who can hear us?' Have mercy on me, O God, have mercy on me, for in you my soul takes refuge. I will take refuge in the shadow of your wings until the disaster has passed. I cry out to God Most High, to God, who fulfills his purpose for me" (Ps. 59:4,7,9 and Ps. 57:1–2). God delivered David out of the hands of Saul. He can deliver you, also.

- Demolish arguments through prayer and speaking the truth in love. The weapons we fight with are not the weapons of this world, according to 2 Corinthians 10. They have the divine power to demolish strongholds, speculations, logic, and pretensions. Through prayer, God can change things and also give us the words to speak and the attitude needed to speak the truth in love.

- Don't retaliate in anger. We read in Romans 12:17 and 19, "Do not repay anyone evil for evil . . . Do not take revenge, my friends, but leave room for God's wrath, for it is written: 'It is mine to avenge; I will repay,' says the Lord." It is natural and appropriate to feel angry if you are attacked—especially if the attack is personal or unfair. Your family will understand your feelings and you can be supportive of them, as well, during this time. However, in public, don't retaliate. Instead, express disappointment at your opponent's tactics. Passionately refute any untruths, but don't get carried away in anger. You will lose credibility and the opportunity to be more professional than your opponent. Take the high road, speaking the truth in love (Eph. 4:15).

- Remember you are in charge of the decisions in your campaign. Outsiders will often give advice on how to "get" your opponent. In the heat of a campaign, it can be tempting to succumb to their offers, but later you may regret it. Don't allow anything to be said or done in your campaign unless you have prayed about it and it passes the "gut check." If it doesn't feel right, don't do it. Any piece sent out or broadcast on the airwaves will contain your name. You will be remembered for years by how you run your campaign. Don't compromise your integrity or personally destroy your opponent in order to win.

- Develop a comprehensive ad making a generalized statement against negative campaigning. This type of ad can counter a series of claims that are baseless (random shots over the bow). Your response "expresses disappointment that my opponent has chosen to run a negative ad" and positively expresses your message and pledge to "run on ideas; not run down my opponent."

- Expose and clarify untruths. Sometimes you have no time to respond, but if you learn of rumors circulating in the blogosphere or coffee shops, nix them. Your opponent is trying to put you on the defensive. Here are some ways to respond:

  > Develop a "truth" newspaper ad, radio spot, or direct mail piece that clarifies the issue. This is what I did with the Social Security accusation in one of my campaigns.

  > Consider using experts or community leaders to verify the truth about your position. Voters often don't know which candidate to believe if they don't know them personally so if you can develop an advertisement featuring people they do know and trust, it will enhance the integrity of your position.

  > Highlight documented facts to back your statements. If you can expose your opponent's false claims using documented records, it will weaken his or her credibility and minimize any future attack.

➤ Consider exposing and clarifying untruths even after the election. Many times candidates send out a negative campaign piece during the final days prior to the election so the opponent doesn't have time to respond. This often backfires as perceptive voters view this as unfair; however, it is still done and was done during one of my campaigns. I went ahead and won by a sizeable margin, but I wanted to set the record straight in case the negative piece might be believed by some. I wrote a letter to my district in a "from the heart" format, listing the claims from my opponent and sharing the factual information about each claim. The claims were about my supposed voting record—issues I'd voted against when, in reality, most of the votes were only on specific amendments of a bill and not representative of my final vote. Some people advised me to ignore the claims, but I wanted my constituents to know the truth. I placed the letter in the newspaper as a paid ad and closed by thanking them for their trust and pledging to continue to serve them to the best of my ability. It felt good to clear the air and begin the new term of service on a positive note.

- Look at the attack as an opportunity to grow. Proverbs 27:17 presents a valuable truth: "As iron sharpens iron, so one man sharpens another." There has never been a political confrontation I've gone through in which I didn't learn something about myself. Use these times to draw closer to the Lord and to examine yourself to see if God is using this experience to refine and sharpen you.
- If accusations are true, confess and renounce any sin. Hopefully, you have examined yourself before filing for office to see if there is anything not pleasing to the Lord in your life, repented of any sins, and are living a pure life before God and man. Second Corinthians 13:5 says, "Examine yourselves to

see whether you are in the faith; test yourselves." If you fail the test, you need to get right with the Lord and correct the situation.

Sometimes, however, opponents bring out information from a Christian candidate's forgiven past. If this happens, the best advice is to follow the wisdom of Proverbs 28:13, "He who conceals his sins does not prosper, but whoever confesses and renounces them finds mercy." God is merciful and so are voters most of the time if a candidate is truthful and forthright with them. What voters will not tolerate, however, is a candidate who lies to them. Admit your mistakes. Share what steps you have taken to correct the problem, and then state how this experience is going to impact your service, if elected. Be humble, sincere, and positive.

- Remember the battle is the Lord's. King Jehoshaphat was a man facing a great battle. He was being attacked by vast armies. He sought the Lord, and God spoke a mighty word of encouragement to him. Let it encourage your heart, also. "This is what the LORD says to you: 'Do not be afraid or discouraged because of this vast army. For the battle is not yours, but God's'" (2 Chron. 20:15).

That's the most important truth of all to remember in the trenches of campaigning and in the daily journey of life. If God is for me, then who can be against me?

CHAPTER 15

IN THE TRENCHES—PART II FORUMS AND DEBATES

S ome of the most common ways for voters to see a contrast between the candidates is through candidate forums and debates. While these can be stressful, the apprehension can be minimized through preparation.

Candidate forums are usually sponsored by an area organization such as the Chamber of Commerce, the League of Women Voters, or sometimes a church organization. All candidates are invited to share about themselves in an opening statement for two or three minutes and then answer a few questions.

Usually, candidates do not address their opponent directly or have an opportunity to rebut comments that are said. Sometimes it is done indirectly by using phrases like, "Unlike my opponent, I support. . . ." or "Contrary to what you may have heard, I do support. . . ." Use these phrases to correct misinformation being presented by your opponent or to clarify something that has been said. However, don't overuse them, or you may sound too whiny or combative. Overall, be positive about what you believe and want to accomplish, and that will get you further than cutting down your opponent.

In my experience, most of the people attending candidate forums are either members of the sponsoring organization or family members of a candidate. Unfortunately, very few members of the public attend, but the media covers these events. This provides you with an opportunity to convey your message through their reports, making the event worthwhile.

Candidate forums

Here are some points to remember if given the opportunity to participate in a candidate forum:

- Understand the format ahead of time. Talk with organizers beforehand to find out the anticipated setup of the tables, chairs, microphones, and podiums. Find out who will be moderating and how long you will have to answer questions. Do research on the philosophy of the sponsoring organization to determine if it will be supportive of your candidacy. If the organization is backing your opponent, you may be facing a setup and will want to decline the invitation to participate. If, however, it is a neutral group, you will want to take advantage of this opportunity to increase your name ID.
- Be prepared. Know what points you want to make and practice saying them. Study the issues and be prepared to address questions on a variety of topics.
- Consider what your opponent might say or how he or she would address questions. Be ready to answer why you believe the way you do and why your position is best.
- Practice makes perfect. Ask trusted family members and friends to help you practice. They should ask you questions to challenge your thinking and give you an opportunity to address issues without the pressure of an audience. Allow them to give you honest feedback on not only the content, but also on your style of presentation.
- Use your words wisely. Building the case for your position by choosing your words wisely is called framing the issue. There's a big difference in perception between saying, "a

woman who has a right over her body" and "an expectant mother carrying a baby who deserves to live." Euthanasia can be described as "death with dignity" or "murdering the helpless." Abortion can be called the "voluntary interruption of pregnancy" or the "killing of a defenseless human being." Words matter. Strategists and marketing agents labor over which words to use in their messages because people's opinions are determined through words. Think through and choose your words wisely before the forum to ensure your words have the greatest impact.

- Deliver your message in a positive way. When you have to tell why you don't like something or why you disagree about a topic, frame the answer by stating what you do believe in or like. This takes practice, but is more effective than falling into the "I don't like . . . because" trap.

For example, to answer the question, "What's your position on abortion?" you could answer, "I'm against abortion and believe it's murder," or you could answer in a more positive way, such as, "I believe every life is valuable and deserves to live. That's why I'm pro-life. I'm also pro-woman, believing we should support and help every expectant mother who is facing an unplanned pregnancy."

If given the question, for example, "Why do you oppose improving our public schools through increased taxes?" you could answer, "I certainly support our public schools but believe there are positive steps that can be taken without depleting the wallets of our families any further through taxes. I am proposing a realignment of funding in the budget to make education the number one priority that it should be. We need to. . . ."

Take time now to think through your positions on issues and how your stand can be presented in the most positive light, and you will leave voters with a favorable impression at the end of the forum.

- Keep answers short, but sweet. Ecclesiastes 6:11 says, "The more the words, the less the meaning, and how does that profit anyone?" Keep this truth in mind during any forum or debate. Practice saying what you want to say in the most concise form possible and the impact will be more potent.
- Look professional. Now is the time to wear the suit and tie. Take time with your appearance as your image very well could appear in a newspaper or TV report. In addition, if you look good, you will feel good and have more confidence during the event.
- Look straight ahead or review your notes rather than looking at your opponent. This technique keeps the discussion less personal and focuses the attention of the audience on the issue, not the interaction between the candidates. Address answers to the audience and the moderator, not your opponent.
- Smile. Look pleasant and be positive. Never look frustrated or let your opponent get you flustered or angry. When the going gets rough, take a deep breath, smile, and don't be afraid to show a little humor, if appropriate. Ronald Reagan was loved by all due to his contagious smile and quick wit. Remember, enthusiasm is contagious.
- Pray! Now is the time to rely on God's wisdom, favor, and promises in His Word to empower you and enable you to speak the truth in love. Review the speaking promises from Chapter 5 and stand on His Word to see you through.

Debates

Sometimes you will have the opportunity to be a part of a true debate. In these cases, you and your opponent will have the opportunity to answer a variety of questions and take turns answering and rebutting the other's comments. If you have a chance to debate, consider the following advice, in addition to the guidelines listed above:

- Make sure you understand and agree to the rules before the debate including time limits, format, physical set up of the room, and agreed-upon procedures. Negotiate acceptable terms if you feel uncomfortable with the proposed format. Will the moderator ask all questions or will there be questions from the audience? Will candidates be seated or stand? Are candidates expected to stay at their seat/podium or will they be allowed to take the microphone and walk around the stage? Make sure you discuss and get agreement on these seemingly minor procedural details ahead of time because they can make a big difference in determining who wins or loses the debate in the mind of the viewer.

- Practice with a mock debate. In his book *How to Run for Local Office*, author and former mayor of Westland, Michigan, Robert Thomas advocates setting up a practice debate at home. "First, make a written list of every possible question that you think anyone might ask you about the campaign or your candidacy. Then, use someone's basement and set it up as if it were a real debate. You will want a table for you, one for your opponent or opponents and some chairs for the audience. If you can, get a sound system with three microphones and hook them up. . . . Then get some of your inner circle, family, and friends to ask you questions just as if it were a real debate, and have one of more of your inner circle "play" your opponent. Have the "audience" ask you any questions they want, including the ones you have written out. . . . If your answers are not quick and correct, keep practicing until they are."[1]

- Prepare a book of sample questions and answers. Robert Thomas also prepared a questions and answers book that he took to candidate forums and debates. He considered every possible question he might be asked, as well as responses his opponent might give to a question. Then he prepared his own answers and responses to the questions and the possible comments by his opponents. When he went to debates, he was well prepared.

At a minimum, you will want to prepare a position paper on your candidacy. This is a paper listing the various issues of the day that might be of relevance to your campaign and your positions on them. This white sheet can be used not only at candidate forums and debates, but also by your volunteers when they make phone calls or encounter the public. Taking the time to think through these responses early will save many headaches later.

- Teach; don't preach. The key to persuading a person is imparting knowledge to him or her. Once people have accurate information, they will often change their beliefs. Sometimes emotion trumps facts and people won't change, but understanding comes from knowledge.

  Hosea 4:6 says, "My people are destroyed from lack of knowledge." It is knowledge that enables wise decisions. And it must be delivered in a positive way. Second Timothy 2:24–26 speaks volumes about how to share the facts of your position: "And the Lord's servant must not quarrel; instead, he must be kind to everyone, able to teach, not resentful. Those who oppose him he must gently instruct, in the hope that God will grant them repentance leading them to a knowledge of the truth, and that they will come to their senses and escape from the trap of the devil, who has taken them captive to do his will." When you gently instruct someone who opposes you instead of getting angry or accusing him or her, you have a better chance of winning the person over. When you teach rather than act resentful, you open the way to change minds and win votes.

- "A gentle answer turns away wrath, but a harsh word stirs up anger" (Prov. 15:1). This proverb is true in life and in the midst of a debate. If the exchange gets heated, try to answer calmly in a gentle voice. Your answer will appear more credible and help dissipate an explosive issue.

- End the debate with a handshake and a smile. Even if things have gotten a little stressful during the debate, it is the professional (and Christian) thing to forgive and forget by extending a goodwill handshake to your opponent. It also is reassuring to the audience to know that no matter your differences or which person wins, a well-meaning person will be representing them.

If you take the words to heart in these last two chapters, you will be prepared for almost any battle. Having the battle plan in place and the offensive and defensive weapons in hand will make the darkness of the trenches less scary. When the smoke clears at the end of the day, you will find yourself still standing and quite possibly with a victory flag in your hand.

Chapter 16

Get Out the Vote

Several months have passed since you signed your name on the line and took the leap of faith to run for office. Since then, you have gone to every chicken and taco dinner in the county. You have worn out two pairs of shoes knocking on doors. You've waded through cobwebbed porches, fought off "friendly" pets, and tripped on uneven sidewalks or stray toys getting to those doors. You've sweated, waved, smiled, walked, and distributed thousands of pieces of literature at parades in your area. You've lined up yard sign locations, raised funds, developed targeted lists for mailings, and built a team of wonderful volunteers who are partnering with you in this effort. Along the way, you've met some of the most wonderful people in the world. You feel blessed by the things that have been accomplished but also admit to being tired, and the election is still three weeks away!

This is the time to heed the words Paul spoke to the Galatians in Galatians 6:9, "Let us not become weary in doing good, for at the proper time we will reap a harvest if we do not give up." These words could not be truer than at this moment. Now is the most important time of your campaign. Everything you have done thus far has laid the groundwork for the crucial activities of the next few days. You need to re-energize and focus on the goal. Election day is in sight.

The pivotal activities of the final three weeks of a campaign are called get-out-the-vote (GOTV) strategies. It does not matter how many people you have met who say they like you. If they don't get out on election day and cast a vote in your favor, it doesn't matter. Your efforts will have been for naught. You have got to get them out to vote.

In order to do this, you have to reconnect with the voters, reminding them that election day is coming and asking them again to vote for you. Sometimes it is hard for candidates or those close to the campaign to believe it, but most people are not tuned in to politics and elections. They have other priorities and are busy taking kids to soccer practices, going to school functions, putting in extra hours at work, or going to the lake on weekends. At best, most voters do not think about elections or candidates or how they will vote until the last minute, despite your many efforts. And, sadly, in many elections over 50 percent of American voters don't even exercise their right to vote on election day despite being registered and aware of the election. Below are some suggested activities to get voters out to vote for you.

Yard signs

Blanket the area with your yard signs no more than four weeks out from the election. This is true for several reasons:

1. If you put them out before then, people will stop seeing them. You want people to notice them and see your name right before the election. If you erect them too early, you lose that impact. Your opponent can get the edge if he is more disciplined in waiting to put them out. It is hard to wait, especially if you have enthusiastic volunteers who want to put them out early to show their support of you. Thank them for their support and ask them to wait to put out the sign but to

display a bumper strip or window sticker on their car in the meantime.

2. Waiting until three or four weeks out minimizes damage or loss. Yard signs can become the victims of thunderstorms, high winds, icing, and other weather-related conditions, which can cause signs to disintegrate or blow over. Damaged or disheveled signs do not project a positive image for you and can reduce their impact. In addition, signs can be vandalized by children (especially near Halloween if the election is in early November) or ripped apart by dogs. In addition, sometimes supporters of your opponent take it upon themselves to "help" out your opponent by stealing yard signs. This, unfortunately, is a too common occurrence. To minimize this, wait to put out your signs.

3. Putting them out in one day near the election sends the message that your campaign has momentum and is the one worthy of support. People will be forced to notice your signs if they are all of a sudden on every street corner in their neighborhoods. They will recognize your name, remember election day is around the corner, and consider voting for you—especially if their friend or neighbor is displaying your sign in their yard.

Check with your local governing authorities to see if they have any ordinances regarding the timing of campaign signs. Some cities prohibit campaign signs from being erected until a given number of days before the election. Determine any local rules before implementing your yard sign plans.

In order to get all the signs out in one or two days, you need to be organized. This is a major undertaking and requires organization and dedicated volunteers. Depending upon your organization structure, you should be ready for this. Perhaps you have Precinct Captains lined up who will be responsible for putting out the yard signs in their areas. Or perhaps you have a Yard Sign Chairman who has recruited several Yard Sign Captains who will divide up the locations and be in charge of placing and removing the signs. Either approach can be effective.

Your campaign will also need to determine beforehand if you will be totally responsible for generating the yard sign location list or if volunteers will help. You will no doubt secure many locations by going door to door and asking people in key locations for their permission to place a yard sign. But volunteers can be responsible for finding yard sign locations, as well. Ask God to "supply all your needs" (including good yard sign locations and volunteers) and He will.

I met a terrific Yard Sign Captain one day during my first campaign when I was going door to door. I almost missed him, as there appeared to be no one home when I rang the doorbell. I had left my pushcard in his door and started across the yard to the next house, when I heard banging from a patio area behind the house. I turned back and walked around the house and found an older gentleman repairing a patio chair. His back was to me. I called out "Hello" several times to no avail. I realized, finally, that he was hard of hearing, and I stepped inside the patio area and stepped to the side so he could see me. I waved. He immediately stopped and came over to visit. We had a wonderful conversation. He supported my positions on issues and was very encouraging of my campaign. I asked him if I could put a yard sign in his yard. He gladly agreed. I thanked him and went on my way.

As I walked along, I began to think about the need for a Yard Sign Captain in his area. My opponent was from this town and I didn't know many people there. The nice man I had met came back to mind. Even though we'd just met, would he be willing to help? I came back by his house later, breathed a quick prayer for favor, found him still working on the back patio, and asked him if he would be willing to be my Yard Sign Captain for his part of town. I told him the responsibilities and, to my wonder and deep gratitude, he enthusiastically agreed.

He became the most dedicated yard sign volunteer I had, plus a dear friend. He not only put up the signs, but also monitored them daily for any damage or vandalism. He repaired the signs immediately if they became torn and stopped his car to get out and adjust them if they started to lean slightly. He even talked to his neighbors about my candidacy, obtained more yard sign locations through his contacts in town, and gave a monetary contribution to the campaign, as well. I'm so thankful for him and thankful God led me to him. God will lead you to similar volunteers.

Once your organization is in place, get all your yard signs to your captains with detailed instructions and their lists of locations. Share with them the target dates for your yard sign blitz. Ask them to put the signs in a visible location on the property, usually beside the sidewalk or along the edge of the yard. Warn them about placing them on restricted areas. Areas along road ditches and edge lines of property can be owned by the city or state and you cannot put signs there. Yard Sign Captains should inquire of the state or city government officials if the proper location is in doubt.

Volunteers should put signs up on the blitz days and monitor them through the final three weeks to determine if any signs need to be repaired or replaced. They should also return the day after the election, or soon after, to remove the signs. While it makes a good impression to put up sharp-looking signs prior to the election, it also makes a good impression to remove them afterward, win or lose. Candidate signs that are abandoned after an election slowly deteriorate, leaving a bad impression on area voters. You don't want your message to turn into trash. Stress the importance of removing the signs in a timely manner to all your volunteers, and you can avoid the disintegration of your image.

Absentee voting

Elections can be won or lost on the votes of people who do not go to the polls to vote on election day. These individuals vote weeks in advance through the mail or in person at the local election authority with an absentee ballot. They are retired couples traveling south for the winter, nursing home residents, college students, military personnel, disabled individuals, and business travelers. These voters can hold the key to the outcome of your campaign. You need to find them, provide them with information about your campaign, and ask for their votes.

The best way to do this is to target people who voted absentee in the past. In Chapter 10 we discussed obtaining information about registered voters from your local election authority. This information includes people who have requested an absentee ballot in the past with their address. You can optimize your chance of securing their votes by sending them a campaign flier along with a personal letter from you asking for their vote. Send the letter a week prior to the beginning of absentee balloting for your election, which could be four to six weeks prior to election day. Check with your election authority to confirm this date, and then contact the voters through the mail, in person by targeting your door-to-door efforts to these individuals just prior to the start of absentee voting, by phoning their homes in person or through your volunteer phone bank, or by conducting a literature drop to their doors with your volunteers.

Other ways to reach potential absentee ballot voters include:

1. Always have absentee voting information and applications with you when going door to door or at public events. This enables you to ask parents if they have a child attending college or in the military who might need an absentee ballot. It allows you to share applications with disabled individuals you meet going door to door. It helps them get the balloting information they need.

2. Visit area nursing homes with absentee ballot applications and ask the administrators who might be interested in voting and if they need an application. Go meet those residents and not only give them the ballot applications, but also introduce

yourself and tell them about your candidacy, asking for their votes.

Inquire of your local election authority to see if they travel to the nursing homes to assist with resident voting rather than sending applications to them. If this is the case, find out the date they will be coming to the nursing home and go there a couple of days before the election officials visit to introduce yourself to residents and share your campaign information. By meeting them a few days before they vote, your message will be fresh on the minds of the residents.

LOUELLA PRYOR
REPUBLICAN CANDIDATE
MORGAN COUNTY TREASURER

Dear Morgan County Voter:

I am writing to you today to ask for your vote and your support in the upcoming primary election. Please take a minute to look over my card I have enclosed. I hope you will agree that I have the experience and the dedication to serve you as Morgan County Treasurer.

Again, I would appreciate your vote on the republican ballot in the upcoming election.

Sincerely,

Louella Pryor

Louella Pryor
Republican Candidate
Morgan County Treasurer

FIGURE 16.1 Sample letter to give nursing home
residents along with a pushcard

3. Look for announcements in local newspapers listing the names of college honor roll students. Recruit a volunteer to check the names with the list of registered voters in your county and write the students a letter. Send them an application and ask for their vote.

4. Have absentee ballot information at your (or your political party's) booth at local fairs throughout the year. Ask people who stop by if they will be out of town during the election and if they need an absentee ballot.

Help individuals obtain ballots and you may get their vote. Target persons voting absentee, and you could increase your final vote count enough to put you over the top.

Yard sign rallies

A creative technique proving highly successful to candidates is a strategy called yard sign rallies or sign waving. This entails getting a group of volunteers to stand at a busy intersection or along a well-traveled thoroughfare holding your sign, smiling, and waving to passing motorists. It doesn't cost anything, yet it increases your name ID in the crucial final days of a campaign plus reminds people to go vote. When people see their friends and neighbors braving the elements to take a stand for you (literally!), it will make a big impression.

Pickup truck signs

Another simple, inexpensive way to increase your name ID and remind people of the upcoming election is through highlighting your large campaign sign in the back of a pickup truck and parking it at a busy intersection or in the parking lot of a popular business in town during the last seventy-two hours of the campaign. The truck could be left at one location for awhile and then moved to another spot in the district throughout the final three days of the campaign.

Chris Benjamin, campaign strategist and Chief of Staff for Missouri House Speaker Rod Jetton, shared a variation of this technique that was successful for one Missouri state representative candidate who lived in a rural district. "He would sit on the tailgate of his parked truck with his sign in the back. He waved and smiled at people driving by. It was highly effective. People saw him, waved, and honked—and got out and voted him into office overwhelmingly."[1]

Reminder postcards

Postcards can be an effective way to remind people to vote. In past elections I have seen postcards used effectively two ways: through the candidate sending them out and through friends sending them to other friends.

When I first ran for office, I tried to implement a postcard system used by a person who had successfully run for state representative from another part of the state. He had gone home after going door to door every day and written a personal note to every person he met that day. He wrote short notes such as, "I enjoyed meeting you while campaigning August 23rd. Your roses were beautiful. I'd be honored to serve you as state representative and ask for your vote November 7. Thank you." He then signed each one and dropped it into the mail the last week of the campaign. As you can imagine, this personal touch elevated him past the incumbent he was running against for an upset victory.

When I tried doing this, it got too burdensome. I physically couldn't do it if I wanted to get any sleep. Variations of this idea could be developed, however, which would accomplish the same thing. Postcards could be printed with a simple message similar to the handwritten note and personally signed by you. A volunteer could make note in the data base of the houses you contacted while going door to door and mailing labels could be printed out for them. The personal touch is lost somewhat, but the basic message is the same.

Another effective way to use postcards is through your supporters. Print up election day reminder cards and ask volunteers to take bundles of ten with them to hand address and send to their friends and family the last week of the campaign. People pay more attention to the opinions of people they know over some mass mailing asking for votes for a candidate. The only cost to the campaign is the cost of printing the postcards, since the volunteer affixes the postage. Printing these cards is money well spent and a very effective GOTV strategy.

Newspaper advertising

If your campaign plan determined that local newspaper ads would be cost-effective in relation to the number of voters you would reach, now is the time to begin running your newspaper ads. Have a presence in weekly papers during the final three weeks of the campaign. Consider the design tips outlined in Chapter 8.

Radio and television advertisements

If your campaign plan determined that local radio, television, or cable advertisements were cost effective, now is the time to begin running them. Longtime political consultant S. J. Guzetta recommends following the "10, 20, 30, 40 plan" in his book *The Campaign Manual*. He advises spending your media budget in the following manner: "Place 10 percent of the dollar amount in the fourth week before the election, 20 percent in the third, 30 percent in the second, and 40 percent in the final week. This spread, in combination with the other media and campaign activities, works most effectively in continuing positive name ID and builds good, steady momentum right up to election day."[2]

Direct mail

Earlier in your campaign you identified the groups of voters that you wanted to target. Hopefully, you have obtained the names and addresses of the individuals you want to target and have prepared and printed direct mail pieces that send specific messages to specific sets of voters. Now is the time to send them. Use your volunteer network to stick mailing labels on them and get them to the post office in time. Alternate the drop dates so voters receive the mail pieces over several days during the final week of the campaign. Drop the last piece, the get-out-the-vote card or letter, so that it arrives the day before the election.

The final weeks of the campaign are also the time for endorsement letters to be sent out on your behalf by a supportive third party. This could be an individual or organization that supports your candidacy and wants to energize its sphere of influence to get out and vote for you. Check with your state's campaign laws to determine if you can have knowledge of the letter or not and what kind of reporting, if any, your campaign needs to do regarding the monies which were spent on your behalf, as this may be viewed as an "in kind" contribution or an "independent expenditure." If it is considered an "independent expenditure," then the candidate cannot have any prior knowledge of the mailing.

Phone calls

If you have not made any phone calls earlier in the campaign, now would be a good time to do so. Phone calls provide vital pieces of information and can make the difference in your race.

The goal of the calling campaign is to locate your supporters and to get them out to vote for you on election day. Chapter 10 outlined how your campaign could initiate calls to develop lists of voters who can be targeted during the final three weeks of the campaign. If your campaign has done this, you should already have stacks of names of voters who support your stance on various issues and who support you. You also know who will *not* vote for you. No more money should be expended on these voters. You don't want to help remind them of election day, as they will be voting for your opponent. You want to locate and target voters who support you.

Four weeks out, set aside your list of voters who *will* vote for you. You will call them during the final days of the campaign.

Use the last month of the campaign to call those voters who indicated they were undecided. You want to give them the information they need to persuade them to come over to your side. To do this, you will want to call the unidentified voters to verify they are still undecided, then proceed. A sample script is below:

Sample Undecided Phone Script

"Hi, Mrs. Jones?" (Always verify whom you are talking to so you'll know later if the information you obtain matches up with the name and address on your list.)

"This is Marilyn and we're conducting a short election survey tonight and wondered if we could ask you a couple of quick questions? It will only take about one minute."

If "No," then say, "Thank you anyway," and go to the next person.

If "Yes," then say, "Thank you. If the election were held today for County Sheriff, would you vote for John Doe or Suzie Meldon?"

If "John Doe" (your candidate) then proceed: "Will anyone in your household need an absentee ballot or a ride to the polls?"

If they need one of these, get the contact information and tell them an absentee ballot application will be sent to them or someone will be contacting them on election day to give them a ride. Say: "Thank you very much. This concludes the survey. Have a good evening."

If they answered the election question with your *opponent* say, "Thank you" and end the call. Place their name in the opponent's pile and don't send them any more information.

If they say they *haven't decided* who they are going to vote for, you could proceed several ways:

1. You could thank them, end the call, and send them some general information about John Doe and then re-survey

---

them again next week to see if the information helped sway them; or

2. You could ask them a question about which issues are important to them such as "Of the following issues regarding the County Sheriff's job, which is most important to you?

    ___ Honesty and integrity

    ___ Job experience in law enforcement

    ___ Criminal justice experience

    ___ Past political experience"

    Then you could send them information targeting that issue and highlighting your qualifications and call them again next week; or

3. You could give them a 'push question' to try to sway their opinion such as, "If you knew that John Doe has been a police officer for fifteen years and Suzie has been a lawyer, would this make you more likely or less likely to vote for John Doe?" Pick your contrasting issue(s) and share it with undecided voters to try to sway them. Call them again the following week to determine if they have decided. Keep doing this until you have a good idea how the undecided voters are going to vote.

Conclude all calls by politely thanking them.

FIGURE 16.2 Sample phone script for undecided voters

Use this information to target the undecided voters during the final four weeks of the campaign and to prepare for GOTV efforts. After making these phone calls, you should have a good list of people who support you. You will also have a good feel for how your campaign is doing and if you need to spend extra money getting your message out or improving your name ID. You should also know the parts of your county or district or city where you have the most and least support. This can be helpful on election day as you try to get your supporters out to vote.

Once you have determined the voters who will support you and have further added to your supporters through targeting the undecided voters, now you can use this information to get out the vote. Line up volunteers to call *supportive* voters every day during the last three days of the campaign and on election day. Optimally, you will call them three times to remind them to vote. Below is a sample script:

Sample Get-out-the-vote Phone Script

"Hello, Mrs. Jones? This is Kevin and I'm a volunteer for John Doe's campaign. As you know, John is running to be our next County Sheriff and has a positive vision to better protect our neighborhoods. This election and your vote are vital to the safety of our community. He wants to remind you that Election Day is this Tuesday. John needs your vote. He looks forward to working for you and thanks you for getting out to vote for him on November 5th."

FIGURE 16.3 Sample get-out-the-vote phone script

Keep track of the calls you have made. If you get an answering machine, then leave a similar message reminding them of the upcoming election and thanking them for their support and vote. Make sure they know every vote is vital and their vote is needed.

On election day add a question to determine if they have voted. If not, then call them back and ask again later in the day. This is an effective way to get out the vote for your candidacy. You may think it is annoying to call people over and over, but it gets results. In order to win, you have to get your people out to vote for you. All the yard signs and well wishes in the world won't amount to anything unless they actually mark the ballot for you. Set up an organized system of volunteers to make these calls the final Saturday, Sunday, and Monday prior to the election and on election day.

Implementing a calling project may not be fun to think about, but it can be one of the most effective strategies of your campaign. Be bold. Be brave. Try it. You will most likely be glad you did.

Text messaging

Text messaging is a way to use technology to get your voters out on election day. You can send a simple GOTV reminder to supporters if you have their cell phone numbers. Use the SMS messaging system discussed in Chapter 9 to reach the most individuals in a short amount of time.

Internet efforts

In today's technologically advanced world, you will not want to neglect spreading the word through this medium. Reminding voters of the upcoming election and asking for their votes could not be simpler or cheaper than through e-mail.

If you have utilized a Web site, you have generated a team of supporters who have e-mailed you. You can send them a series of e-mail messages prior to the election similar to your direct mail pieces. Every day for the week prior to the election, your supporters can receive a targeted message reminding them of your stance on various issues and asking them to not only vote for you, but also to help spread the word.

A single e-mail message can be multiplied indefinitely if your supporters will send it on to their friends via the Internet. It is a terrific way to get out the vote.

E-mail messages should be focused and eye catching. You can do this through creative fonts, graphics, color, and pictures. Be careful about sending too many pictures or graphics, however. A large amount of graphics can slow down the transmission, making the recipient wait on the other end or clogging up their in-box. This will not be appreciated by receivers and can dampen their desire to pass it along to their friends.

A simpler way to catch their attention is by the creative use of colored text and bold fonts. Ask a technically gifted volunteer to help you design these e-mail messages. While it is good to send out well-written e-mail messages, it is even better to do it in a way that projects professionalism.

Take time to write effective titles for your message. Many people choose to open or delete a message based on the message in the title. Try to "hook" the readers with a comment relating to why the election is important to them or designed to tweak their curiosity. Examples might include: "Family under attack"; "Jane shares insider results from phone survey"; "Election going down to the wire"; or "Jane's opponent went too far." These titles will invite readers to learn more.

Use the Internet to help get out the vote.

Literature drops

Literature drops can be another effective way to get people out to vote and are fairly easy to do. Teams of volunteers go door to door in your targeted precincts (those favorable to your political party and the swing precincts) the weekend before the election, blanketing the doors of the homes with campaign literature or a get-out-the-vote door hanger. Volunteers don't need to knock on the door. They just leave the election reminder.

The type of literature to drop at the door depends upon your preference and budget. Overruns from earlier printings of direct mail pieces, brochures, and pushcards can be used by themselves or with a bright-colored sticker affixed to the front reminding them to vote. A special card or door hanger could also be printed with a specific message about your candidacy and a reminder about the upcoming election on Tuesday.

Get-out-the-vote efforts can make the difference between victory and defeat on election day. They build momentum and amplify your earlier efforts. Even though you may be weary, finish the race strong by sending effective e-mail messages, blanketing your district with yard signs, reaching absentee voters, using the media effectively, and waging an aggressive phone campaign during the final weeks of the campaign. You will be glad you did when you cross the finish line on election day.

CHAPTER 17

ELECTION DAY

lection Day is finally here. You've run a hard race with your opponent. One of you will cross the finish line first and earn the privilege of serving the people of your area. Hopefully, that will be you. Polls will close in a few hours, but the race is not done yet. You have several hours to do last minute campaigning that can make the difference. Election day activities fall into three categories: influencing voters once they reach the polls to vote for you; getting people to the polls; and election night activities.

Election poll coverage

People need to see your name as they walk into the polling site to vote. You would think that voters would know who they are going to vote for prior to arriving at the polling site, but that is not always the case. Many times voters come out to vote for a specific candidate, such as for president or governor. They have seen the television ads for these high-profile races and formed an opinion they want to register. However, they are not as informed about races further down the ticket. They may not have paid attention to your race nor formed an opinion about who would be the best candidate. These individuals are the voters you must reach on election day.

The most common ways to connect with these voters is through having campaign signs at the polling places and through personal contact with you or a volunteer.

Signage at polls

As part of your yard sign distribution plan created prior to Election Day, obtain a list of polling sites and get volunteers to put up four signs at each election polling site prior to the beginning of voting. This usually means someone has to get up very early in the morning or stay up late at night if putting up the night before. Don't put signs up the night before unless you are sure they will remain undisturbed until the next day.

Before election day, check the rules for placement of campaign signs. Usually campaigning must be conducted at least twenty-five feet from the door of the polling site. Some polling locations prohibit signage, so check with your local elections official prior to Election Day to ensure every sign is used effectively. If a polling site, such as a church, does not allow signage on its property, then try to locate a site nearby that will. The goal of adequate signage near the poll is to imprint your name on the minds of undecided voters prior to their entering the election booth. Most people will vote for someone whose name is familiar over someone they have never heard of. Seeing your name on your sign prior to entering the election booth may be just the reminder they need to vote for you.

Personal contact with voters

Even better than seeing your sign at the polling place is seeing you. You should spend the day traveling between the most important precincts to greet the voters as they go in to vote. Pick out the precincts with the largest number of voters who vote for your political party. Wear your name badge and look pleasant as you greet voters. Don't force handshakes, but smile and nod at voters as they enter. If someone approaches you, feel free to extend your hand, look them in the eye, and say, "I'm John Doe, running to be your next County Sheriff. I'd appreciate your vote."

You cannot be at every location at the same time. You will have to rely on volunteers to help fill in the gaps. Ask supporters to represent you at the polls on election day. Give them a campaign T-shirt and plenty of campaign brochures. Ask them to hand out your information to interested voters. This can make for a long day, so recruit enough volunteers so no one has to give more than a couple of hours of their time. Take time during the day to stop by all the polling sites where you have volunteers. Give them a bottle of water and perhaps a snack and thank them for the sacrifice of their time and effort to help your campaign. Make sure they know how much you appreciate their partnership in this effort for better government.

Train them to effectively target voters. Make sure they know to stand back twenty-five feet from the door of the polling place. Have them smile at voters and if a voter makes eye contact and looks at their campaign shirt or literature, use that as an opportunity to say something like, "Hi, here's some information about John Doe, running for County Sheriff. He'd appreciate your vote." Ask the volunteers to hand the person the literature and back away unless the voter has questions.

I've found in my years of working the polls that many people don't want to be bothered when they come to vote. If they are looking down or walking quickly toward the door, just smile and don't bother them. Your approach could turn them against you. Undecided voters, however, will often look for more information. Once they get inside and are standing in line, they may look at the brochure your volunteer gives them and that can make all the difference once they enter the booth.

Getting your supporters to the polls

Election day is the time to get your supporters to the polls. This can be done through giving rides, phoning, monitoring vote counts, and GOTV neighborhood efforts.

Rides to polls

While going door to door or making campaign phone calls, you or your volunteers might have found individuals who need rides to the polls. Hopefully, you have secured a volunteer who is willing to give them rides and they are doing so throughout the day. While there are usually not a lot of people who need rides, every vote counts, so try to set up some provision to help your supporters get to the polls if they cannot drive themselves.

Phone calls

Today is the most important day for your phone volunteers. They have the important task of using the information they have gathered over the previous months to generate a large turnout for your campaign. Throughout the day, volunteers should be calling the people who have indicated they are going to vote for you to get them out to vote. Make sure the volunteers have a list of polling sites along with a precinct map in case a voter needs to know where to vote.

A sample election day script might look like this:

Sample Election Day Phone Script

"Hi, Mrs. Jones?" (Always verify who you are talking to so you'll know if the information you obtain matches up with the name and address on your list.)

"This is James, a volunteer with the John Doe for Sheriff Campaign. We just wanted to remind you that today's Election Day. Have you had a chance to vote yet?"

If "Yes," then say, "Thank you. John appreciates your support and looks forward to working for you making our community safe."

If "No," then say, "John needs your vote. Today is the day we have a chance to make a positive change in our community's law enforcement leadership. Will you be able to get out and vote soon? Do you need a ride? Do you need information on polling site locations?"

If the person needs a ride, then say you'll connect him/her with a volunteer who will provide a ride. If the person needs information on where to vote, use the map and poll site list to assist him/her. If the person plans to vote, close by thanking him or her for the support.

FIGURE 17.1 Sample election day phone script

The volunteers should keep calling the supporters until all have said they have voted. This may entail calling the same household multiple times throughout the day. The voters may get annoyed, but it works. Even on election day, many families get busy with life and don't get around to voting even though they have good intentions. The reminder phone calls help them focus on their earlier goal of helping to elect you. Most will find a way to get to the polls if reminded and if the caller is courteous.

Monitor vote counts

Another way to get people out to vote is to monitor the vote count totals from target precincts. Refer back to your door-to-door precinct priority list. The precincts most important to target were ones with a large number of voters who typically vote for members of your political party. You need these precincts to have a big voter turnout. Ask volunteers who are manning these precincts to occasionally ask voters leaving the polling place what number of voter they were. Election judges usually say this number as a person signs in. This gives you an idea of how many people are turning out to vote in this crucial precinct.

Are these precincts coming out to vote in numbers you had hoped for? In your initial campaign plan, you determined the number of votes needed in order to win by looking at a past election similar to yours and seeing the total number of citizens who came out to vote. You then took 51 percent of that number to determine the number of votes you would most likely need in order to win. This is a good start, but you can go further in this analysis. You can figure how many votes you need *by precinct* by listing all the precincts in your district, along with the number of people who voted from that precinct in the earlier election and figuring what 51 percent of those voters would be. This would be a general guess of how many votes you need from each precinct. However, precincts differ in their political makeup. You may need to get 55 percent of the vote in more supportive precincts to make up for the 45 percent vote you will get in less favorable precincts. Look at past races where a person from your party won. Use those numbers as a beginning point to determine the various percentages from each precinct that might be needed in order to win. Fine-tune the numbers to adjust for the candidate's place of residence, results from your calling program, and other factors, such as where you've gone door to door, which might change the breakdown of percentages for your particular race. The end result should add up to at least 51 percent in order to be elected. This is all an educated guessing game, but one you can use to monitor votes on Election Day. Your analysis may look something like this:

Precinct	Number who Voted in 2006	51% Votes Needed	Percent Voting for Candidate A 2004	Percent Voting for Candidate B 2006	Number of Votes Needed to Win
1	385	196	55%	52%	211 (55%)
2	400	201	25%	36%	160 (40%)
3	694	353	51%	53%	367 (53%)
4	71	36	67%	60%	48 (67%)
TOTAL	1550	786			786

FIGURE 17.2 Sample precinct analysis to determine
voter turnout and votes needed to win

You can see by the example that this plan counts on getting the same amount of support that Candidate A from the same political party did in 2004's similar election from Precincts 1 and 4 (55 percent and 67 percent). It counts on increasing the vote in Precincts 2 and 3 through going door to door and other means of communication with those precincts. Throughout the day you can see what the total voter count is in those precincts. You need a heavy turnout in Precinct 3 in order to win. Last minute literature drops can help increase this turnout.

Election day literature drops

Teams of volunteers can be used to help increase voter turnout in precincts supportive of you or your political party in past elections. Ahead of time election day reminder cards or sticky notes can be prepared, saying something like:

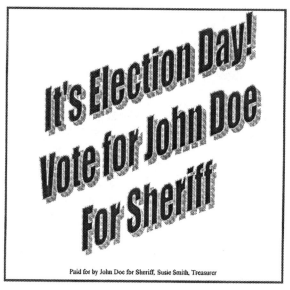

Paid for by John Doe for Sheriff, Susie Smith, Treasurer

FIGURE 17.3 Sample election day sticky note

Volunteers can go to targeted households, leaving these reminder notes on doors. Targeted households could be:

- Voters whom you have identified through your calling program to be supportive of you plus any undecided voters; or
- Households with more than one registered voter; or
- All registered voters in that precinct.

The target you choose is determined by how sophisticated your campaign has been in gathering information earlier. No matter which way you target, your team can help remind people of the election and get them out to vote on election day in your targeted precincts.

Election night activities

The polls have closed. The race is done. Now is the time for waiting and then, hopefully, celebrating. Depending upon the size of your race, you will probably want to have some sort of election night watch event. Whether it be in someone's home or at a local community hall, having somewhere to go on election night provides an opportunity for your supporters to be with you and you with them as together you learn the outcome of your efforts. It provides you an opportunity to thank them for their sacrifice, their partnership, and their support. Most importantly, it provides you an opportunity to publicly thank your family for all they have done to support your campaign. Too many times family members are left out of the race. It's not intentional but just happens as more and more attention is focused on the candidate during the race. The spouse and children soon get left out and can begin to feel disenfranchised by the entire process. What started out as a partnership ends up as a one-man or one-woman show.

Dr. Tom Barrett talks about this phenomenon in his book *Walking the Tight Rope*.[1] He describes campaigning as running a marathon. Both the candidate and his spouse are running parallel marathons—similar in distance, but very different in reality. The candidate is running his or her race with the encouragement, assistance, and support of others. The spouse is running his or her race mostly alone. Too many times the spouse is not even recognized at the end of the race. Dr. Barrett writes:

> All along what had secretly sustained this runner (the spouse) was the hope that her husband would notice her sacrifice. She had hoped he would be aware of the loneliness and difficulty of her back-alley marathon. She had hoped he would acknowledge the necessity and importance of her race to him and their family. She had hoped he would pour honor and recognition upon her as a winner. She had hoped he would love her and thank her for her efforts.

But he didn't.

He was too excited about being in the winner's circle.

Remember to recognize and thank your family during the election night festivities. Make a list ahead of time of all those people you want to thank so that you don't leave anyone out. In that list, consider thanking the Lord. Remember who has enabled you to be where you are tonight and bring Him praise.

Think about what you would like to say to the media if interviewed. The media will often ask you for a quote. Be prepared to send a positive message to the voters and your opponent. What you say can set the tone for your future.

In addition, win or lose, you will want to thank the voters. Save enough money in your budget to place a final ad in the newspaper or on the radio after the election thanking them for their support. It will leave a positive impression in the minds of voters and get you started on the right foot, if elected.

Personal reflections

If you are like me, you probably will experience a myriad of thoughts and emotions as you await the results and look back on the past months of campaigning.

I can still remember clearly my first election day. I knew it had been God's will that I run. Through prayer, I had felt God's call to put my name on the line and to run the best campaign I could. What I didn't know was whether or not it was God's will that I *win*. I had grown as a person through the campaign, had met so many wonderful people I never would have met otherwise, had learned about important issues, and had had several wonderful opportunities to minister to people and share the love of the Lord. Perhaps these were the reasons God had called me to run, rather than to serve in office.

I remember pondering one of my favorite axioms as I drove from polling site to polling site throughout the day:

Face the worst;

Expect the best;

Do the most;

and

Leave the rest.

I had to face the worst—I could lose. That is the nature of elections. Someone wins and someone loses. I had to accept the fact that I could lose and remind myself that if I did, it wouldn't be the end of the world. God still had a plan for my life—a good plan—and would use me wherever He placed me, if I was willing and obedient.

While facing the worst, I needed to stay positive and expect the best. There was no reason to dwell on the possible negatives.

The third part says to do the most. I felt good that I had done the most I possibly could. It wasn't a perfect campaign, but the Lord had provided people to come alongside to help and given me the energy needed to accomplish almost everything I wanted to accomplish. Ecclesiastes 9:10 advises, "Whatever your hand finds to do, do it will all your might." No matter the outcome, I knew I could sleep well knowing I had done all I could do with the resources and time the Lord had given me.

Lastly, I was reminded to leave the rest. Resting in the Lord is the privilege Christians have in whatever we do. We are to do our part and God will do His part. We can rest in the assurance that whom God calls, He enables. He will make a way, if it is His will for our lives. Proverbs 21:31 puts it in perspective, "The horse is made ready for the day of battle, but victory rests with the Lord." I had done my part. Now was the time to leave the rest in God's righteous hands.

When the votes came in that night, I had won overwhelmingly with almost 60 percent of the vote. I walked into the election night event sponsored by my county's political party to cheers from supporters who had seen the results on the big television screen and were awaiting my arrival. It was a surreal moment as I realized I was going to be my district's new state representative. I had been given a new ministry—representing and helping the people of my area to improve their lives, and making a difference for the One I represent. It was a moment I will never forget.

I pray your election night will be as memorable. I hope this book has given you the help and insights you need to successfully campaign for public office through running God's way. May your campaign and public service make a difference, both in this life for the people you serve and eternally for those touched by your service.

ACKNOWLEDGMENTS

This writing of this book would not have been possible without the support and assistance of many wonderful individuals. Some of the individuals who helped this dream become a reality include:

My wonderful husband, Lowell, and daughter, Tiffany—You've encouraged me from the beginning of this project. Thank you for your support, your love, and your partnership in this effort. I couldn't have done it without you. You're the best and I'm so thankful for you!

My parents, Ted and Virginia Zellmer—Thank you for your support and your prayers in what God has called me to do over the years. I am so blessed to be your daughter. Thank you for always believing in me.

Missouri State Representative Brian Baker, Missouri House Speaker Chief of Staff Chris Benjamin, former U.S. Senator Jim Talent, Political Director Danny Pfeifer, and Missouri State Senator John Loudon and wife, Gina Loudon, PhD—Thank you for the hours you spent reading the manuscript and the time you gave to share your ideas. Your input was invaluable.

Kelly Schrock—A large portion of the chapter on the Internet reflects your expertise and insights. Thank you for sharing your technical know-how and for believing in the project.

Missouri State Senator Delbert Scott, Missouri State Representative Danie Moore, Missouri State Representative Brian Baker, former Missouri State Representative Connie Cierpiot, Cass County Treasurer Steve Cheslik, Johnson County Clerk Gilbert Powers, Morgan County Treasurer Louella Pryor, former City Alderman Barbara Walters Rafter—Thank you for sharing your campaign materials with the readers of this book. I know your examples will be helpful to others as they chart the course of their campaigns.

Mary Cheslik and Chad Middaugh—Thank you for the time you gave to work on the graphics in this book. Your expertise is so appreciated.

Pastor Randy and Gloria Evers—Thank you for your encouragement and words of wisdom over the years. It's a blessing to have a pastor and his wife who are willing to take a stand for righteousness and who support others who are called to service in the public arena. Thank you.

All my friends and family who supported this project—Your encouragement is so appreciated and your prayers have helped make this vision a reality. Thank you for the time spent in prayer for this book and for your friendship. I am humbled by your gift.

Bill Day—The Lord used you to start this all. Thank you for believing in me and asking me to run for state representative. It has been an honor to serve. My prayer is that many others will have the same opportunity through the blessing of the Lord and the strategies outlined in this book.

Appendix A

Fourteen-Month Campaign Timeline

Campaigns go through five distinct stages. The focus and activities change with each phase. Below is a sample guideline candidates can use to keep their campaigns on track. It assumes a November election. If the election is held at a different time, adjustments should be made accordingly, beginning fourteen months out from the election.

Pre-announcement stage—getting ready

When: During the six months before filing for office, starting August of the year prior to the election.

- Pray.
- Write personal bio for announcement.
- Encapsulate the reason you are running into one sentence.
- Secure campaign treasurer.
- Choose name of campaign committee.
- Recruit campaign team (chairmen of various projects).
- Decide campaign colors.
- Decide campaign logo.
- Write announcement press release.

- Secure mailing lists.
- Develop computer database of potential partners.
- Write and send letter to friends, telling decision to run and inviting their partnership in the efforts.
- Write fundraising letters, but send them later:

  - To friends and family;
  - To coalitions (business, pro-life, gun owners, other)

- Buy wardrobe updates.
- Get price quotes on yard signs, direct mail pieces, postage, pushcards, media buys, etc.
- Get bulk rate permit.
- Write campaign plan.
- Develop a budget.
- Gather important dates (major events, parades, fundraising events, etc.)
- Secure voter registration database.
- Secure past election information.
- Do precinct analysis to determine priorities.
- Set up door-to-door schedule.
- Secure census/demographic information.
- Secure copies of past contributors to other elected officials' campaigns.
- Explore Web site development.
- Secure e-mail addresses of like-minded citizens.
- Write and print pushcard.
- Print stationery, envelopes (business and fundraising), volunteer cards, and postcards.
- Decide if going to secure a headquarters and do so, if need be.
- Determine issues through talking with others, prayer, phone surveys, newspaper search, etc.
- Research the issues.
- Gather contact information for media outlets.

- Have professional photo and family portrait taken.
- Order bumper strips and any other campaign material.

Announcement and early campaign stage—launching

When: Spring of campaign year—three months February–May

- Pray.
- File for office.
- Send announcement press release.
- Make personal visits with editors of local newspapers.
- Send fundraising letters to friends and family and coalitions.
- Follow up with fundraising letters:

  ➢ Phone calls; and
  ➢ Set up meetings with "100 Club" members.

- Advertise/hold kickoff fundraising event.
- Consider forming a team to raise funds for you.
- Order signs.
- Recruit volunteers for team.
- Secure billboards and traveling bus signage, if desired.
- Begin going door to door.
- Secure phone bank location(s) for later use.
- Get absentee ballot list and application.
- Write absentee letter to send later.
- Plan parade entries.
- Conduct candidate analysis:

  ➢ Opponent's background, strengths, weaknesses, positions on issues; and
  ➢ Your background, strengths, weaknesses, positions on issues.

- Have good pictures taken in casual settings reflective of your campaign issues for literature.

- Hold a headquarters kickoff.

Full-time campaigning stage—building stage

When: Three months—June, July, and August

- Pray.
- Go door to door every day except Sunday.
- Hold a summer fundraising event.
- Participate in area parades.
- Attend summer community events.
- Be visible at 4th of July celebrations handing out fliers, balloons, or giving free drinks of water from a booth with a pickup truck parked in a visible location with your large campaign sign in the back or taped to the side.
- Prepare debate/forum issues—statements and responses.
- Erect large campaign signs if ordinances allow.
- Send out press releases on issues/events.
- Raise funds:

  ➢ Send another letter to friends and family outlining specific needs of the campaign and how they can help meet those needs;
  ➢ Follow up with phone calls; and
  ➢ Meet with "100 Club" candidates.

If have a primary election:

- Pray.
- Put yard signs out.
- Run your absentee plan:

  ➢ Send letter to those who normally vote absentee in the primary;
  ➢ Target door to door to those who normally vote absentee; and
  ➢ Visit nursing homes.

- Have supporters send out postcards.
- Send a direct mail piece to likely voters.
- E-mail about your candidacy.
- Go door to door to targeted households that normally vote in primary elections.
- Place media ads.
- Conduct Election Day plan:

  ➢ Yard signs at polls;
  ➢ Phone calls to likely voters;
  ➢ Literature drops; and
  ➢ Greet voters at the polls thanking them for voting and introducing yourself *after* they exit the polls. Ask for their vote for the general election.

After Labor Day stage—full court press

When: September

- Pray.
- Go door to door every day except Sunday.
- Design and print direct mail pieces.
- Design newspaper, radio, and cable advertisements.
- Hold final fundraising event.
- Send press releases regarding issues or candidacy.
- Send fundraising letter. Appeal for getting your campaign over the top.

Get out the vote—the home stretch

When: Last five weeks of the campaign—October and early November

- Pray.
- Send last fundraising letter, if needed.

- Put yard signs out the last three or four weeks of the campaign.
- Run your absentee plan:

  ➢ Send letter to those who normally vote absentee;
  ➢ Target door to door to those who normally vote absentee; and
  ➢ Visit nursing homes.

- Send direct mail pieces on a staggered basis the last two to four weeks of the campaign.
- Go door to door to targeted households.
- Have supporters send out postcards.
- E-mail about your candidacy.
- Place media ads.
- Conduct Election Day plan:

  ➢ Yard signs at polls;
  ➢ Give rides to the polls;
  ➢ Literature drops;
  ➢ Phone calls to likely voters; and
  ➢ Greet voters at the polls.

- Hold Watch Night event.
- Thank family members and campaign partners, win or lose.
- Thank God, win or lose.

After the election—thanking

When: During the week after the election

- Pray.
- Take down and store/dispose of campaign signs.
- Place Thank You ad in local newspapers and on radio.
- Write and send personal thank you letters to your campaign team.
- Write and send thank you letters to all volunteers.

- Write and send thank you letters to financial partners.
- Take down campaign headquarters.
- Store campaign materials.
- Serve with distinction whether as an elected official, if elected, or community leader, if not, bringing glory to God through your words and actions.

SIX-MONTH CAMPAIGN TIMELINE

Campaigns go through five distinct stages. The focus and activities change with each phase. Below is a sample guideline candidates can use to keep their campaigns on track. It assumes an April election, such as for school board or city council. If the election is held at a different time, adjustments should be made accordingly, beginning six months out from the election.

Pre-announcement stage—getting ready

When: During the one month before filing for office, starting November of the year prior to the election.

- Pray.
- Write personal bio for announcement.
- Encapsulate the reason you are running into one sentence.
- Secure campaign treasurer.
- Choose name of campaign committee.
- Recruit campaign team (chairmen of various projects).
- Decide campaign colors and logo.
- Write announcement press release.
- Secure mailing lists.

- Develop computer database of potential partners.
- Write and send letter to friends, telling decision to run and inviting their partnership in the efforts.
- Write fundraising letters, but send them later:

  ➢ To friends and family;
  ➢ To coalitions (business, pro-life, gun owners, other)

- Buy wardrobe updates.
- Get price quotes on yard signs, direct mail pieces, postage, pushcards, media buys, etc.
- Get bulk rate permit.
- Write campaign plan.
- Develop a budget.
- Gather important dates (major events, parades, fundraising events, etc.)
- Secure voter registration database.
- Secure past election information.
- Do precinct analysis to determine priorities.
- Set up door-to-door schedule.
- Secure census/demographic information.
- Secure copies of past contributors to other elected officials' campaigns.
- Explore Web site development.
- Secure e-mail addresses of like-minded citizens.
- Write and print pushcard or brochure.
- Print stationery, envelopes (business and fundraising), volunteer cards, and postcards.
- Decide if going to secure a headquarters and do so, if need be.
- Determine issues through talking with others, prayer, phone surveys, newspaper search, etc.
- Research the issues.
- Gather contact information for media outlets.
- Have professional photo and family portrait taken.
- Order bumper strips and any other campaign material.

Announcement and early campaign stage—launching

When: Two months—December and January

- Pray.
- File for office.
- Send announcement press release.
- Make personal visits with editors of local newspapers.
- Send fundraising letters to friends and family and coalitions.
- Follow up fundraising letters with phone call.
- Order signs.
- Recruit volunteers for team.
- Secure billboards and traveling bus signage, if desired.
- Secure phone bank location(s) for later use.
- Get absentee ballot list and application.
- Write absentee letter to send later.
- Plan parade entries.
- Conduct candidate analysis:

  ➢ Opponent's background, strengths, weaknesses, positions on issues; and
  ➢ Your background, strengths, weaknesses, positions on issues.

- Have good pictures taken in casual settings reflective of your campaign issues for literature.

Full-time campaigning stage—full court press

When: One month—February

- Pray.
- Go door to door every day except Sunday.
- Attend community events.
- Prepare debate/forum issues—statements and responses.
- Design and print direct mail pieces.
- Design newspaper, radio, and cable advertisements.

- Erect large campaign signs if ordinances allow.
- Send out press releases on issues/events.
- Raise funds, if needed:

  ➤ Send another letter to friends and family, outlining specific needs of the campaign and how they can help meet those needs; and
  ➤ Follow up with phone calls.

- Run your absentee plan:

  ➤ Send letter to those who normally vote absentee;
  ➤ Target door to door to those who normally vote absentee; and
  ➤ Visit nursing homes.

Get out the vote—the home stretch

When: Last month—March

- Pray.
- Put yard signs out.
- Go door to door to targeted households.
- Have supporters send out postcards.
- Send direct mail pieces on a staggered basis the last two to four weeks of the campaign.
- E-mail about your candidacy.
- Place media ads.

Election month activities—GOTV and thanking

When: April

- Conduct Election Day plan:

  ➤ Yard signs at polls;
  ➤ Give rides to the polls;
  ➤ Literature drops;

> ➤ Phone calls to likely voters; and
> ➤ Greet voters at the polls.

- Hold watch night event.
- Thank family members and campaign partners, win or lose.
- Thank God, win or lose.
- Take down and store/dispose of campaign signs.
- Place Thank You ad in local newspapers and on radio.
- Write and send personal thank you letters to your campaign team.
- Write and send thank you letters to all volunteers.
- Write and send thank you letters to financial partners.
- Store campaign materials.
- Serve with distinction whether as an elected official, if elected, or community leader, if not, bringing glory to God through your words and actions.

PUSHCARD EXAMPLES

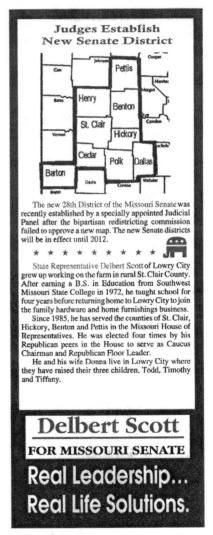

FIGURE C.1 Example of an eye-catching pushcard with
map of new district on the back

Danielle "Danie" MOORE

For State Representative

The Right Leader...
for the _Change_ We Need.

As a community leader and former educator, Danie Moore has the experience to fight for:

★ Improved education for all our children
★ Affordable, accessible and transferable health care
★ Upgraded roads, highways and bridges

LOCAL EDUCATOR

Danie is a retired high school teacher. She taught English and French in the Fulton Public Schools for 26 years, twice receiving the Excellence in Education Award. Danie served two terms as President of her local Community Teachers Association and is a life-time member of the Missouri State Teachers Association (MSTA). She also serves as President of the Kingdom of Callaway Retired Teacher Association, is a member of Delta Kappa Gamma Society International and sits on the board of directors of the Missouri Literacy Association.

MISSOURI UPBRINGING

★ *Central Methodist College in Fayette, Bachelor of Arts Degree*
  University of Missouri, Columbia, Graduate Studies
★ *Elsberry High School, graduate*

CALLAWAY COUNTY COMMUNITY SERVICE

★ *Ecumenical Ministries Board of Directors*
★ *Callaway County Farm Bureau*
★ *TEAM CAL Transportation Task Force*
★ *Kingdom of Callaway Historical Society*
★ *Fulton Optimist Club, Board Member*
★ *County Health Coalition*
★ *Callaway County Literacy Council*
★ *Chamber of Commerce*

FAMILY LIFE

Danie and her husband, Lisle, have two children and four grandchildren. Together they own Target Masters, a training and recreational facility for law enforcement and shooting sports enthusiasts. They are members of the NRA and Ducks Unlimited. They attend St. Peters Catholic Church.

FIGURE C.2 Example of well-designed pushcard

Re-elect

STEVE CHESLIK

Cass County Treasurer

T
R
U
S
T
W
O
R
T
H
Y

D
I
L
I
G
E
N
T

✓ Masters degree in education from CMSU

✓ Middle School Math Teacher (1988-2000) and High School Soccer Coach (1988-1995) at Raymore-Peculiar

✓ Cass County Treasurer (2001-present)

It is an honor to be your Cass County Treasurer. I will continue to serve YOU with integrity and I would appreciate your vote on August 3rd and November 2nd!

Steve Cheslik

Responsibilities of office:
- ♦ Receipting, disbursement, and investment of county funds
- ♦ Payroll for county employees
- ♦ Informing commissioners of county's financial status
- ♦ Custodian of school funds

Accomplishments in office:
- ☑ Implementation of internet banking
- ☑ Diversified investing
- ☑ Financial analysis and prediction for commissioners
- ☑ Direct deposit of county payroll checks
- ☑ Reducing unnecessary office staff hours

All of these have been done with this goal in mind:
TO PROTECT & STRETCH THE TAX DOLLARS OF THE HARD WORKING CITIZENS OF CASS COUNTY!

Steve and Mary Cheslik reside in Harrisonville with their six children: Rachel, Sarah, Micah, Brianna, Tyler and Samuel.

Community involvement:
- ➤ Active church member
- ➤ Youth soccer coach
- ➤ Active member of Harrisonville Kiwanis
- ➤ Life Choice Center for Women auction volunteer
- ➤ Cass County Republican Club Treasurer

VOTE ☒ **STEVE CHESLIK**
Cass County Treasurer

Paid for by Committee to Elect Steve Cheslik, Karen Helzer, Treasurer

FIGURE C.3 Example of pushcard for a candidate for county treasurer.

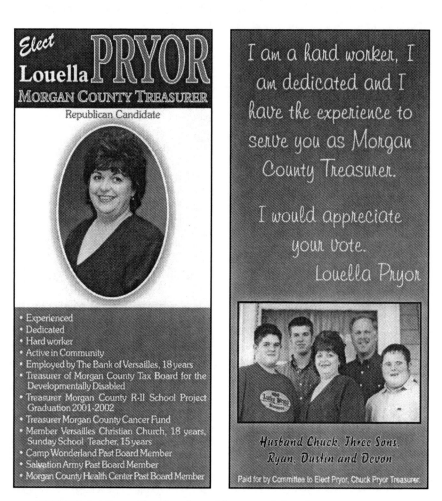

FIGURE C.4 Example of pushcard for a candidate for county treasurer

Proven Leadership
For the 124th District

DEDICATION: Working hard for our community.

INTEGRITY: Following through on her promises.

LEADERSHIP: Aggressively pursuing your concerns in Jefferson City.

It has been an honor and privilege to serve you as your State Representative for the past two years. I have worked full-time for the citizens of the 124th District and have dedicated my time and energies to make a positive difference for the people of this area. I hope that I have earned your confidence and support in reelecting me as your State Representative. Your vote on November 5 will be appreciated.

Thank you,

Vicky Hartzler

THE RIGHT VISION
THE RIGHT VALUES

VICKY HARTZLER

A Person We Trust:

- Public School Teacher for 11 years.
- Director of Senior Citizen activities and youth programs for many years.
- Vice-president of Cass County Farm Bureau.
- Children's teacher at the Harrisonville Mennonite Church

A Recognized Leader:

- Freshman Legislator of the Year for Constituent Services.
- American Legislative Exchange Council Task Force on Education.
- Honored by the National Federation of Independent Businesses for her support of Missouri jobs and small businesses.
- Honored by Eagle Forum for her dedicated work for God, Family, and Country.

A Voice for our Community:

- **Public Safety**—Vicky has taken an aggressive approach against crime believing our children should live in safety.
- **Taxes**—Vicky will continue working to reduce the tax burden and to cut unnecessary spending.
- **Education**—Vicky supports quality education and has fought for education policies which are grounded in the basics and rooted in local control.
- **Family**—Vicky believes strong family ties are the basic building blocks of society. She is fighting to improve the adoption process, making the blessing of family available to all.

THE RIGHT VISION
THE RIGHT VALUES

Paid for by Vicky Hartzler for State Representative Committee, Loretta Fifer, Treasurer

---

FIGURE C.5 Example of pushcard

DIRECT MAIL EXAMPLES

THE DIFFERENCE IS CLEAR!		
Issues	**Brian L. Baker**	**His Opponent**
EDUCATION	• Increased school funding by $143 million—Source: HB 1002 • Endorsed by teachers and school boards	• No record
SMALL BUSINESS	• Authored the Small Business Fairness Act—Source: HB 978 • Endorsed by the Missouri Chamber & NFIB	• No record
FAMILY VALUES	• Supported the Marriage Amendment—Source: HJR 42 • Endorsed by Missouri Right to Life	• No record
SENIORS	• Voted to give seniors property tax credits—Source: SB 730 • Voted to get seniors prescription drugs—Source: SB 1160	• No record

RE-ELECT

BAKER

State Representative, 123rd District

www.BrianBaker123.com

Paid for by Citizens for Brian L. Baker - Brenda Curvey, Treasurer

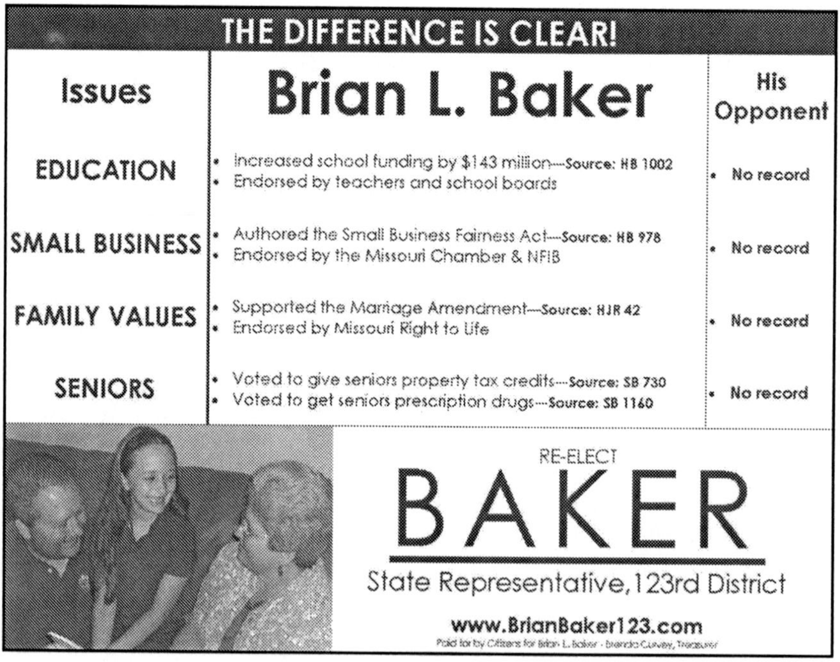

FIGURE D.1 Example of a contrast piece comparing the stands
on issues between two candidates

VICKY HARTZLER

...Fighting for Senior Citizens

Vicky Hartzler respects and appreciates the wisdom of her grandmother, Izola Zellmer, and other important seniors in her life. She knows how important it is for seniors to receive that Social Security check in the mail and wants to ensure it is there for our future. She believes it is vital that Congress take steps to *preserve* and *protect* Social Security. That's why Vicky asked federal officials to intervene for us in Washington, D.C. *She stands up for us!*

Vote November 3 for **Vicky Hartzler** She's a Representative that has your best interests at heart!

VICKY HARTZLER
State Representative

Vicky Hartzler has a heart for senior citizens. As a board member of the Cass County Council on Aging and former director of senior citizen activities for the Harrisonville Parks and Recreation, Vicky understands and cares about the issues important to seniors. She fights for us at home and in Jefferson City.

Vicky...

* Vicky is fighting for property tax relief for senior citizens and co-sponsored legislation to help low income elderly stay in their homes.

* Vicky co-sponsored legislation to fully deduct veteran's pensions and worked to ensure only veterans are admitted into veterans' cemeteries.
* Vicky said 'No' to efforts to take money away from veteran's homes.

...with your best interests at heart.

* Vicky was instrumental in securing more money for Meals-On-Wheels and established grants to replace outdated kitchen equipment at senior nutrition sites. She will continue to support legislation to ensure seniors receive the services needed to live independently.

* Vicky is a vocal supporter of retired teachers co-sponsoring legislation to increase benefits. She initiated a project to honor former one room teachers and and capture their stories.

FIGURE D.2 Example of "Inoculation" direct mail piece sent to senior citizens to ward off possible attacks claiming Vicky Hartzler was going to dismantle Social Security.

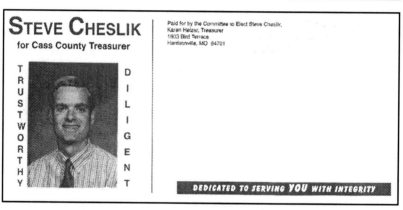

FIGURE D.3 Example of general issue direct mail piece

Environmental regulation, unfair competition, and outdated roads and bridges threaten the future of our rural economy.

That's why now, more than ever, we need a representative like *Vicky Hartzler.*

This election day, cast your vote for the future of our rural way of life...

Vote Vicky Hartzler for State Representative.

Farmer's Rights

☐ As a part of lifelong farm family, Vicky Hartzler recognizes the importance of property rights — that it's in a farmer's own interest to care for their land.

Farmers don't need state bureaucrats without first-hand agriculture experience, telling them what to do.

Promoting Agriculture

☐ Vicky Hartzler understands we need a state department of agriculture that cuts through the red tape and promotes ag exports and value-added products like ethanol and livestock processing — businesses that boost agriculture and related jobs.

Improving Infrastructure

☐ As a teacher, Vicky Hartzler believes our kids deserve a quality education.

Vicky also believes we need better roads and bridges in our part of Missouri.

As our state representative, Vicky Hartzler will fight for our fair share of state highway and education funds.

Protecting The Family Farm

☐ The movement of corporate agriculture into Missouri has many of us fearing for the future of the family farm.

Vicky Hartzler feels strongly that corporate farms should not be given any exemptions, breaks or abatements that would give them an unfair advantage over family farms.

Paid for by
Vicky Hartzler for State Rep Committee,
Ed Buhl, Treasurer
P.O. Box 771
Harrisonville, MO 64701

Bulk Rate
U.S. Postage
PAID
Permit #18
Harrisonville, MO

"...because the future of our rural way of life is at stake."

FIGURE D.4 Example of an issue-based direct mail piece sent to a targeted audience

This Tuesday, Let's Vote *Vicky Hartzler*, State Representative.

In the election this Tuesday, let's elect a representative with the values we trust and the leadership we need...

Vicky Hartzler supports private sector health care reform, not more government bureaucracy.

Vicky Hartzler will protect our farms and businesses from burdensome government regulation.

Vicky Hartzler is working for new solutions to get criminals off our streets.

Vicky Hartzler is fighting to ensure our kids get the quality education they deserve.

Vicky Hartzler.
The Right Vision.
The Right Values.

...Let's elect *Vicky Hartzler*, State Representative.

What's the first thing you should Do this Tuesday, November 8th?

Paid for by
Vicky Hartzler for State Rep. Committee
Ed Bohl, Treasurer
P.O. Box 771
Harrisonville, MO 64701

Bulk Rate
U.S. Postage
PAID
Permit # 18
Harrisonville, MO

Go Vote for <u>Vicky Hartzler</u> For State Rep!

FIGURE D.5 Example of a get-out-the-vote direct mail piece.

Appendix E

Newspaper Advertisement Examples

FIGURE E.1 Example of using candidate's last name to build a campaign theme into a series of newspaper advertisements

FIGURE E.2 Example of general ads for a county office.

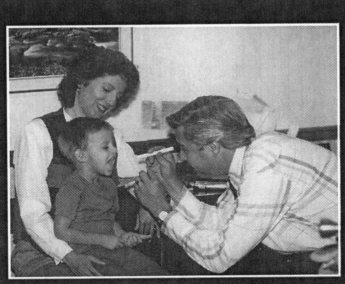

VICKY HARTZLER ON HEALTH CARE

"Socialized health care is not the way to fix the best health care delivery system in the world. We can achieve quality, affordable health care through common-sense, market-based reforms."

Citizens Concerned About HealthCare:

"If Mrs. Hartzler can carry qualities as a representative as well as she does as a person, she'll make one of the best representatives the district has ever had." —Richard Price, M.D., Harrisonville

Vicky Hartzler's Health Care Goals:

- Reduce health care costs;
- Ensure each person has the right to choose his or her own doctor;
- Ensure health care coverage is accessible to everyone, including those with pre-existing conditions; and
- Accomplish results through private-sector reforms rather than government-controlled bureaucracies.

Paid for by Vicky Hartzler for State Representative Committee, Ed Bohl, Treasurer.

FIGURE E.3 Example of ad using reverse printing and endorsement quote to make an impact.

Do you ever feel like you are standing alone?

Not me. I believe there are as many voters in Johnson County that believe the way I do, as there are beans in this field...That there is no room in the county for negative campaigns. That there is no room for gossip, innuendo, and politics as usual. I stand firm in my convictions, and so can you be electing Gilbert Powers for County Clerk. Isn't that the kind of values you want for your county government?

Elect Gilbert Powers For County Clerk

"I would appreciate your vote on November 8th for County Clerk."

Paid for by the Committee to elect Gilbert Powers for County Clerk, John T. Price, Treasurer

FIGURE E.4 Example of a response ad to negative campaigning by opponent

ENDNOTES

Chapter 2

1. Do You Make Your First Impression Your Best Impression?, http://entrepreneurs.about.com/cs/marketing/a/uc051603a.htm (accessed January 12, 2007).
2. Dress for Success, http://www.uwm.edu/-ceil/career/jobs/females. htm (accessed January 12, 2007).

Chapter 3

1. Webster's New Collegiate Dictionary, 1977, G. & C. Merriam Co., pg. 1362.
2. Brian Baker (Missouri state representative), interview by Vicky Hartzler, August 3, 2007.

Chapter 4

1. Mike Klesius, "21st Century Rough Riders," *Campaigns and Elections,* December 2006, 26–32.
2. Robert Thomas, *How to Run for Local Office,* (Westland, MI: R & T Enterprise, Inc,.1999), 9.

3. Chris Benjamin (Chief of Staff for Missouri House Speaker Rod Jetton), interview by Vicky Hartzler, August 14, 2007.
4. S. J. Guzzetta, *The Campaign Manual,* (Alexandria, VA: Political Publications, 2006), 43.
5. Ibid.
6. Ibid.
7. Ibid.
8. Ibid, pg. 41.
9. Chris Benjamin, ibid.

Chapter 5

1. Diane Ullius, "Crossing a Bridge of Shyness: Public Speaking for Communicators," EEI Communications–EEI Press, eeicom.com, http://www.eeicom.com/eye/shyness/html (accessed February 22, 2007).

Chapter 6

1. S. J. Guzzetta, *The Campaign Manual,* (Alexandria, VA: Political Publications, 2006), 61–62.
2. S. J. Guzzetta, *The Campaign Manual,* (Alexandria, VA: Political Publications, 2006), 62.

Chapter 7

1. S. J. Guzzetta, *The Campaign Manual,* (Alexandria, VA: Political Publications, 2006), 109–110.

Chapter 8

1. Chris Benjamin (Chief of Staff for Missouri House Speaker Rod Jetton), interview by Vicky Hartzler, August 14, 2007.
2. Robert J. Thomas, *How to Run for Local Office,* (Westland, MI: R & T Enterprise, Inc,.1999), 86–87.

Chapter 9

1. Waldo Jaquith, "Reinventing the Wheel," *Campaigns and Elections,* December 2006, 102.
2. "Internet Usage Statistics for the Americas." 2007. Internet World Stats, http://www.internetworldstats.com/stats2.htm (accessed April 5, 2007).
3. Stuart Shepard, "Now Entering the Blogosphere," *Citizen,* (March 2007), 10–11.
4. Ibid.
5. Stuart Shepard, "Moving Pictures Move People," *Citizen,* (February 2007), 10–11.
6. Ibid.

Chapter 12

1. "How Your Learning Style Affects Your Use of Mnemonics" *Mind Tools: www.mindtools.com/mnemlstylo.htm* (September 12, 2007).
2. Ibid.

Chapter 13

1. Chris Benjamin (Chief of Staff for Missouri House Speaker Rod Jetton), interview by Vicky Hartzler, August 14, 2007.
2. Cathy Allen, "How to Ask for Money," *Campaigns and Elections,* April 1998, 24.
3. S. J. Guzzetta, *The Campaign Manual,* (Alexandria, VA: Political Publications, 2006), 242.

Chapter 14

1. S. J. Guzzetta, *The Campaign Manual,* (Alexandria, VA: Political Publications, 2006), 48.

Chapter 15

1. Robert J. Thomas, *How to Run for Local Office* (Westland, MI: R & T Enterprise, Inc., 1999), 81–82.

Chapter 16

1. Chris Benjamin (Chief of Staff for Missouri House Speaker Rod Jetton), interview by Vicky Hartzler, August 14, 2007.
2. S. J. Guzzetta, *The Campaign Manual,* (Alexandria, VA: Political Publications, 2006), 170.

Chapter 17

1. Thomas J. Barrett, Ph.D., *Walking the Tightrope,* (Vienna, VA: Business/Life Management, Inc., 1994), 62–64.

INDEX